# Wade Cook's Stock Picking Handbook

# Wade Cook's Stock Picking Handbook

## Liberty Network, Inc.

**Printed in the United States of America**

**Distributed to the trade by Midpoint Trade Books**

For Library of Congress information, please call the publisher. "Wade Cook's Stock Picking Handbook: Subtitle One: How to Invest in the Stock Market; Subtitle Two: How to Trade in the Stock Market."

ISBN 0-9745749-0-2

"This publication is designed to provide general information in regard to the subject matter covered. It is sold with the understanding that the publisher is not engaged in rendering legal, accounting, or other professional services. If legal, accounting, or other professional services are required, the services of an independent professional should be sought."

From a declaration of principles jointly adopted by a committee of the American Bar Association and the Committee of the Publisher's Association.

Edited by Brenda Sutherland and Carrie Cook

Published and Distributed by Liberty Network, Inc.
1420 NW Gilman Blvd. #2131

Issaquah, WA 98027

1-866-579-5900  425-222-3764 (fax)

Distributed to the trade by

Midpoint Trade Books

212-727-0190

Printed in United States of America

10 9 8 7 6 5 4 3 2 1

TO LAURA–

My Love, My Life.

# Acknowledgements

Wow! This past year has been a challenge. The market has shown signs of a rebound, so the message in this book is so very important and timely. My loyal staff has been wonderful. Sometimes adversity strengthens resolve and distinguishes people as their character shines through and literally "saves the day." I am also grateful for John Childers who has been so supportive in this work. Thanks again to my gracious wife Laura and my supportive kids. They sure make my life worthwhile.

# Table of Contents
## Book 1

## Book 2

# Preface

I'm really into the question: "To whom are you listening?" So I thought at the very beginning of this book I would introduce myself through the following paragraph. I think you need to know a little about me and what my thoughts are towards the stock market.

I have attended many seminars in my life. I have learned that I would much rather listen to a boring speaker who really knows his business, than listen to an exciting speaker who does not walk the walk. There is so much more to be learned from someone who has been in the trenches—a foxhole sergeant, if you will—than from someone who has only an academic background without useful experience. If I am going to receive training, I want to receive training from someone who has been there. Think about your own life. Is it not true that virtually everything you have learned—and learned how to do well—has been taught to you by someone who was experienced in that area? We do not learn to drive a car by only reading a driver's education manual. At some point in time you have to get behind the wheel and learn how the gas pedal, the brake and the gear shift work. You have to learn how to maneuver in and out of traffic. You also need to learn defensive driving. In essence, it means that it is essential to have "OJT" or On the Job Training.

It would be naive to think a person could learn how to fly a Boeing 757 by only studying the manual, without any simulation or hands-on training, then get into the seat and fly the plane. In fact, sometimes a co-pilot will sit in the right chair for a decade or two before he can move to the left chair as captain. Just imagine boarding a plane and a pilot says over the intercom, "Ladies and gentlemen, welcome aboard. I am a brand new pilot and I have never taken off before. Sit back, buckle up and enjoy the flight." Most of us would scramble for the exit. Why is it then that we trust our money with someone who doesn't have proper experience? Why is it we choose to handle our own money without the experience level necessary to handle it wisely and most effectively?

*Experience is a hard teacher, because she gives the test first, the lesson after.*     ~ Vernon Law

One of the advantages of thousands of our students have is to learn from my good deals as well as my bad deals. Boy have I made some mistakes. They have really been doozies. But one of the major aspects of

# Preface

my personality is when I get kicked in the teeth on a trade I will try to figure out what went wrong and why. I look at whether I should have traded—or not—as well as how to correct the problem. I use negative experiences to better myself in order to prepare myself for the next trade.

Because I am in the trenches everyday and working many stock market transactions each month, I constantly try to figure out better ways to do better trades. By this I mean better entrance points and better exit points. By the way, just a quick little play on words, sometimes in my seminars when I talk about technicals as a way of knowing when to get in and to get out of a stock, I spell it TechNEEcals. The two large E's stand for Entrance point and Exit point. A theme I whisper in my brain to myself almost everyday, "there has to be a better way." I take this from the Bible, 1 Corinthians 12:31 "But covet earnestly the best gifts: and yet shew I unto you a more excellent way."

Let me give a real world example, one not from the stock market, to illustrate this point. We have become quite an Arabian horse family. My two teenagers are very talented. Every summer we go to Regina, Saskatchewan, Canada for the Royal Red Arabian and Half-Arabian Championship Horse Show. A few years ago we had to stay on the opposite side of town from the fair grounds where the horse show was being held. I did not know my way around town very well, but I did get a map. I looked at the freeways and some of the better highways, and made it around the town for the first and second day in about 16 to 18 minutes, depending on the red lights. After I dropped off my family to warm up the horses, I went off exploring and made the trip in less than 14 minutes. The next day I decided to take a different road that looked better on the map and I got the trip down to 12 minutes. I was proud of myself. I had knocked off 4 or 5 minutes. I was at the fair grounds talking to someone who was a native of Regina and told him how I hit Prince Albert Street for a while and then used the loop to the fair grounds. He responded "Why are you going that way?" I asked him if he had a better way. He then showed me on the map a better way. Sure enough when I tried it, the trip only took 8 minutes. My point is that talking to someone who has been there in the trenches, helped me find short cuts I would never have found on my own.

I bring tens of thousands of trades to the picture. From the time I wrote my first book about the stock market, Wall Street Money Machine, I have done thousands of trades. Many have been good and some bad, but as a student of the stock market first, I have learned many valuable lessons.

My mission in life is to help people build a more quality life. I have chosen cash flowing the stock market as the arena for my attention. It does require full attention. For years I was an investor in real estate. I made my first fortune in real estate. I am still doing real estate transactions, but fewer and at a much higher price range than before. I now choose to use the stock market as my arena for building cash flow simply because of the "functionality" of the stock market. I do not mean to say that the stock market is easy. In fact it can be one of the toughest professions you will choose to engage in. I do however mean, because the infrastructure exists, that it is easy to trade. It can be done in your back bedroom, on a computer, a laptop, or in your car while you are going about your normal business. It does make the perfect part time job. If I could trade in real estate while on my phone and in the car like I do the stock market, I would probably do a lot more real estate deals. I simply cannot buy an option on a piece of real estate, wait for it to go up in value, and three weeks later sell that option at a profit, or get out at a slight loss, over the telephone. Such a methodology does not exist! I have used the analogy before of Snickers candy bars. I love Snickers candy bars. If I could call the food warehouse and find out a case of Snickers is going for $60, and put down $2 as an option to tie up a case, or $200 to tie up 100 cases, and then as the case of the candy bars rises in value, sell my $2 option (to buy the candy bars) at $3, or $300 making a nice profit, I would. Again such a way of trading cannot be done. But the stock market allows this type of trading. You can be an investor in the stock market and buy stocks for what I call a "right-term hold." You could become a trader in the stock market and literally use it as your family's part time business. You buy wholesale, sell retail and take the profits home to pay the bills.

Again what I bring to the table for your benefit, is years of experience, tens of thousands of trades and a dedication and passion for the learning process—a process I turn into the "Tell, Show, Do" teaching method to help my students get through the learning curve in a more effective manner.

## Trade Suitability Is Good

I firmly believe trade suitability is not only worthwhile but also very necessary. Let me tell you how important this is to me as a teacher of seminars. I have people sign an agreement stating they acknowledge I and my fellow instructors are just that, we're instructors, not professional stockbrokers, or financial professionals in any manner. We do not give specific advice on what any one of our students should be engaging in. We teach formulas with which people can then work with their stockbrokers, find out if the formula is suitable for them, and then have their stockbroker help them find stocks or options that fit the parameters of that particular formula.

It really is that simple. We are part of the team. I believe we are the most important part because we help people establish a foundation. We love the educational process. We teach people the correct principals and then let them govern themselves. The discipline to govern yourself wisely, especially as a novice investor, is usually lacking in most people. That is why it is so necessary to work with a good stockbroker for trade suitability.

This is also one of the reasons why I do not like Internet type trading accounts. Yes, the firm had you fill out the same documentation as to what types of trades you are going to do, and disallowed you from doing certain types of trades, and the trade you are about to do was okayed by them, but on a day-to-day basis, where is the oversight? Where is the camaraderie? Where is the sounding board to bounce ideas off

# Preface

of? I know many of these firms have support rooms where you can talk to an actual stock broker, but how can a group of stockbrokers who only talk to you from time to time, be up on your particular situation?

That is what you get with your own stockbroker. You get to know him/her, and they get to know you. They know what you like and don't like. They discuss your risk level with you—how much risk you are willing to take in any given situation, and what type of reward you are looking for. They help you balance risk and reward. If you do not have a dedicated person to help you, you are left on your own, and left to your own devices, you may go astray very quickly.

John Wooden, the former coach of the UCLA basketball team, and also known as the Wizard of Westwood said a very important thing to his players. Now remember these players are young college basketball stars. In their own mind they are the cat's meow. I cannot imagine any one of his players, traveling across the country to a far away city, 8:30 at night, the time they should go to bed because they have practice the next morning, actually wanting to go to bed. They want to go out and party. John Wooden said to these young players, "Discipline yourselves and others won't have to." What a powerful statement. I suggest that statement to all of us. Again, as a new investor most of us do not have the required discipline and therefore we need a live, passionate, courteous and knowledgeable stockbroker helping us decide which trades are best, when and why, and then implementing the how-to's for us in an effective manner.

Remember, this book is actually two books – *How To Invest In The Stock Market* and *How To Trade In The Stock Market*. I hope you enjoy and use both.

**Book One**

# How to Invest in the Stock Market

# Book 1

# 1

# Sailing into Profits:
# Stock Investing Made Easy

The quest for good investments in just not that tough once you know a few basic rules. These rules are just not tough to learn and use. First of all, let's define the term, "good investment." It is simply an investment that makes us money. There is no other reason to invest.

Now, what does, "make money" mean? This is not an easy question to answer. Remember the ad on TV? "We make money the old fashioned way—we earn it." Recently, I had a run in with a government bureaucrat. They can't stand it when I tell people that they can "make money" in the stock market. I further explain that the way to make cash money is to trade, not invest; to treat the stock market like a business. They don't get this. You will get it, because you're not a government type. No, honestly, I think they think I'm showing people how to print counterfeit money on a press in the basement. That must be their idea of "making money."

Treating the stock market like a business simply put means that you buy a stock or option at wholesale prices, wait for it to grow in price and sell it for a higher price. They do this a bunch of times, pay their employees, rent, electricity, advertising, et cetera. If there is any money left over, they make a profit. They do this well, and if we own a stock in McDonalds (MCD), our stock just might go up in price, say from $26 to $29 over a period of time. They make money, so might we.

Safeway, Microsoft, Caterpillar and the New York Times each have their own business model, each their own way of making money. We can own stock in any of these companies and in ten thousand more.

> *"Twenty years from now you will be more disappointed by the things that you didn't do than by the ones you did do. So throw off the bowlines. Sail away from the safe harbor. Catch the trade winds in your sails. Explore. Dream. Discover."*
> - **Mark Twain**

## Share the Risk

For centuries, explorers, entrepreneurs and merchants have sought out investors to join in their ventures and share the risks. Most people were not willing to shoulder all of the risks. These adventurous types would either borrow the money, sometimes second mortgage their entire future; sometimes they would give up part of the ownership and sell equity to others. This equity is stated as stocks or shares. We, the investor with Columbus or Magellan or Marco Polo, hope to share in the spoils-the profits at the end of the venture.

Most original enterprises were short-lived-they ended at some point in time. Then, with certain levels of success achieved, entrepreneurs, sometimes the banks or big money, would want a more continuous operation. Companies were founded to take on more and more ventures. They grew as they expanded. They grew, as they became better at making profits.

> *"A ship in port is safe, but that's not what ships are built for."*     **- Grace Murray Hopper**

These enterprises were private, in that a few investors, a few families, owned all of the shares. Later, exchanges formed. Here, the owners could put all or part of their shares up for sale. Stocks were "listed" and a "warehouseman"-a specialist in that stock-would conduct the buy and sell. Soon, with partial lots being sold, hundreds of people now owned stock. The more the merrier.

It was a way for the small guy to own ten shares of "Intergalactic Transport." He could not afford thousands of shares, as in one-quarter of the company, but ten shares was within his reach.

> *"The man without a purpose is like a ship without a rudder-a waif, a nothing, a <u>no man.</u> Have a purpose in life, and, having it, throw such strength and mind and muscle into your work as God as given to you."*     **- Thomas Carlyle**

## Dividends

What did he want from his ten shares? At first, these people wanted part of the profits. Management would figure out the profits, how much they needed to keep on hand and divide the profits to the shareholders, according to how many shares they owned.

Dividends were elusive, sometimes paid out, sometimes held back. And sometimes there was not enough money for any type of dividend payout.

One year later the company decided to keep all of the money and use it to send eight ships to the orient for silk and spices, selling Old World wares along the route. They were only going to send two ships, but decided those eight ships would create a dominance in that marketplace.

There arose such hope for extra profits-a desire for more dividends-that the stock almost tripled within a year. This increase in stock prices was far above what you would have received as dividends. You were angry at first, you wanted the money. But now, wow, management is looking to the future. Your stock is way up. Should you sell now? But wait, what if the "ship comes in," and the profits are even more than expected? What will the price of your shares go to in that case?

*"He that will not sail till all dangers are over must never put to sea."*        - **Thomas Fuller**

A few weeks later, bad weather reports come back from the far-off Pacific Ocean. Maybe the company's ships won't make it. The stock drops in value. It's now only two times what you paid for it. Should you sell?

Yes, you say, I'll sell two of my shares. You're glad you don't own 100% of a small company, because it's different to sell a part, but this stock market business does present a unique way of dealing. And just as soon as you sell the two shares, the other eight double in value again. Why? Because, even though the weather reports were bad, the current cargo brought in by the last few ships arriving from the same area sold for much more money than anticipated. And your ships are heading out to the same source.

*"I find the great thing in this world is not much where we stand as in what direction we are moving: To reach the port of Heaven, we must sail sometimes with the wind and sometime against it-but we must sail, and not adrift, nor lie at anchor."*    - **Oliver Wendell Holmes**

Your eight remaining shares are doing well. Again, keep them or sell them? The company announces a two for one split of the shares. The company will give as a dividend this time, not cash, but additional stock. Your eight shares will become sixteen. The price is cut in half also, but you notice the price now moving back up. Only a month or so before the first ship is expected back, your shares continue to rise, as more people want into the deal.

Blue skies are here again, but one investor who owned 5,000 shares, now 10,000 after the split, is in financial trouble. He has to sell all of his shares. This creates a big supply and he keeps lowering his price. Finally, his shares are all sold, but what a price! Your stock is back to the price it was before the split.

However, the expectations of profits and reward are immediate, and again the stock surges forward. You sell two more shares, leaving you with fourteen. They are up nicely, but another company files a very large lawsuit against the company you have invested in, and the government wants more taxes. The stock tumbles again, giving back all the gains of the last month. You sell four more shares. Still a nice profit, but not what it could have been last month.

The ships? They're now a week out and the stock goes up double. The news of the lawsuit is old news now. A resolution or settlement could be years away, and the company just purchased more ships from a bankrupt former competitor.

And, could this be?  Another stock split?  Your ten remaining shares become twenty shares and the news rolls on.

*"The Pessimist complains about the wind, the Optimist expects it to change; and the Realist adjusts the sails."* — **Author Unknown**

## What about now?

The times they are a-changing, but everything in the shipping business would find its counterpart in software, transportation, wireless phones and office supplies.  In virtually every situation, or in the anticipation of an event, the stock moves.

Today, few companies pay dividends-about 8% to 12% on a regular or irregular basis.  A small percentage of people buy stock for dividend payouts.  Most people want their stocks to grow in value.  That's where the perceived value is.  Now, anything real or perceived that would affect the profitability of the company, now or in the future, will affect the stock price today.

So do we need to polish our crystal balls?  Hardly.  Every one of us can tell which way the wind is blowing.  We can see blue skies, and see the clouds gathering in the North.  We can use our God-given instincts to connect the dots.

Here are some specific things anyone can do to make better choices.

1) Follow earnings.  I mean, really study related news.  Find out if what you're reading or listening to is a report about current (just ended, so really past tense), blended (say six months back, six months future), or future-usually the next twelve months or the next fiscal year.

2) Now see if there is earnings growth.  Check the earnings for the previous two years, giving you three in all.  Do you see the trends?

3) Still with earnings, see if the earnings have been growing from operations (sales) or from acquisitions.  It's easy to buy a company at the end of the year and have its large earnings show up on the books.

4) Are earnings affected by one-time expenses-charge-offs, restructuring changes, bad investments, etc.?

5) Compare with P/Es of other stock in the same field.  All of these can be checked out on-line or from a good stockbroker.

6) Study the management team, their mission and their passion.

7) Check the debt ratio–lower is better

8) Check the book value, or break up value. A stock at two to three times book is not uncommon. Look for better bargains.

9) Consider options so you have less at risk and better leverage.

10) Know beforehand how you'll manage the downside in case something goes wrong.

11) Always ask the question: What else could I be doing with my time and money?

## Let's Go Fishing

As I write this I am on a plane flying home from Dallas. I was just interviewed by Pat Summerall for a news play on Fox News Channel. While at the airport I randomly selected a few magazines and newspapers to use in writing this section. Our mission: to find great stock. Listed below are several ways I get turned on to these companies. Notice I didn't say turned on by the companies. A mention of a company is a start.

Now the studying begins. Here are my problems with basing my decisions on a new release of information.

1) You don't know the agenda of the writer. Many companies hire PR firms to tout their stocks.

2) The writer usually has a bias and a limited viewpoint.

3) The article is old. Maybe the magazine has a web site for quicker information.

4) Many people try to "pump and dump" a stock. They own it but want you to buy it.

5) The information is incomplete.

So, why do I read about some of these companies and act on the information? Because I'm always learning. The real companies of tomorrow may be in someone's garage today.

If you've read the information regarding ships, earnings, as well as determining value, in my last release, Two Bad Years, and Up We Go!. then his first quote from Personal Finance Magazine will set the tone.

"Quietly with little fanfare, the torch of stock market leadership has passed to a different breed of company-not large, not well know, but potentially very rewarding. The big household-name growth stocks, which led the stock market for much of the '90s, have done little to enrich their owners since March 2000, and in some cases have done much to impoverish them. The new stock marker leaders are solid companies, with real products or services (not just hopes or concepts) and a history of profitability. They are underfollowed by analyst and modestly valued. Most important from my point of view, these stocks sell for reasonable multiple of earnings, revenue, and book value." (Page 49-50)

The author mentioned ten stocks. I will not list them here as you can read the article yourself. It's the April, 2002 Edition, p. 49. I do wan to list excerpts from this article so you can get a feel for the words used. Notice on page 51 the references, or the inference to earnings.

"The evidence suggests that over lengthy periods, small-company stocks typically deliver the best returns."

"I search for companies with a solid business, reliable management, and low valuations."

"The price-to-earnings ratio should ideally be less than 18."

"The price-to-book value ratio should be less than 3 as well (optimally less than 2)."

Now on to the companies:

"The war against terrorism highlights the need for outstanding intelligence. Surely, that incident emphasized our need for eavesdropping equipment."

"Orders tracked up nicely late in 2001, rising 19 percent over the same period in the prior year."

"The company is debt-free, and the stock sell for 1.6 times book value and 1.3 times revenue."

"From $24 at the end of 1999, the stock rose to about $61 in mid-2001. Since then it has sunk back to about $45. At today's price,... sells for 12 times earnings and 1.4 times book value."

"The company has grown its revenue an average 40 percent a year for the past five years and is sitting on a pile of cash-$361 million."

Can you see that most of these comments point to future profitability? Now a caveat. In one of his paragraphs, the author said:

"I bought Massey for clients in January 2001, about a month after its creation. In my opinion, it's still a good purchase today."

We need to do more homework. What does he own? Is he really trying to sell his stock when it gets a little higher?

Next, Worth Magazine is one of my favorites. I read it all the time. There are usually several pages on what professional money managers are buying. Again, I offer the some cautions.

Kevin Landis of Firsthand Funds on Enterasys Networks (ETS), Worth Magazine, 36.

"This network-hardware maker delivered a one-two punch scandal-weary investors in February: It delayed its fourth-quarter earnings release to sort our revenue irregularities and said it was the target of a confidential SEC inquiry. But the potential rewards from this attractively priced stock, down more than 60 percent, outweigh the current risk. Suspect revenue is confined to the Asia-Pacific unit and is worth only about 2 percent of the total. I expect 50 percent growth in sales, which were $217 million in the third quarter, by late 2003, fueled by product rollouts. That should drive the stock as high as $20."

Chuck McQuaid on Mohawk Industries (MHK), Worth Magazine, 36.

"The world's second-largest carpet manufacturer was busy keeping house during an industry downturn last year. It paid down $281 million in debt, acquired top ceramic tile company Dal-Tile, and successfully launched its first line of wood flooring products. As demand picks up this year, these new product lines, along with lower raw material prices and reduced interest expenses, should help 18 percent earnings growth. Trading is just 14 times my 2002 earnings estimate of $4.20 a share, the stock is a good buy."

Jim McCamant on Interneuron Pharmaceuticals (IPIC), Worth Magazine, page 36.

"The promising biotech company has put its failed diet drug, Redux, behind it. Pagaclone, the drug it's developing with Pfizer, targets anxiety disorders, the most widespread psychiatric illness in the United States. Thus far, the drug has produced fewer side effects than the competition. Positive results from Phase III testing for panic disorder and Phase II testing for generalized anxiety disorder, along with data from trials of Tropsium, an overactive-bladder treatment, should help double the stock price in 18 to 24 months."

Martin Whitman on AVX (AVX), Worth Magazine, page 36.

"Profits have stalled at this leading electronic components maker, which is being hurt by pricing pressures brought on by an inventory glut at distributors and end-product manufacturers. But with more than $500 million in net cash, the company should be able to weather this economic downturn. Seasonal demand helped increase the number of units it sold in the third quarter, which ended last December. And the long-term outlook for its products sold: They are used in myriad electronic devices, from cell phones to automobiles. At a recent $18.36, the stock is a good buy.

It trades at less then eight times AVS's long-term earnings power of $2.34 a share, which it should attain within three to five years."

Virtually everything in these brief comments points to earnings. Some are putting problems behind them. Others are expanding. Still one other is waiting for an industry turnaround.

NEXT: These are front page Wall Street Journal snippets from April 15, 2002. Notice all news points to earnings-up or down.

"FLEETBOSTON PLANS to put its Robertson Stephens investment bank up for sale and slash its $3,5 billion venture-capital portfolio by 29%."

"Congressional investigators are demanding that J.P. Morgan turn over documents relating *to* complex transactions with Enron."

"Citigroup's net jumped 37% on a huge gain from the sale of shares in its insurance unit, but core earnings trailed forecasts."

"Bank of America's profit rose 17%, boosted by its consumer unit, but the firm offered a dour outlook for the rest of the year."

"Intel agreed to pay $300 million to settle a patent fight with Intergraph over the Pentium chip."

"GE will cut 7,000 jobs this year in its GE Capital Services unit in an effort to reduce costs and move more functions to the Internet."

"Continental reported a $166 million loss. U.S. airlines are expected to post collective first-quarter losses of over $2 billion."

And this is just one day's newspaper.

NEXT: Brokerage firm reports and how they can affect a stock.

The first two examples show how positive news affected the stock. Novellus Systems (NVLS) reported earnings April 15th (after market) for a loss of $0.02 versus the expectations of a loss of $0.09. The company also stated that forward quarter 2 earnings will exceed current estimates. The stock closed around $50.40 on the next 15th and opened up the next morning at $53.90.

**NVLS**

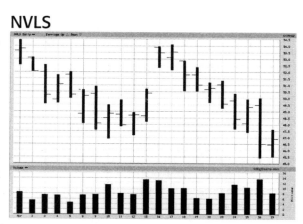

## MERQ

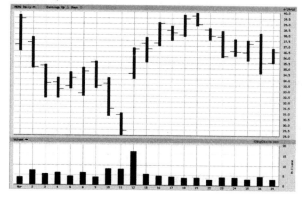

Mercury Interactive (MERQ) reported earnings April 11th (after market) of $0.14 versus expectations of $.011; $0.03 better than expected. The stock closed on the 11th at $29.44 and opened up the next day at $36.70.

The next two examples show how negative news affects the stock

## NET

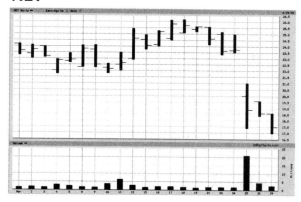

Network Associates (NET) disclosed on March 26th that the SEC has issued a 'Formal Order of Private Investigation' into the company's accounting practices during the year 2000. The stock closed on the 25th at $25 and opened up at on the 26th at $22.23.

## PSFT

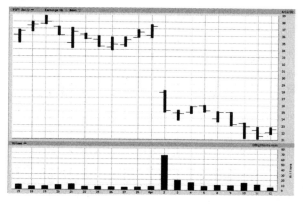

Peoplesoft Inc. (PSFT) reported that 1st quarter software sales were $130-$135 million. This result was about a 15% drop from a year ago. This drew a lot of attention due to the fact that they hit their projections every quarter of the previous year. The stock closed on April 1st at $37.37 and opened on the 2nd at $25.16.

NEXT: Forbes Magazine.  Forbes is full of stories about companies and people.  I like it, because of the biographical approach.  In the back there is a section titled Money and Investing.  There are usually good stocks mentioned.

I also check Money Magazine from time to time.  I read my local newspaper and Money section from USA Today.  There is great information in Investor's Business Daily and Baron's.  I also watch CNBC or Bloomberg while I'm dressing to get a feel for the pulse of the market.  Often times I hear of a company I want to check out.

Also, just as this book was off to press, I was watching CNBC and mentioned these comments to my broker.  He is very astute.  He said, "Wade, no one cares about the numbers.  They're focusing on the comments about the numbers."  Get it?  Perception becomes reality.  We can read and listen to those opinions and make appropriate plays.

## *"THE PRICE OF A STOCK TODAY, IS BASED ON THE ANTICIPATION OF FUTURE EARNINGS."*

# 2

# What Makes Stocks Go Up

## Fear And Greed

Virtually every movement in the stock market is created by one of two human emotions: fear or greed. This aspect of stock market movement cannot be overemphasized.

Remember, when you buy a company you are buying it for "fear" or "greed" purposes. If you really believe a company has the potential for making a lot of money, your purchase would fall under the greed category. Conversely, you sell because of fear. Yes, you've been greedy; your stock is up, so you sell before it goes back down. In short, fear and/or greed is/are the underlying emotions of all stock movements.

## The Law Of Supply And Demand

I was getting ready to go play basketball and my young son of 14, just about 15, came in to see me while my wife and I were talking. We were discussing some reports I had just read about the up-trending market, of which I have just written a new book. He said to me, "Dad, what makes stocks go up?" We only had a few minutes to talk so I basically told him that stocks go up and down because of the law of supply and demand.

I continued briefly that there are only so many stocks in any one company, and when there are many people who want a particular stock, the price of the stock will have the tendency to go up. Conversely, when a lot of people do not want the stock but want to sell the stock, it will have the tendency to go down. All I had time to explain was that there was a middleman, like a warehouse. In this case it would be either the Specialist on the New York Stock Exchange or the Market Maker on NASDAQ. That person is the middleman in buying and selling stocks, similar to a warehouse in buying and selling groceries. For example: at a certain time of year if there is a big demand for oranges, and the warehouse is getting low, they could raise their price and people would be willing to pay the higher price because they want oranges. There is a demand for them. If the oranges have aged, or if nobody wanted them for whatever reason and if they were sitting there not selling, then the warehouseman could lower the price in order to create a price level where people would want to finally buy.

## 2-What Makes Stocks Go Up?

This law of supply and demand, while simplistic, still answers most of what goes on in the marketplace everyday. As a matter of fact, to make it even more simplistic, let me share with you what my stockbroker frequently tells me. I know that he is very busy and when I call him about the market and/or a particular stock and it is up to $30, I usually ask the question "Well what caused that?" He is probably at that point in time typing away to get the stories or related information about the stock so he can give me a good answer. But while he is doing this he has this cute little answer he gives in a non-committal way. He says "More buyers than sellers." Within that simple statement are deep implications. Conversely when stocks go down he answers, "More sellers than buyers."

Many years ago when I was teaching real estate seminars and other aspects of wealth accumulation from maintenance to retirement, I would frequently tell people that one of the keys to wealth is to own things that other people want to own. I am sure that anyone reading this has owned something that has no value to anyone else. It could be an old car in the garage. It could be a 20-year-old mink coat. It could be a host of other things you have laying around the house. They have no value because nobody else wants them.

The way to accumulate wealth is to constantly accumulate things that other people want. In those instances I was primarily talking about real estate. We would discuss the areas of town; we would think hard on the type and size of houses; and also look at the quality of the house—how well it would hold up over the years—and then come to a conclusion that there is a certain type of property that could be purchased at the current time, which, in the near future and in the far out future, would probably still be in demand by a lot of other people. If that area of the town grows, say, as the population grows, or as improvements are made to the property, then additional demand will be created and the investment will pan out and have the highest likelihood of staying profitable. But, if we buy real estate in a bad area of town, or buy a horrible property that is not only hard to maintain but virtually impossible to make profitable or improve upon, then our investment is probably not going to pan out because we have something that not too many other people want.

As we turn to the stock market it is substantially the same wealth principal, yet obviously in a different arena. One of the keys to wealth accumulation, especially if you want to do it in a little bit more rapid manner, is to buy stocks that a lot of other people want.

There are different types of stocks, let me make a quick list:

1. Cyclical—these are stocks that either go through a two or three year cycle of expansion and bust, or a cycle completed a lot faster, say within calendar quarters throughout the year.

2.  Value stocks—these stocks, compared to the other stocks in their sector or in the market place, are low priced. One calculation for this low price is the price to earnings ratio, or P/E. P/E basically determines how many dollars we are spending for one dollar of earnings. This is a barometer of how well the company is doing because we can get the P/E on any stock and determine if the stock is undervalued or over valued. Other measuring sticks would be the debt ratio, the dividend yield, and the book value of the company. Basically these would be categorized under the fundamental approach to looking at stocks, which is a way of measuring the health of a company.

3.  Growth Stock—I would put virtually all value stocks under the growth stock category, but there is a separate category for pure growth stocks. These are the ones that in any industry have the highest likelihood of increasing in price, because the company has the highest likelihood of being profitable not only now but also in the future. These are companies that have a great product that is in its early stage of development and marketing. Other companies are expanding into competitive areas they have not formerly been. Other companies are dominant in their field, and virtually have a monopoly-like aspect to them.

    Many mutual fund companies and financial professionals specialize in these growth stocks and they are constantly putting out lists of them. They are not only easy to find, but they are easy to study. I love growth stocks, but as you can tell from the last five or six years in particular, there has been such a rapid increase in business innovation that some of these stocks have faltered as of late. What seemingly were great growth stocks have not grown at all and some have even declined in value. Please see chapter five.

4.  Income stocks—some stocks are purchased for the dividends. Dividends are usually paid out on a quarterly or annual basis. Some large companies have *MIPS*, or *Monthly Income Preferred Securities.*

Underlying all four of these approaches to me is a fundamental principal of finding value, or bargains. I go looking for stocks that have the highest likelihood of going up so I can answer my son's question that the law of supply and demand takes over and if I want to get in the way of a large demand, then I simply need to look for great companies that have current cash flows, and the highest likelihood of continuous cash flows with the probability of earning large amounts of money. All in all the most basic fundamental aspect of the stock market in increasing the value of any company, is not just earnings but the anticipation of future earnings.

# 2-What Makes Stocks Go Up?

*"The current stock price is based on the anticipation of future earnings."*     *–Wade Cook*

You can take any one of the four types of stock listed above and fit the particular stock you are looking at into a test model. You can pose the following questions: is this company going to make money? And, as the company starts to make money and the stock starts to move up, will that create a momentum in and of itself? Will there be a likelihood that many people will be attracted to this stock and want to get involved and own it?

One of the core aspects of all of this is a company that has a product that is easy to explain. They need a management team who can concisely put forth what the company is doing and then run the company at maximum efficiency. We don't have to go in and run these companies, but we can sure look at them and analyze them. Part of this is a fact which does not readily meet the eye: that is the float.

The stock float is simply the number of shares issued and outstanding. In certain SEC guidelines, even outstanding options or warrants to buy the stock need to be included. Let me put this in perspective. New investors often ask this question: "If this stock is $40 and that stock is $30, isn't the $40 stock better?" OR, "Isn't the company with the $40 stock better? " This question just shows a lack of understanding. Yes, it may be a better company, but the price of the stock is irrelevant to the discussion. The $40 stock may be in a company with 10,000,000 outstanding shares on the float. The market capitalization of the whole company is four hundred million dollars. The $30 stock is in a company with 1,000,000,000 (one billion) shares outstanding. Its market cap is thirty billion dollars.

The price of the stock, in-and-of itself, gives an incomplete picture. It can only be used in math formulas to determine other things, like the P/E ratio.

The float would signify not just the amount of stock that the insiders or founders own, but the complete public float. Even though there is a high demand for the stock, with so much supply (for example, in the billions of shares) the demand is overwhelmed by the huge amount of stock available. The stock hardly moves at all with good news or even bad news.

A few years ago Dell Computer (DELL) did multiple stock splits. Seemingly they were doing stock splits about every twelve months and it felt like they were going to continue to

**DELL**

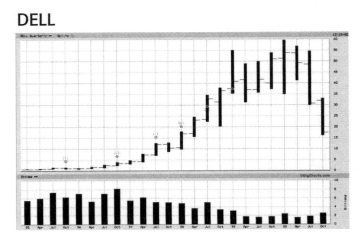

do so. Not only were stock splits becoming popular—I mean by that, the splits themselves were a specific reason for buying the stock—but DELL was very prominent in the industry with all types of advertising in many mediums and with a great business plan. They also had a charismatic leader and good management team and it seemed like it would never end. But as we all know "this too shall end."

Notice this five-year period of time in the chart. DELL stock, after it did the split, would run back up to near its pre-split high. But remember that if there are 300 million shares of stock before a 2 for 1 stock split, there are 600 million shares after the split. After the next 2 for 1 stock split there are 1.2 billion shares and after the next 2 for 1 stock split there are 2.4 billion shares. (These numbers are a general example and do not relate to Dell.) Now the situation changes. People have stocks that have doubled and tripled and quadrupled in price. They have so many shares in their portfolio, that they can sell some and still maintain a large position. There is so much supply and not enough demand to absorb all the new stock.

Each time Dell did the split, even though it went up, the stock price did not go up as high as the previous high before the stock split. As a matter of fact you see a down trending high from one split to the next. Each time it did a split the highs would continue to be lower. This is about the time when we determined that this game was over. I had made a lot of money on several of these stock splits but when we saw this huge supply and the stock not recovering to its previous highs, it told us there were too many shares on the float to be absorbed.

# *JUST FOR LAUGHS:*

# *INVESTMENT IDEA*

If you had bought $1,000 worth of Nortel stock one year ago, it would now be worth $49.

- With Enron, you would have $16.50 of the original $1,000.

- With Worldcom, you would have less than $5 left.

- If you had bought $1,000 worth of soda pop one year ago, drank all the pop, then turned in the cans for the 5 cent deposit, you would have $107.

- Based on the above, my current investment advice is to relax, have a soda and recycle.

# 3

# Looking for Good Stocks

The most frequent question I am asked at my seminars around the country is how to find good stocks. I teach at a lot of high schools, either in their business or their math classes, or sometimes I get to speak to the whole assembly. Those young students more than likely are not going to be able to play some of the more advanced cash flow strategies like option spreads and going long on calls and puts. But, they can buy certain amounts of stock. One young man I talked to worked at Safeway and he was able to buy about 10 shares of Safeway stock every month. Over the couple of years that he had been doing this the stock had almost doubled in value. I hear stories like this all of the time. He had an inside track because he worked there.

Many other people look at the stock market and it bewilders them because there are so many choices. That is the purpose of this chapter, to narrow down and help all of us decide which stocks are worthy of our attention and our investment. I think one of the most fundamental ways of looking at the stock market is to view each company as if you personally were looking at buying the company yourself. Now some of these companies are in the billions of dollars, so most people cannot go out and buy even 1/10th of a billion-dollar company. However, we can buy the gas station on the corner, or the convenience store a couple of miles away.

Let's look at buying a particular business in our neighborhood. We need to look at the health of the business, and use whatever measuring sticks are available. A common term is "show me the books." This means you would look at the income and the expenses of the company to determine if is has made a net profit, will continue to make a net profit, and further develop its sustainability. In real life, because of the complexities of the tax code, earnings and net profits are not necessarily related.

For example, in a publicly traded company the net profit would be calculated before taxes. The earnings are usually calculated after taxes. So when you talk about earnings per share, this is the net earnings of the company minus the taxes and other charge-offs, etc. These earnings of a particular publicly traded company would then be used to calculate the earnings per share, or the P/E. (See P/E calculations later).

Back to our little corner grocery store: we would want to know if it has the ability to sustain its current earning capacity. When we buy a company we are basically trading our cash for a glorified job. A lot goes into that decision. Our purchase buys the future of that business, not the past. The past is only one indication, or factor, to use in the decision-making process.

## Each Business Has Its Own Problems

One of my most common topics in my business seminars is to help people find a business that has the kind of problems that they like to deal with. Every business has unique problems. If you like people problems then you might want to have a company that deals with people type situations. If you like mechanical problems, and are good at solving mechanical problems, you might want to buy a car garage and manage and/or work as a mechanic there. If you like hardware and software computer problems, then find a type of company that matches your ability to fix these types of problems. In short, pick a company that you would have an affinity for, just based on what problems you enjoy solving. It would be silly to buy a business that you do not know anything about and have no desire to learn anything about.

Let's relate this to bigger companies in the stock market. These companies also have business plans, a theme or a mission that is easy to decipher. However, some companies' business plans are very complex. Their product or service is meant to fill a need, solve a problem and make people's lives better. Some companies are "conglomerates" and have dozens or even hundreds of different subsidiaries like General Electric (GE), TransAmerica and even CISCO (CSCO). Even General Motors (GM) owns numerous other businesses that feed into the main business.

The question you need to ask is, "do I understand how this business makes money?" Sometimes when you look at a company and read their financial statement, you still have that lingering doubt, or that continuing question of "what is it that they do?" "How do they make money?" The business plan or mission of the company should be easily recognizable. If you do not understand what a company does to make money then you probably should steer away from it.

## Debt

When we buy a neighborhood business, we usually own it lock-stock-and-barrel and have some incurred debt in order to acquire the business. But, just like most small businesses have long-term and short-term debt, so do large companies. I touted debt avoidance for years. Americans and American companies should avoid debt. Debt is a killer of business. In my own life the times that we have struggled as a business were when we had excessive debt. Simply put, because debt is the killer of business, even if you have a company that is viable and has the potential for making good money, excessive debt can ruin that company.

Our company for example, has struggled the last few years, but relatively speaking we have not had a huge amount of debt. For years we had the philosophy that if we could not pay cash for something we did not buy it. We put $600,000 into a phone system and paid cash. We spent a million dollars on a computer system and paid cash. We avoided the high interest repayment expense. Summary: debt is a really good monitor for looking at the health and viability of a company.

There is a quick way to determine a reasonable amount of debt. It is not infallible and definitely not the only measuring stick. It is how much debt exists as a percentage of the market capitalization. Let's explore this: A stock is $30, there are 100,000,000 shares outstanding, therefore the total market cap is $3,000,000,000. Yes, three billion dollars. Your one hundred shares are a small part, but hey, you're glad to tag along.

What is a good debt ratio? There is no set answer. A side question: is the debt serviceable? Is the company current? Is the debt short-term (must be paid within one year), or long-term (usually secured and over one year)? Let's look at the simple answer without all of these other implications and ramifications. 30% maybe 40%. This means this company would have debt of $900,000,000, to $1,200,000,000. 40% of three billion dollars is 1.2 billion dollars.

Now, let's move up the percentage and see where your fear factor kicks in. What if the company had two billion dollars in debt? That's 60% of the stock price as debt. That's high. And think, some companies have debt of 80% and 90%. On the other hand, some companies have debt of zero percent, or 10% to 20%.

Let's make it more personal to you. Let's use 40%, which is not uncommon. Your $30 stock has $12 of debt against it. Are you okay with that? For me, I don't like debt over 40%. Once it gets above 50% to 60%, then it's just too scary for me. Any stockbroker can give you the current debt ratio.

Another way this debt is stated is a "times" number. This method is on most stock brokers' computers. They'll tell you the stock price is three times debt. Debt is $10 per share. Therefore $30 is three times $10.

Okay, let's put this in perspective and bring up a few more points. You want to own stock in a healthy company. You want the stock price to go higher. The debt is high, but guess what? That last $100,000,000 loan was taken out to build new factories because they cannot produce their FDA approved drug fast enough. Another company borrowed $40,000,000 to beef up their marketing campaign and expand their sales staff. All of these should increase sales and bring more profits to the bottom line. Debt could be good if all of these plans pan out. You see, everything ultimately comes down to management. Remember, "Bet on the jockey, not on the horse." Can this particular management team pull it off and repay the loan?

Next. Many times an event like buying another company, or acquiring new jets or gates for an airline, or two companies merging should be seen as good. The stock should go up. But, hold it! On the news announcement, the stock goes down. It might stay down for six months to a year or so. Why? Because most of these events are accomplished with debt. I know I have written this before, but today's stock price is the anticipation of future earnings, and if debt holds down earnings, or is perceived to do so, the stock price goes down now.

Debt is real. Future profits are "blue sky"—they are somebody's guess. The loan has to be repaid. Interest expense is real. Everything else is a hope and a dream. Now, a year later, sales are up. The debt is being paid down; the stock moves back up.

Debt is not the main weather vane. Earnings are. Debt is the rust that just may stop your weather vane from turning the right way. It could potentially bog things down. Let's hope management has some WD-40 handy.

## Asset Valuation

Back to the purchase of the convenience store down the street. Every business has assets. This one has an ice cream machine. The owner paid $6,000 but it's now worth $2,000. We're okay with this. However, he has an antique machine, which he picked up for $1,000, and it's now worth $5,000. This is a wild comparison to prove a point.

He paid $1,000 a few years ago and has been expensing it out. This means depreciating it. Big words for a basic report, but this is important. One would think that if you pay $1,000 for a business item that the $1,000 would show up as an expense. You would subtract it from income and adjust your profits down. You would have a lower net profit and therefore pay fewer taxes. "Not so fast," says the IRS, you can't take the whole $1,000 this year. You have to "spread it out." Equipment can be "depreciated" over three, five, or ten years, some even longer.

Back to the owner. He has written off $600. His adjusted cost basis is $400. That's how it's carried on his books. But, it's now worth $5,000. If he sells it he will have a $4,400 capital gain and more taxes to be paid. Before that, though, he carried it at $400 (and going down).

The importance of this discussion is dramatic when we see how a company carries assets on its book. I think we can all agree everything we buy goes up or down in value. Rarely does anything stay the same. MicroHard, Inc. spent $300,000,000 to acquire XYZ Co., another $100,000,000 in a stock swap for JKL Co., and $80,000,000 cash for DEF Co. Was the purchase or merger an outright purchase? Did they over pay? Have some of these companies gone up in value? Are some losers, therefore ready to go out of business?

Well, just about "yes" to all of these questions. The $300,000,000 XYZ Co. is now only worth $150,000,000. The $100,000,000 is now worth $1,000,000,000 and is set to be spun off. MicroHard might pocket over $800,000,000 cash and still own some of the new stock. Oh, and the $80,000,000 venture in DEF has gone belly up. Too bad.

The only issue here is how companies carry assets on their books. The following is excerpted from other books and internet site.

*This is my attempt to shed light on the process of expensing assets gone sour. First of all, let me restate some of the nomenclature of the current era. One can frequently read financial reports with the words, "one-time expense," or "one-time charge." Also used are expressions like, "non-recurring charge," and even "one-time write-offs" or "write-downs." A similar statement is "restructuring change."*

*This is simply a process of taking an investment and turning it into an expense. These investments are usually in the form of business purchases, as in Boeing buying McDonnell Douglas. Sometimes these investments are stock or partnership unit purchases in other companies. Once in a while these investments are in divisions or subsidiaries a company has started, still holds, or has spun off. Also of note is the term "blue sky," or someone's guess as to the value of an existing business or part of it. This term "blue sky" is often associated wit the value of employees—say, the business they create. News reports of 28,000 people being laid off may contain additional facts that the company is "taking a $200,000,000 charge for blue sky." One last charge or write-down could be from the discontinuance of a product line or the loss of a copyright or lawsuit.*

*All of the above "items" are carried on the company's books as some type of investment. It is listed in the financial section under assets. It could be "non-marketable securities," in the case of stock ownership in another company. It could be "real estate" or "business owned" in other cases.*

*One interesting side note with extensive dynamics is just how the asset is carried in relation to its real value. According to Generally Accepted Accounting Principles (GAAP), an asset is carried on the books at the cost (basis) or market value, whichever is less. This offends the sensibilities of most non-accounting types. "You mean the $1,000,000 apartment building, which has been depreciated to $800,000 but is worth $2,000,000 or more, can only be listed on the books at $800,000?" The answer: YES.*

*Adjustment to these asset values should be adjusted to each SEC filing—with each financial statement, so long as there is a substantial or noticeable change since the last filing. Let's explore this. Company A is a*

20% investor in Company B. Company A has purchased 5,000,000 shares of stock at $1 per share. It's been two years. Company B is doing great, but needs more money. The next offering (PPM) is for $20,000,000, but this time the shares go for $2 each. Yes, Company A's shares in Company B might now be worth $2 each, but they still have to be carried on the books at $1 each, or $5,000,000.

Now, let's go the other way. Company B is not doing too well. It needs more money. This time, shares (the same type) are offered at 50¢ each. Now, sadly, Company A's investment is reduced to this amount. It's a $5,000,000 investment is now valued at $2,500,000. We'll get to the other $2,500,000 in a while.

All of this is done, regardless of the fact that Company B goes public in one year and the stock goes out at $14 per share. Remember: Cost or Market—whichever is less

Let's return now and see how an investment, carried on the books under assets, becomes an expense. Then we'll explore the stock valuation and tax implications. There are two basic financial documents in every SEC filing. Yes, there could be hundreds of back-up documentation forms and pages, but these have a genesis in either the Income Statement (some might still call it the Profit and Loss Statement) and the Financial Statement. This Financial Statement, once again, lists assets and liabilities, and then the net worth at the bottom.

Once an asset has shrunk in value, or if either inside accounting or outside auditors feel that the asset is no longer viable, a decision is made to write it off. Quite simply, it disappears from the asset column (all or part of it) and finds its way to the expense side of the income statement. It is treated, pretty much, like any other expense.

Now, two things have happened. One, the company's net worth is less. Two, the company is now making less money. Let's explore this aspect first.

A $1,000,000,000 write-off could seriously reduce the current profit, or earnings of the company. Many people follow earnings. They base their stock valuations on earnings. It takes a savvy investor—ever a student of *the market—to read behind the headlines. For example, a few years ago JDS Uniphase (JDSU) had headlines reporting a "$7.9 billion" loss. The stock tanked. If you were to read the report, you would have read that it had operating income of 2¢ a share. "How," you ask, "can a company which is making money report a $7.9 billion loss?" Simple. They just wrote off $7.9 billion worth of investments purchases and "blue sky."*

*Boeing was set to announce fairly good earnings one quarter awhile back. The stock rose nicely over the previous nine months, but especially so in the two to three weeks before their earnings announcement. Then, suddenly, they announced a $280,000,000 charge-off—a non-recurring item—from their previous purchase of McDonnell Douglas.*

*Awhile ago, Microsoft announced quarterly earnings of only $1,200,000,000—a noble feat by any measuring stick. If you read on, however, you would have found a $1.3 billion charge-off for "poor investments." I guess some of their dot.com escapades didn't pan out—like who hasn't had bad dot.com investments? Are you getting these numbers? That's $2,500,000,000, in net earnings without the charge-off. And this $2.5 billion is after taxes.*

## Taxes And Write-offs

*Let's stick with the Microsoft example. $1,300,000,000 as an expense creates a $455,000,000 tax savings at a 35% tax bracket. That's money the company can use to expand and grow and further build shareholder value.*

*Oh, and if an expense is large enough, it could wipe out all the net income this year, create an NOL (Net Operating Loss), which can be used to offset net profits from previous years or in the future years. That's right! A loss could generate a return check from the IRS.*

*To recap: earnings are bad, the stock might go down; earnings are bad, there might be substantial tax savings. Do you see why it's so important to read further on in these news reports and try to ascertain the true health of the company?*

### String It Out Or Take It Now

*Obviously, not all investments a company makes are accomplished all at once. Likewise, a company's investments do not all go south simultaneously. Many companies write these bad assets off over a period of time, but there has been a dot.com fiasco of late, in epic proportions.*

*Everyone, even if not directly invested in by a company, has felt the high-tech downturn. Imagine now, that you're on the Board of Directors. You have the auditor's report and some of your investments don't look too hot. In fact, some are worthless. You know it's going to look bad so what do you do? First choice: string out the bad news. Take some now, some next quarter and if possible, some at the end of the year, or next year. Second choice: pile on the bad. Get the bad news out of the way. Take the hit now and get on with life.*

*As of late, many companies have taken huge write-downs. And while for some companies, these investment write-offs are complete, others are still holding some bad assets, while others have assets which haven't completely soured yet. These "one-time expenses" occur all the time. They have just been more pronounced lately.*

*Also note another phenomena waiting in the wings. Just because a company has written off an investment doesn't mean that it no longer owns the investments. It's carried on the books, at a new zero-basis. What if, just what if, there is a Phoenix? What if the asset can be sold, or the start-up eventually makes it? I know it's rare, but life has many mysteries. In this case the company re-books it as an asset (especially in the case of publicly traded stock) or claims the profits as income.*

## Blue Sky

Another aspect of looking at a small private business would be to look at the assets you are buying. Are they "blue sky assets" or are they "hard fixed assets?" Fixed assets are capital-type investments like land and buildings. Here, you would look at the machinery or equipment type assets, then the inventory assets and lastly the "blue sky assets." Every business for sale has some level of blue sky or basically what is considered as the owners equity. Again, what you are buying when you buy a business is a glorified job. You are looking at what the business will make.

Now, to further this discussion we need to talk briefly once again about price earnings ratios (P/E ratio). If you were to sell your small business, netting around $100,000 a year, you would contact a business broker or real estate agent and probably sell it for about one- to one-and-a-half-times net earnings. You might be able to get up to two time's net earnings on a good day. Further in your calculations, would be how much inventory you have, minus how much debt you have. If you have a small company netting $100,000 a year, you might sell that company for about $150,000. What this means is that someone is willing to give you $150,000 now for the potential earnings of your business.

You ask the question "Why not more?" One answer could be to ask another question: "Why should anyone pay more?" If they had $400,000 or $500,000 they would probably buy a better business than the one you have for sale. On any given day, a business will sell for what someone is willing to pay for it.

Taking your company public is a very expensive and difficult process. However, stock in a publicly traded company in your type of business is going for twenty times earnings. A small company netting $100,000 would in theory trade for around twenty times its net earnings—in this case it would be about $2 million, not $150,000. Twenty times $100,000 is $2,000,000. Look at this number another way: If you had $2,000,000 in a bank at 5% interest, you would earn $100,000. Investors are willing to buy stock in a company for about the same numbers. The risk is the stock could go down in value, but the hope is that it will go up. "Wow," you think: "I'd rather own 40% of a $2,000,000 company, than 100% of my private company."

You would own 40% of a $2 million company; or $800,000 as compared to $150,000. You can see why there is a tendency for a lot of small companies to go public from the owners' point of view. However, it does not mean that you as an investor should invest in every company that goes public.

Look at companies and put yourself in the driver's seat. Why? Because you are. A lot of things we will discuss throughout this section will come into play, but the long and the short of it is that people (you) buy stock in companies with good earnings.

## Book Value

Book Value is a determination of a company's value based on the break-up and sale of the components. The Book Value is easy to find out—just call your broker, or most good computer programs (stock search) will list this value. It is not uncommon for a company's stock to be trading at two to three times Book. Many are at eight and ten times Book Value.

Let's look at this a little more closely. I can't stress enough, though, that the listed Book Value is how the assets are being carried, according to GAAP, and according to those values as of their last Quarterly Filing. Take a look at how many banks have been buying up regional banks. Granted, banks have odd reporting requirements. They carry loans on their books a certain way. These loans, plus assets, make up their Book Value. Their stock is at $20, but the Book Value is at $24. Their stock is at a discount to Book Value. They are a target for a takeover. Conversely, another bank's stock is at $14 and the Book Value is $10—AND it's still a target. Maybe even more so. Why? Because the true value of its assets is larger in real life than how they're being characterized on their books.

...And finding out the Book Value is a start. Let's now explore what to do:

1) Do more homework. If we like the book value, and are considering investing, then look closer at their SEC filings. (www.edgar.gov).

2) Think whether or not they are a take-over candidate or not. What is someone else willing to pay?

3) If there is a great book value compared to the stock price, still determine the debt level. This may make it prohibitive to be taken over.

A few real life examples. At the time I wrote this chapter, Enron was in bankruptcy, Global Crossing also, and an American icon was there too, K-Mart (KM). Look at the book value of each one, as of March 18, 2002.

These values will change, but first let's explore K-Mart, probably the one with the highest likelihood of being reconfigured, bought out, merged, or in which assets will be purchased. In Bankruptcy nothing makes sense. The power-players (usually the debt holders) rule.

Look again at the stock price of $1.50 and a book value of <u>$11.00</u>. In many companies it's the complete opposite. A book value of $12 often supports a stock price of $30 to $50. And think—"cost or market, which ever is less." K-mart could have bought land and built a building back in the 1960's for $2,000,000. The property

**KM**

*As of this writing, K-Mart's January '01 year-end book value for the trailing 12 months was 11.73 per share*

## ENRNQ

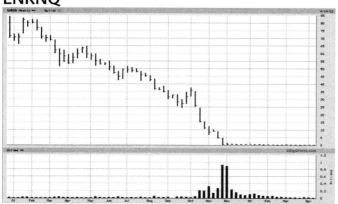

*As of this writing, Enron's January '01 year-end book value for the trailing 12 months was 11.40 per share.*

## GBLXQ

*As of this writing, Global Crossing's January-01 year-end book value for the trailing 12 months was 7.76 per share.*

is now worth over $10,000,000 with improvements. The reported book value could be substantially lower than the value in the real world.

But… And this will get your heart racing. The creditors take over, the court trustee configures a plan, and if K-Mart doesn't come out of Chapter 11, a senile judge could disallow all shareholder's interest, a new company formed, with key people and creditors owning 90% of the new stock and 10% going to raise new money. Maybe 100% of the old shareholders will be jammed into 5%. (That's right, five percent) of the new company.

This happened to me with another K—as in Circle K (the convenience store chain). We were wiped off the slate. Sometimes I like these bankrupt companies because the stock price goes up on news—good news and bad news—but not when they first go into bankruptcy or when they are coming out of bankruptcy. Too much going on that puts me out of control. You as the reader will have the luxury of hindsight to see how the K-Mart situation plays out.

*If one does not know to which port one is sailing, no wind is favorable.*          ~Seneca

*OUR PURPOSE IN LIFE SHOULD BE TO BUILD A LIFE OF PURPOSE.*

*WADE B. COOK*

# 4

# Follow Earnings:
# The Infamous P/E Ratio

Because earnings are so important for good choices in selecting great stocks, let's spend a little more time on this topic.

A P/E ratio is a formula. The stock price divided by a company's earnings (the back-slash is for division). Let's say you have a stock at $30 and they announce earnings of $1 per share. We can't do the math yet. Most of these announcements are made quarterly (10Q's). In fact three times the reports are quarterly, and the year-end quarter will also produce the full year's totals. These numbers can be found in the company's 10K. Let's go ahead and work the ratio but it will not be complete. For this calculation, let's pretend the $1 is the annual earnings per share. Yes, we're pretending. $1 of earnings is then divided by the current stock price and we get an earnings ratio of 30. If the stock price is $15, the ratio would be 15. If the stock price is $60, the P/E would be 60. This 60 is where a lot of companies on Nasdaq have their P/E ratios.

$$\frac{\$30}{\$\ 1} = 30$$

Let's stick with the $30 stock price—a P/E of 30. Not bad, but again, not totally true. In some way we have to mentally extrapolate this $1 and make it an annual number. Could we not use the three past quarters? Yes, but we own the future, not the past. You might think, if this company makes $1 per quarter times four, there would be $4 of earnings per share. Again, this might not be accurate. Rarely does a company have even quarterly earnings. The earnings per quarter are usually different. It usually goes something like this: first quarter $1, second quarter .75 cents, third quarter .75 cents and fourth quarter .50 cents. The total for the year is $3. I'm trying to keep this simple. Now do the division.

$$\frac{\$30}{\$\ 3} = 10$$

# 4-Follow Earnings: The Infamous P/E Ratio

A P/E of ten is a good number, as all the other stocks in this sector might have P/Es of 16, 18, or 28. When you read certain corporate reports, the wording can be very deceiving. You don't know if the writer is talking about trailing earnings, blended earnings, future, or forecasted earnings. But it's not that tough to get a handle on it. If you're online, using company info, or if you call your broker you will be given the trailing twelve-month earnings. And these ratios are updated instantaneously on their computer. They use the last SEC filed earnings report and a software program divides it, even as the stock price is moving. Look at the above ratio. If the stock moves to $33 (with year-end earnings at $3), then the P/E would be 11. A P/E ratio is good for determining a) if the company is making money and b) how it compares to other stocks?

A perspective: Historically, all stocks have had an *average* P/E of 15.5. Today's P/Es are a little higher. On any given day the 30 combined stocks on the DOW, or DJIA have an average P/E of 19.2, or 19.6. We usually just round off to 20. NASDAQ has averages in the mid 30's and 40's. New high-flying companies and companies which are expanding could carry P/Es of 60 to 90.

Most of you have heard of the DOT.Com Bust. (In California they sometimes refer to this as the DOT-BOMB). In fact, only 9% of Internet companies failed. 91% made it in some shape or form. Even if your favorite company made it, the stock may have gone from $280 to $18. Some P/Es were at 904, or 109. I saw one at 2,200. That is the bubble that had to bust. Expectations of earnings growth were unreasonable.

You see, everything returns to the norm. If a stock is trading at a high multiple, like 904 <u>times</u> earnings, one of two things has to happen:

1) The earnings grow to justify this high stock price, <u>or</u>

2) The stock price will fall and get back in line with where it should be. What I call the "norm."

One way to be careful is to look for great companies with low P/Es. Let me give a perspective on this from a cab driver's point of view. I learned awesome lessons of life and finance as a cab driver. Those thirteen months served me well.

A few years back I used AOL's P/E as an example in my seminars. It proved an important point. This was before the merger with Time-Warner. Its P/E was 608! I used the sale of a small business netting $100,000 and how a private sale would generate $150,000 to $200,000. If this company went public, and *if* the stock traded at 20 times earnings, or a P/E of 20, it would go out at $2,000,000.

Let's look at a P/E of 608. This means investors are willing to pay $60,800,000 to get at $100,000 of earnings. It's so ridiculous; it is a wonder how these stocks got so high. It was like TULIPBULBS.com. We as Americans paid astronomical prices for these stocks. They were way up in the stratosphere and something had to give. The bubble burst. Stock prices plummeted. Everything returns to the norm. We should learn to find solid growth, good earnings, reasonable expectations and great management.

The following lists will consist of several indices, or groupings of stocks. I offer this here so you can judge for yourself. Obviously these charts are a snapshot in time. You can get current information quite easily. Check out www.B4UTrade.com for many investor aids to help you.

## DOW JONES INDUSTRIAL AVERAGE (DJIA) — 30 stocks

| Ticker | Name | Price | P/E Ratio | AVERAGE P/E |
|--------|------|-------|-----------|-------------|
| AA | ALCOA INC. | 30.11 | 48.74 | 4.89 |
| AXP | AMERICAN EXPRESS CO | 48.16 | 20.92 | |
| T | AT&T CORP. | 20.15 | 18.07 | |
| BA | BOEING CO | 37.30 | 106.83 | |
| CAT | CATERPILLAR Inc. | 76.90 | 23.84 | |
| C | CITIGROUP Inc. | 49.44 | 16.53 | |
| KO | COCA-COLA CO/THE | 44.14 | 25.52 | |
| DIS | THE WALT DISNEY CO. | 21.50 | 39.81 | |
| DD | DU PONT | 40.50 | 21.82 | |
| EK | EASTMAN KODAK CO | 22.94 | 14.11 | |
| XOM | EXXON MOBIL CORPORATION | 38.48 | 14.93 | |
| GE | GENERAL ELECTRIC CO | 28.93 | 20.90 | |
| GM | GENERAL MOTORS CORP. | 43.54 | 8.96 | |
| HPQ | HEWLETT-PACKARD CO | 25.50 | 30.42 | |
| HD | HOME DEPOT Inc. | 35.50 | 19.46 | |
| HON | HONEYWELL INTERNATIONAL Inc. | 28.77 | N/A | |
| IBM | INTL BUSINESS MACHINES CORP. | 93.20 | 21.19 | |
| INTC | INTEL CORP. | 30.80 | 53.54 | |
| IP | INTERNATIONAL PAPER CO | 39.14 | 123.63 | |
| JNJ | JOHNSON & JOHNSON | 49.79 | 23.38 | |
| JPM | JP MORGAN CHASE & CO | 36.44 | 24.73 | |
| MCD | MCDONALD'S CORPORATION | 24.48 | 29.31 | |
| MRK | MERCK & CO., Inc. | 49.71 | 15.49 | |
| MSFT | MICROSOFT CORP. | 28.78 | 28.86 | |

| | | | |
|---|---|---|---|
| MO | PHILIP MORRIS COMPANIES Inc. | 44.90 | 7.95 |
| PG | PROCTER & GAMBLE CO | 95.50 | 23.64 |
| SBC | SBC COMMUNICATIONS Inc. | 21.70 | 9.46 |
| UTX | UNITED TECHNOLOGIES CORP. | 83.21 | 17.70 |
| WMT | WAL-MART STORES Inc. | 58.95 | 30.83 |
| MMM | 3M CO | 74.52 | 25.89 |

NASDAQ. We have taken only a random selection of the 100 NASDAQ stocks. For the most part, we selected every fifth listing; however since a few had no earnings, we then selected the next closest well-known company on the list with a P/E. These companies include: Genzyme, Immunex, Microsoft and Yahoo!. These one hundred NASDAQ stocks trade in a trust (SPDR) known as the Q's (ticker QQQ).

| Ticker | Name | Price | P/E Ratio | AVERAGE P/E |
|---|---|---|---|---|
| AMZN | AMAZON.COM Inc. | 58.30 | N/A | 136.83 |
| AMAT | APPLIED MATERIALS Inc. | 21.00 | N/A | |
| BGEN | BIOGEN Inc. | 38.90 | 29.19 | |
| CEPH | CEPHALON Inc. | 46.76 | 14.75 | |
| CTAS | CINTAS CORP. | 42.23 | 27.55 | |
| CMBT | COMVERSE TECHNOLOGY Inc. | 19.45 | N/A | |
| DELL | DELL COMPUTER CORP. | 35.82 | 35.89 | |
| ESRX | EXPRESS SCRIPTS INC-COMMON | 58.20 | 22.42 | |
| GENZ | GENZYME CORP-GENL DIVISION | 49.69 | 44.93 | |
| IMNX | IMMUNEX CORP. | n/a | 58.38 | |
| IVGN | INVITROGEN CORP. | 62.86 | 50.73 | |
| MXIM | MAXIM INTEGRATED PRODUCTS | 44.80 | 49.51 | |
| MSFT | MICROSOFT | 28.78 | 28.86 | |
| NVDA | NVIDIA CORP. | 16.90 | 74.77 | |
| PSFT | PEOPLESOFT Inc. | 20.72 | 32.41 | |
| RATL | RATIONAL SOFTWARE CORP. | 14.66 | 48.87 | |
| SSCC | SMURFIT-STONE CONTAINER CORP. | 15.10 | 309.41 | |
| SNPS | SYNOPSYS Inc. | 28.19 | 36.07 | |
| VRTS | VERITAS SOFTWARE CORP. | 35.82 | 189.67 | |
| YHOO | YAHOO! Inc. | 42.90 | 118.83 | |

HIGH TECH STOCKS: Ticker: (XCI)

| Ticker | Name | Price | P/E Ratio | AVERAGE P/E |
|--------|------|-------|-----------|-------------|
| AMD | ADVANCED MICRO DEVICES | 13.40 | N/A | 44.74 |
| AAPL | APPLE COMPUTER Inc. | 24.35 | N/A | |
| AMAT | APPLIED MATERIALS Inc. | 21.00 | N/A | |
| ADP | AUTOMATIC DATA PROCESSING | 38.84 | 23.70 | |
| CSCO | CISCO SYSTEMS Inc. | 21.00 | 38.59 | |
| CPQ | COMPAQ COMPUTER CORP. | 10.28 | 114.22 | |
| CA | COMPUTER ASSOCIATES INTL Inc. | 24.67 | N/A | |
| CSC | COMPUTER SCIENCES CORP. | 41.11 | 16.55 | |
| DELL | DELL COMPUTER CORP. | 35.82 | 35.89 | |
| EDS | ELECTRONIC DATA SYSTEMS CORP. | 21.84 | 27.95 | |
| EMC | EMC CORP/MASS | 14.45 | 375.00 | |
| GTW | GATEWAY Inc. | 6.38 | N/A | |
| HWQ | HEWLETT-PACKARD CO | 25.50 | 30.42 | |
| IBM | INTL BUSINESS MACHINES CORP. | 93.20 | 21.19 | |
| INTC | INTEL CORP. | 30.80 | 53.54 | |
| MU | MICRON TECHNOLOGY Inc. | 12.54 | N/A | |
| MSFT | MICROSOFT CORP. | 28.78 | 28.86 | |
| MOT | MOTOROLA Inc. | 13.87 | 43.44 | |
| NSM | NATIONAL SEMICONDUCTOR CORP. | 37.91 | N/A | |
| NOVL | NOVELL Inc. | 6.14 | N/A | |
| ORCL | ORACLE CORPORATION | 12.28 | 30.05 | |
| PALM | PALM Inc. | 24.35 | N/A | |
| SGI | SILICON GRAPHICS Inc. | 1.16 | N/A | |
| STK | STORAGE TECHNOLOGY CORP. | 25.33 | 21.10 | |
| SUNW | SUN MICROSYSTEMS Inc. | 3.54 | N/A | |
| 5TXN | TEXAS INSTRUMENTS Inc. | 25.58 | N/A | |
| COMS | 3COM CORP. | 6.93 | N/A | |

# 4-Follow Earnings: The Infamous P/E Ratio

DRUGS (Pharmaceuticals) Ticker: DRG

| Ticker | Name | Price | P/E Ratio | AVERAGE P/E |
|--------|------|-------|-----------|-------------|
| AMGN | AMGEN Inc. | 67.14 | N/A | 43.29 |
| AZN | ASTRAZENECA PLC-SPONS ADR | 45.35 | 25.25 | |
| BMY | BRISTOL-MYERS SQUIBB CO | 25.34 | 20.93 | |
| LLY | ELI LILLY & CO | 62.04 | 28.61 | |
| FRX | FOREST LABORATORIES Inc. | 47.28 | 26.01 | |
| GSK | GLAXOSMITHKLINE PLC-ADR | 43.57 | 16.96 | |
| IVX | IVAX CORP. | 19.03 | 33.73 | |
| JNJ | JOHNSON & JOHNSON | 49.79 | 23.38 | |
| KG | KING PHARMACEUTICALS Inc. | 15.67 | 334.52 | |
| MRK | MERCK & CO., Inc. | 49.71 | 15.49 | |
| PFE | PFIZER Inc. | 30.67 | 42.20 | |
| PHA | PHARMACIA CORPORATION | n/a | 24.38 | |
| SGP | SCHERING-PLOUGH CORP. | 16.27 | 20.36 | |
| WYE | WYETH | 45.76 | 11.15 | |
| ABT | ABBOT LABORATORIES | 42.01 | 26.41 | |

INTERNET STOCKS, Ticker (IIX): As the Internet stocks formed a rather large list, we started with number two, and selected every third company on the list from that point on.

| Ticker | Name | Price | P/E Ratio | AVERAGE P/E |
|--------|------|-------|-----------|-------------|
| AOL | AOL TIME WARNER | 15.75 | N/A | 47.22 |
| BRCM | BROADCOM CORP. | 31.40 | N/A | |
| CIEN | CIENA CORP. | 6.48 | N/A | |
| DCLK | DOUBLECLICK Inc. | 11.64 | 95.30 | |
| EBAY | EBAY Inc. | 58.99 | 101.48 | |
| FDRY | FOUNDRY NETWORKS Inc. | 24.48 | 52.04 | |
| ITWO | I2 TECHNOLOGIES Inc. | 1.70 | 5.80 | |
| JNPR | JUNIPER NETWORKS Inc. | 17.60 | N/A | |
| NOVL | NOVELL Inc. | 6.14 | N/A | |

| | | | |
|---|---|---|---|
| PALM | PALM Inc. | 24.35 | N/A |
| Q | QWEST COMMUNICATIONS INTL | 3.59 | N/A |
| RSAS | RSA SECURITY Inc. | 17.02 | N/A |
| SEBL | SIEBEL SYSTEMS Inc. | 12.39 | N/A |
| SUNW | SUN MICROSYSTEMS Inc. | 3.54 | N/A |
| VRSN | VERISIGN Inc. | 14..85 | N/A |
| WBSN | WEBSENSE Inc. | 23.69 | 29.57 |

OIL AND GAS, Ticker (OSX)

| Ticker | Name | Price | P/E Ratio | AVERAGE P/E |
|---|---|---|---|---|
| BJS | BJ SERVICES CO | 33.71 | 37.29 | 47.91 |
| CAM | COOPER CAMERON CORP. | 45.14 | 57.60 | |
| GLBL | GLOBAL INDUSTRIES LTD | 4.80 | N/A | |
| GSF | GLOBALSANTAFE CORP. | 23.57 | 26.84 | |
| HAL | HALLIBURTON CO | 24.35 | 163.38 | |
| NBR | NABORS INDUSTRIES Inc. | 38.69 | 46.79 | |
| NE | NOBLE DRILLING CORP. | 34.50 | 26.20 | |
| RDC | ROWAN COMPANIES Inc. | 26.08 | N/A | |
| SLB | SCHLUMBERGER LTD | 50.47 | N/A | |
| SII | SMITH INTERNATIONAL Inc. | 37.47 | 44.02 | |
| TDW | TIDEWATER Inc. | 27.58 | 19.43 | |
| RIG | TRANSOCEAN SEDCO FOREX Inc. | 19.92 | N/A | |
| VRC | VARCO INTERNATIONAL Inc. | 16.84 | 22.23 | |
| WFT | WEATHERFORD INTERNATIONAL | 37.36 | 30.41 | |
| BHI | BAKER HUGHES Inc. | 30.73 | 52.86 | |

Have you seen opportunities? We could go on with Transportation, Advertising, Media, Travel, Food, Gold and too many other lists to mention.

Do your homework. Find value. Go for growth, but also learn trading formulas to generate more cash on the stocks you choose.

# 4-Follow Earnings: The Infamous P/E Ratio

## Earnings

Before we look at historically low P/Es formed in the marketplace right now, we first should discuss earnings and earnings per share, or P/E. The earnings of a company are its bottom line—they are the profits (after taking out dividends to shareholders of any preferred stock and after taxes).

To figure the earnings per share, we take the number of shares outstanding and divide it into earnings—hence we get earnings per share. Earnings are very important and are that which the company uses for dividend payouts, for investment in growth, for excess debt reduction. This figure is most often used by lending institutions for calculation of new debt paybacks.

Earnings should be from sales, and not from one-time phenomenons like the sale of a division, or a bad investment charge off. Many sources list earnings per share: Barron's, Investor's Business Daily, most local newspapers with financial information, and most computer on-line services.

In determining your stock purchases, you'll not only want current figures, but you'll want to know where the company has been. Does it have a history of increasing earnings? Did they increase, then slow down? We need to understand why the earnings per share are what they are.

The P/E is a very important number. I teach this from coast to coast. "When in doubt," I say, "follow earnings." Yes, the other measuring sticks are useful, but not as important as earnings. Think of it. Some companies just don't need a lot of assets to produce income. Some need a lot of assets and other forms of overhead.

The P/E is stated in terms that let us figure how much each dollar of our stock purchase is making. If the company's stock is trading at $80 and it earns $8 per share, it has a multiple of 10. If it's making $4 per share, it has a multiple, or P/E of 20; 20 times $4 equals $80. Another way would be to divide $4 into $80 and get 20, or a P/E of 20. In this case, what we're saying as investors is that we are willing to accept a 5% cash flow return (even though we may not actually receive the $4 or the $8); 5% of $80 is $4.

As I've said, P/Es are very, very important. We need to understand how to use them—and how to keep them in perspective. Let me give you a cab driver's take on this. A P/E stated as dollars just says how much you're paying for each dollar of earnings. If a company has a P/E of 42, you're paying $42 to get at one dollar of earnings. Likewise, if the P/E is 8, it means you're paying $8 to get at one dollar of earnings.

To decide if a P/E for a particular company is good, we need to: (1) pick a number we're happy with—say, "I'll buy any company with a P/E under 24," or (2) compare it to the market as a whole, or (3) compare it to stocks in the same sector, say high-tech or pharmaceuticals.

Let's look at (2), as (1) is self-explanatory. Standard and Poors has an index of 500 stocks. It's called the S&P 500. The combined P/E for these companies is in the thirties. You compare your company to this number and get a feel for how well it's doing.

You could also look at a smaller picture and compare your stock to other companies in the same business. There are so many variables in trying to get a handle on this information. One problem is that different reporting services use different time periods. For example, one newspaper may use "trailing 12 months" numbers to figure a company's P/E. It could be accurate to the last decimal, but is it appropriate to make a judgment solely based on where a company has been? Are we not buying the future—what a company will earn? Some figures are on projected earnings. If we only used this number, would that be complete—as if anybody knows what a company will actually earn? Yes, analysts (for the company or independent) can make their best guess, but they often fall short or overstate earnings.

Probably the best gauge would be to take a blend of the "trailing" and the "projected earnings." Many papers report it in some combination: say, trailing 12 and future 12 months. Many use six months back and six months future.

A couple of thoughts:

1. I have been such an adamant proponent of caution in buying stocks. So many investors get caught up in the hype of it all. Yes, I agree we all have to recognize the sensational and buy into it a little—but very little. "Follow earnings, follow earnings," I shout. People who have attended my seminars and even some of my employees have drowned me out. Let me give an example by way of a story.

   Iomega (IOM) is a high-tech software company. Years ago, the stock reached new highs and kept going up. They announced a stock split (I really like stock splits) and the stock soared. I got in at $14 and $16 and sold out at $30—a really nice profit. The stock went to $50. The hype was still in the air. I bought some $40 options, even though I knew the stock was way overpriced. I got out in days with a double on some and a triple on others. The stock went over $60 and headed for $80.

   Everyone was getting in—in both stock and options. I stopped. These numbers put the P/E over 100. I think it hit 120 times earnings at one time.

   At my seminars, in my office, and on W.I.N.™ (our Internet subscription service) I shouted, "I am not playing," "the bubble has got to burst," and "it's way too high." "Yes, I might miss out, but this high price can't be sustained." Also, I had been following Iomega for some time as a nice, little, volatile, covered call play, and this time around

I wasn't going for it. This all happened between the spring of 1996 and the fall of the same year.

It's hard to buy a stock at $50 when you were buying it for $14 just months before. Yes, its earnings were up a little, but not that much. The price was not justified.

It did another split. It was a 2:1. The stock split down to the $30 range and went back up to $40. This is when it was at 120 times earnings.

I held no positions, but everyone around me did no matter how hard I tried to stop them. I calculated the stock (based on earnings and a little hype thrown in) ought to be around $23 per share. I was throwing in about $10 per share for the "Internet hype" value. It was really a $12 to $15 stock.

This next part will seem like a joke, but it's true. When the stock was way up there, analysts for the company were trying to justify the high price. They actually made comments like: "The price isn't so high based on projected earnings three years from now." That's right, three years. Talk about hype. But tens of thousands of people bought into it.

Guess what? It fell to $30, then to $24—almost overnight it was at $16. Then it trickled on down to $13. It rebounded to $13$^1$/2 to $14$^1$/2 and I started jumping back in. I bought stock, options, and sold puts. I loaded up. I sold out within weeks, before and when it hit $27.

I'll play this type of stock a lot, but not when the price is too high. One of the questions you must ask is this: what must the company do to sustain this price? The hypesters that run up a stock are gone; and it could take years to recover from buying too high. Be careful! Follow earnings!

2.  The market is crazy, and if not totally wacky, at least hard to understand. This example has played out recently in scenario after scenario. Here's a typical example: a stock is at $60. An analyst (someone with what kind of education? What kind of real-world experience in running companies? What kind of motivation?) Projects that in the next year the company will earn $3 per share. He/she calculated this by taking numbers supplied by the company, et cetera, et cetera and putting the numbers through some kind of filter—possibly what other companies in the same field are saying or doing, and comes up with the $3. This is a P/E of 20 and not bad for this sector. He/she recommends the stock as a buy. Not a strong buy, just a buy, and thousands of investors

and funds start to buy. The stock goes up to $62 on this recommendation, but within weeks it's back down to $60.

Let's thicken the plot a little with more information. Last year the company earnings were $2.90 per share. For this type of business this was a nice profit. The year before it was at $2.40 per share and the year before that it was $1.50 per share. It has had a nice increase. Time passes and the actual earnings are $2.97 per share. The analyst was off 3¢ and the stock falls to $52, dropping $8 off its value. You think I'm joking, but I can show you a long list of this same story played out repeatedly.

The company is profitable, it's growing, it's earning millions—more than the previous year-but alas, the stock gets killed.

*AS A GENERAL RULE THE MOST SUCCESSFUL MAN IN LIFE IS THE MAN WHO HAS THE BEST INFORMATION.*

*BENJAMIN DISRAELI*

# 5

# Trader vs. Investor/Buy and Hold is a Strategy Whose Time has Come and Gone

Let's discuss whether you are an investor or a trader. There is a world of difference between the two. An investor would be considered a "right-term" person. A trader is someone who is using the stock market for a more immediate reward. In real estate I purchased some rental properties to hold for four to ten years. But I made bigger money, especially at the beginning of my career, in short term plays. By that I mean; buying a house on Monday and fixing it by Tuesday or Wednesday, putting it up for sell on Thursday, and hopefully closing by the next Monday or Tuesday. I became very good at this by only purchasing properties that I could turn over quickly.

In the stock market there is a similar method. You look for short-term trades to generate income. This is a business type income. I have often said on radio and TV shows that we need to treat the stock market like a business. If you do so, you will be considered a "trader." One side benefit is that all the expenses of trading would be expensed out or tax deductible if you meet the requirements. Another potential side benefit would be that you would hopefully make enough money with short-term trades (meaning three-day to three-month trades) to pay your bills each month and have enough to take home as well as enough to put into slightly longer "right-term" trades, or move away from the market to real estate, oil, or other investments.

Yes you can be an investor and a trader at the same time. You could dedicate part of your money to each enterprise. One is a very active enterprise, which requires an active involvement; the other requires a passive involvement. Nevertheless each one requires its own level of expertise; each type requires a certain amount of homework and dedication to know the investments you are holding for each purpose.

"Buy and Hold" *can* work if given 30 years or more, but I feel that there is such a better way. Yes, position trading is more work, but the results are definitely worth the effort. The hold period must be appropriate. It must fit your risk tolerance, your own particular stage in life and your own cash flow needs. You can get your money to work harder as you learn to deploy money the way you would in any other business. Trading is a business—a business that can support your family. All you have to do is change your expectation level and learn how to "work" your money better. The past correction in the marketplace, seen as risky by some, provided great opportunities for others. It provides investment opportunities, as well as trading opportunities.

These two strategies are symbiotic. As you develop skills as a trader you will learn to choose better investments. Conversely, the study and search for good investments will net many trading opportunities. To get good at both methods we need to find, study, practice and work each formula and then find stocks or options to fit the formula.

## Trade Suitability

A good stockbroker can make or break an investor, especially a beginning investor. I have often said *"one computer can take the place of 50 men, but no amount of computers can take the place of one good man."* Obviously this refers to women as well since many women are entering this profession.

A stockbroker is like a coach. This comparison cannot be complete, but there are enough similarities to bring up a worthwhile discussion. A coach ascertains where his players are. What their skill level is. How fast they learn. How proficient they are at connecting the dots in general, and down to particulars. A coach brings out the best in each player, recognizing how that player fits into the team. A coach knows teaching methods: he knows which ones will work for each player. A coach knows the opponent-their strengths and weaknesses. A good coach sees the whole battlefield.

In many areas of our lives, I suggest that we have to be the coach *and* the quarterback, and *not only* the coach on the sidelines, but also the coach up in the box. A wise person learns what his responsibilities are and what the responsibilities are of those around him. During one of my seminars I mentioned to my audience that when you look in the mirror, you are "You, Incorporated." You are your own corporation; you are the president, vice-president, secretary and treasurer. You are the Board of Directors. You define your mission in life. You set in motion everything that is going to happen. You are the one dealing with all the situations, pondering possibilities, and seeing them through to completion.

In the other areas of life, we have the ability to surround ourselves with proficient people. In the stock market, you can surround yourself with people who are proficient at doing trades: people who are good at the "how-to's."

Often times I have discussed priorities and the importance of setting right priorities. While I am not big on setting goals, I am definitely big on setting priorities and doing the best thing that I should be doing at that particular time. In life, quite often people try to divert us from that which is truly important. Many people are not successful because they are constantly diverted. The real question is: "are the *how-to's* more important or are the *why-to's* more important?" This leads me to a discussion of leadership and management. I have heard it said that a manager is a person who does things the right way, a leader is a person who does the right things. Many people are good at doing things the right way. This can be sheet rocking or working with sheet metal, or any other business or career. To me management is knowing the "how-to's." But if we seriously want to achieve greater success, we need to be a leader, especially a leader of our own lives. Leaders know the "why-to's" and do the right things.

A manager knows how to conduct stock market trades in the most effective manner. A leader makes sure that the right trades are being done. A leader makes sure that everything is kept in perspective and the overall financial goal is well thought out and effectively implemented. Most of us do not have the luxury of being a leader all of the time. We are often called upon to be a manager and a leader simultaneously. For example, a simple thing like driving a car: a leader makes sure a car is going to the right place, a manager makes sure it is driven safely to that place. In many cases we are both a manager and a leader.

When it comes to investing and trading in the stock market, notably at first, we may need someone else on our team who acts as a leader. Until we know what we need to know about particular trading styles, we might have to call upon our stockbroker to help us determine the direction. Later, when we have become more adept at the "operating at my highest level" concept, we can just use the stockbroker to conduct and perfect certain trades the right way. But until we reach this point, we are going to cross back and forth between the leader and management roles.

This chapter is dedicated to the beginning investor, and at a certain level, the intermediate investor. I want to bring up points which all investors can use. I offer the following information on working your accounts better.

## Filling Out the Forms

When you go to a stock brokerage firm to set up an account, they will give you several forms to fill out. They want to know all about your financial situation. They also want to know what experience you've had with different types of trades. They will ask you which type of trades you wish to conduct in the account. You will then sign your name at the bottom of the form.

Their trade suitability department will go over your application and then determine what types of trades they will allow you make in your account. Most brokerage firms will allow you to buy stock and mutual funds and bonds. Another level of trading would be options, for example, long call options and long put options, which means that you actually own them. Another level, which might be the 2nd or the 4th item on the page, will be writing covered calls. Possibly the last item will be selling puts, usually listed as selling "naked puts," or selling "uncovered puts."

If you are a new investor, one with little experience and one without a large amount of money, they will allow you to do only a few types of trades. If you have a lot of money, but little experience you also will be limited. If you have a lot of experience and a relatively small amount of money, you will probably be allowed to do the trades, but many brokerage firms today will not even take on an account unless an individual has a large amount of money. For example, some accounts require $25,000 of available cash to do spreads and naked puts (this is one of my favorite strategies). It definitely is a bullish strategy. It should not be used in down markets, or with a down trending stock, but it is a way of capturing profits now by taking on the responsibility to have a stock put to us if the stock is below a certain price). Many brokers see this as too much risk exposure; therefore they require more cash.

Whether you use stocks or the more leveraged options, you need to develop a style that fits you. A wise stockbroker can help immensely. This style should deal with the following four aspects of trading:

1) Is it learnable by you? Do you understand how it works? Are you aware of the ins- and-outs? Do you know when to use this particular strategy, when not to, and when to exit each trade?

2) Is your broker up on it or does he/she just know about it? Maybe you should simulation trade with them.

3) Is the strategy too risky for you? Is the risk acceptable compared to the potential reward, or possible loss?

4) Your time is important. Does this style require constant monitoring or can you put it in place and let it ride?

Let me pose three diametrically opposed points of view, or ways of investing:

## *"RISK A LITTLE TO GAIN A LOT"*

### *OR*

## *"RISK A LOT TO GAIN A LITTLE"*

### *OR*

## *"RISK A FAIR AMOUNT TO GAIN A FAIR AMOUNT"*

Of course you'll probably say, risk a little to gain a lot, but there is oh so much more! Sometimes you risk a little but gain nothing. Sometimes you put a lot of your money on a particular stock hoping to gain a few dollars; but you find your stock doubling in six months.

There are two basic "securities" you can use: stocks (ownership in equities), or options—a right to buy or sell a stock at a fixed price, on or before a certain date. Options allow you to "leverage" in and only put up part of the money. They are low cost. Yes, they also limit your risk, but still should be used sparingly, as they expire. You buy time, and if the stock doesn't move within that time frame, you will lose. You should make sure you understand options. Fortunes are made, fortunes are lost. Also if you're going to trade options, only work with an experienced stockbroker who has been around the option block a few times.

Stocks, on the other hand, are less volatile than options; and while the quick profits are not there, neither is there an expiration date. If you make a mistake and buy a stock too high, or if the stock goes down, time will often bail you out.

Back to our broker. I really like this questioning process. I believe that our stockbroker should be a really good tactician, very proficient at keeping us out of trouble and helping us see things we don't see. When you read the first paragraph or two of this trade suitability section, you will see my analogy of what a coach does. From this, determine what it is you want your stockbroker to do.

The brokerage firm calls this "trade suitability." This means determining if the type of trade is right for you. As you grow in expertise and competence in any particular strategy and especially as your account starts to grow, you will be able to add to your repertoire of available strategies. But, at the beginning, what you will be able to do in your account might have some severe restrictions. To me this is acceptable.

Hopefully your coaches/brokers in the stock market will do several of the following:

1) They bring deals to the table. They will learn what you are looking for and spend time finding stocks and options that fit the types of trades you hope to do.

2) They will keep abreast of what is going on in the market place. They are good at connecting-the-dots and seeing announcements and pre-announcements as well as becoming efficient at the anticipation of news announcements.

3) They like, indeed might I say love, being a stockbroker. They like the mechanics of conducting good trades.

4) They have paid for extra software programs or computer systems to make sure they are getting trades, not only in a timely manner, but also at good fill prices. These software programs can cost way over $1,000 a month. Most large brokerage firms will not pay for their new stockbrokers to have access to this level of trading. They may think they are really good, but they do not have experience with the high tech gadgetry that is available in this business. If you have a new retail stockbroker, they may be very limited on what they can do.

5)  They love teaching. I know this sounds strange, but we all need to continually be in the educational mode. The target for making profits in the stock market is always shifting. A wise person realizes this but also surrounds himself with people who have the same realization and hopefully people who are very good at explaining things. That is my point: some people might know something but do not know how to convey knowledge about it. Other people are very good at bringing their customers up to speed and educating them in such a manner that everyone is on the same page.

6)  They will not do unauthorized trades. You can give them authorization, and might I add in writing, to conduct certain trades up to a certain dollar amount. You could also do those trades yourself by putting buy orders and sell orders when you cannot be accessible.

7)  They have a great reverence for the stock market. They have been through good times and bad times and know that sometimes making profits in the stock market is just as much an art as it is a science.

## Seven Reasons "Buy And Hold" Doesn't Work

There are seven major reasons and numerous minor reasons why "Buy and Hold" is a flawed strategy. As you read these I ask that you ponder your own situation. Yes, at the end of this chapter, I'll give a great new way to succeed at all of these methods, but you need to find yourself. You need to figure out what you're going to do with this new information. You need to find a better way for you. My general comments have to filter down to your specific situation. The seeds of your future success will be found in the soil of the problems I'll introduce.

1)  SELLING INVESTMENTS FOR THE FUTURE. I've always had a problem with people selling things which they don't own or use. Stocks are the same. We're always getting sold the next "hot stock." Once the brokerage company's allotment is gone, they're on to the next deal. That's the way they operate. They get commissions and can't pay their bills without selling. We should be careful not to buy into the hype. Let's buy their $14 IPO and get out at $20—not wait for it to go to $100.

OR, let's sit it out. They are selling an investment that will do its thing out sometime over the rainbow, when they won't be around to be responsible for it.

*"It's like the Wizard of Oz. You learn that the Big Wall Street Guys are hiding behind the curtain, peddling a contraption to generate enough noise and sound to be convincing enough to keep you afraid and away from the truth."*
                                                                    *– Tim W., VA*

Think of it. They sell a stock to you at $70. It goes to $75, then sits for years at $50, with dips down to $40. They do damage control: "Remember, Fred, this is your hold position. We have a 25-year horizon on this stock. Oh, and it's for your retirement."

Let me get my cash flow jab in here. You can pay the bills, buy a new home, and buy all the "Buy and Hold" investments you want once you have built up your income. Concentrate on developing a system of cash flow enhancement first. One simple example: write covered calls on existing stock positions. Many of you, with a few hundred shares or a thousand shares of stock, are leaving untold thousands of dollars on the table every month. You could sell calls against your covered stock position, and generate cash.

2)   THEY DON'T PRACTICE WHAT THEY PREACH. We're asked to follow people who do not do what they tell us to do. The average mutual fund—you know, the ones with dozens of their managers traipsing on and off of CNBC—*changes 30% of its stock holdings every year.* They want to get their money in the way of money flows. They want to get a few of the next hot rising stocks. What about you? You *could* hold an investment way past its peak. Its start up and then the rise to higher values becomes past tense. The person who sold you the stock probably sold their position two years ago, and has been in and out of three other positions during that same time.

Every company exists somewhere along the road to oblivion. How many of the current Dow stocks (The Dow Jones Industrial 30) were there at the beginning? Only two, and they are substantially different companies now than when they first hit the list. If indices change their components all the time, *why don't you?*

Current companies last about 40 to 50 years. They are taken over, or sold. They sell off parts (spin offs). They mutate. They change. They become obsolete.

Many great companies have a four to five year growth span. Some companies find that the only way they can keep growing is to acquire other companies. Sometimes it works.

In the dot.com era this was the case. From Amazon.com to Cisco; from VeriSign to Microsoft; companies grew their revenues by acquiring other companies—never mind the fact that they were acquiring another "stupid business" idea. Lately, we've seen huge "charge-offs," or one-time expenses. Companies carried these purchases on their books as an asset and now expense it—move it to their income (profit and loss) statement. Tax savings are good, but earnings suffer and their stock prices go down.

*Again, a cash flow note: these earnings surprises (one time, out of the blue charge-offs) *create bounce opportunities.* Play stocks or options on the bounce.

However, on a more somber note: great leaps in wealth, especially leaps founded on a dream or on a thought that double-digit growth will continue forever, are usually followed by a major correction. Call it a bear market if you want. If all of these stocks surrender back part of their growth because of the "talk," and there is a lot of bad-mouthing going on, these companies, while already negative, pile on their bad investments, write them off, adding more fuel to the fire. It gets to be a self-fulfilling prophecy. *It will get better when a bottom is hit.*

Some stocks will never recover. Others will take years. Yes, earnings rise and fall, retreat and rebound—or not; and generally, stock prices follow earnings. From now on, I want to chase earnings, but even more importantly, I'll look for at least a three year history of earnings. I want to see earnings improvement. I'm also going to pay more attention to the Feds interest rate and monetary policies. If they raise rates, stock prices fall. If they lower rates, stock prices rise slowly and sporadically. Internal and external forces all have a certain power. The real question then is this: is the power real and is it sustainable?

3)  OUT OF CONTROL. For years, I've said, "You can't get rich being out of control of your money." Then I take my cash and buy Apple Computer stock and I'm out of control. A purchase of stock in Apple (AAPL) in 1989 at $19 would have seen the price go up shortly and then down and not recover to $19 until 1997. During this time, the market rose a lot. This is one of the greatest brand names in the world. It is also a classic blue-chip, "Buy and Hold" type stock.

J C Penney is similar. The stock was $20 in 1988, and $18 in 2001. Xerox (XRX) was $8 (adjusted for splits) in 1988 and $5 in 2001. Polaroid was over $20 in 1988 and 50¢ awhile ago. That's right, 50¢. Even Eastman Kodak, a great company, had stock in 1988 at $40 and is now just above $30. Wow, can we afford to keep following the advice of these so-called financial professionals?

And, think about dividends, a share of the company's profits. We also have no control over these. Up or down, paid out or held by the company—we're not in the Boardroom making decisions about dividends.

If you choose investments wisely and baby-sit them, you might be able to stay rich by being out of control, but you can't *get* rich being out of control. Wealth accumulation is a straightforward concept. I call it "cash to asset to cash." Take whatever cash you can get together, put it into an asset and get it back to cash as fast as you can. Money into cream and sugar into ice-cream and back to cash. If you don't do this well yourself, invest in companies that do it well. Far too many of us go cash to asset and forget the third step—back to cash. Then we sit and wonder "What happened?" We make it in our business and lose it in their business.

4) INNOVATION CREATES OBSOLESCENCE. The rapid addition of innovative improvements and the introduction of whole new hi-tech gadgets has seriously shrunk down the life of many companies.

In the hi-tech arena, names come and go in two to three years, not 30 to 40 years. Improvements have come at a dizzying speed. There is always some kid in a garage wanting to upset the status quo. We benefit as a society—our workplace and methods increase our output—but the particular stock we own in HI-GROUP Inc., might get pummeled by a new start up.

Many years ago, a good friend and fellow real estate instructor spoke of getting in the way of progress. He showed how downtown areas, once the busy and exciting part of the city, gave way to close-in building programs. Then the suburbs sprang up and became a life unto themselves. Some suburbs expanded and became cities of their own. His point was that the excitement is always on the fringe—like a fire set in the middle of a field. The fire burns outward and the heat is on the edge, usually way away from where the fire started.

Not until a new development, a sports arena, or hospital, or mall/condo complex is built in the central city will there be a revival. Then the whole process starts over.

Corning (GLW), the old "bowl in the oven" company is an example. It's an "old economy" company. A new fire was lit with "glass," or fibre optics. It got widely profitable again, but even now, with so much competition, and a slowdown in the hi-tech (speed of light transmission), its stock is having a tough time.

IBM has remade itself. Microsoft is into Internet Service, games, banking and too many other divisions to mention. In other places, banks are selling insurance and investments. Everyone is trying to rekindle their fire.

Our job is not that tough. We can read about and watch the new developments. We can see industry leaders emerge, buy into their industry, but sell when the tides change—in six months or two years. We need shorter-term horizons, because, just as companies peak, so do our investments.

5) MANAGERS CHANGE. We'll explore the changing nature of investments from two angles. The first, in regards to a particular company a), the second in regards to mutual funds b).

a) I've constantly espoused the investment philosophy of betting on the jockey, not the horse. An "A" management team, a team from the trenches, with experience and foresight, can take a "C" level product or service and make it a winner. If not, an "A" team will find a new product, fix the old problems, gather good people around them and in short, make it better.

A new team, hired on after a company has been devastated, could be just the fire needed to re-ignite a company's prospects. The problem is, most fixes take time, and often just as the problem is getting fixed, they move on. It's the cycle of life—from a stock market point of view. But note, it is a cycle and *change is the only constant!*

b) For years, I've shown how mutual funds change the character of their make-up. A growth fund mutates into a small-cap fund. A bond fund starts with overseas debt, then convertible debentures, then ends up with stock.

Usually, changes in mutual funds happen when there is a management change. Each person has his/her own personality, and the fund will eventually take on that personality. The question is, is it right for you? Tax ramifications are a concern. Do you want long-term growth (or attempts) as compared to high yield investments? What are your needs and will your needs change?

I suggest you build your own mutual fund. One benefit is to avoid fees and year-end surprises. If in doubt, buy SPIDERS® like SPY, DIA, QQQ and MDY. These are trusts which own stocks. Fees are relatively low and you can choose the sector, or general area of investments which you think will do the most good. Note that even these stocks form rolling patterns. You can better your portfolio by buying on dips and selling at peaks. Also, you can sell options on some of these stocks to generate cash against your stock position. That's cash in your account in one day.

The concern we should have is to better monitor our investments. Get rid of the losers. Let the winners run. Don't hold an investment past its prime. Now you must be thinking that this statement is an irony: Wade is criticizing change, yet telling us to change.

Yes and no. I'm not criticizing change. Trust movement. I am criticizing people who advertise for our money and then do different things with it. I like corporate changes. We just have to figure out if the change is good or bad. If the pros are constantly trying to better their hand, then why shouldn't we?

6)  NO "GREAT COMPANY" IS SAFE. Investment dollars always flow. Today, as always, money is looking for innovation. It doesn't mean that a $90 stock can't double and go up to $180, but what about a $9 stock that goes to $90? Look for great potential.

Debt also flows to its best use. Sometimes companies issue debt and so be it—people are happy with 4% of 14% returns—other money, though, wants a piece of the action—or equity.

The good ol' boy network of even 20 years ago has a whole new group of players. Mergers, acquisitions, buyouts and takeovers have new players. Money has always flowed to the bold. Look at little *Capital Cities, Inc.*, buying out the giant *ABC*. If you think your big solid blue chip company is immune from these attacks, it's time to rethink. Go for the bold.

Here's our problem: as small investors, the money moves behind our backs. We're the last to know. Big money is fickle and most big money investors are impatient. We finally hear about the great deal and jump in just as others are jumping out. Have you ever thought that the major brokerage firms' big advertising push to sell out a certain stock could be its way of unloading their position? There is no substitute to study, reading the news and watching trends.

7)  LONG-TERM CAN BE TERMINAL. We are not long-term people. Our personalities don't work like that. We move homes. We change jobs. We drive different cars, buy new clothes, and change hobbies. Just as we change individually, the whole country changes.

Popular products come and go. Styles change. New cars are introduced. Vacations are different. Food is different. And everything I've written about in these two paragraphs provides products or services sold in publicly traded companies.

We can invest, but we can also *trade* in change. Invest means to "gain ownership"—again, for the most part we're out of control. Trade (*not* day trading) means to capture profits by getting money in the way of movements. I call this "position trading."

Let me share briefly some of the benefits I see in position trades:

(1) Formulas/techniques can be identified and studied.

(2) Movements and patterns, say the five times to trade as a stock goes through a stock split, can be learned.

(3) You can practice, (also known as "simulation trade") before you use real money.

(4) It works or it doesn't. You don't have to wait years to build wealth.

(5) These trades develop real profits—to let you retire or better your retirement. The profits are cash, not someone's guess about value. It's cash to pay the bills.

(6) This cash can be used to buy other, longer-term (four months to 48 months) positions.

(7) Virtually every investment position, once you understand my nine formulas, has a purpose—a beginning, a middle and an end.

(8) You can live a better lifestyle. My aim has always been to help people fit a trading style to a wonderful lifestyle, not the other way around.

The strategies become the workhorses. I've long said, "I teach formulas and then find stocks which fit the formulas." Here's a back-up statement. I was watching a football game, and the commentator said, "The coach's methods are proven, some of the players are not." So it is with stocks. The formulas are proven, some of the stocks are not.

## Become A Semester Investor™

To sum up, "Buy and Hold" doesn't work as it's being promulgated by the so-called bigwigs. It is an ineffective way to build wealth. Even real estate eventually peaks. You could buy an apartment complex, live off of it, take care of it, and watch it grow. At some point, though, with your basis low, and more "deferred maintenance" needing done than you have the inclination for, it might be time to move on. Let new money fix it up.

To everything there is a season. A time to buy, a time to sell. A time to dump losers, a time to capture profits. This time is a season, like a semester in school—a beginning, mid terms, and an end.

I propose you look at investments with a new "term" outlook. Become a Semester Investor. Think in terms of months, rather than years or decades. Pay more attention to your holdings. Make your money work harder and be prepared—totally unemotionally—to move on.

A SEMESTER INVESTOR does the following:

a) Knows what is wanted from each investment.

b)  Position trades: gets money in the way of movements—both up and down.

c)  Uses leverage (options) to advantage.

d)  Learns and uses selling positions—for instance, calls and puts—to generate income.

e)  Weeds the garden better, unloading stocks past their usefulness.

f)  Learns cash flow formulas to a "T." Precision produces profits.

g)  Avoids fads—sticks with fundamentals like earnings, low debt, revenue increases.

h)  Diversifies into formulas.

i)  Does not "dollar cost average" down. He/she waits for support levels, and then trades on timely upswings.

j)  Knows the quarterly "news-go-round" and measures not only the quantity but the *quality* of news. (See the *Red Light, Green Light* Home Study Course by Wade Cook)

k)  Questions everything. The "why is more important than the "how."

*The person who knows how will always have a job. The person who knows why will always be his boss.*
*-Diane Ravitch*

l)  Keeps increasing his/her skill level. Education is a way of life.

*If money is your hope for independence, you will never have it. The only real security that a man will have in this world is a reserve of knowledge, experience and ability.*    *-Henry Ford*

m)  Is self correcting—always improving.

*Discipline yourself, and others won't have to.*    *-John Wooden*

n)  Surrounds himself or herself with like-minded winners.

*KEEP AWAY FROM PEOPLE WHO TRY TO BELITTLE YOUR AMBITIONS. SMALL PEOPLE ALWAYS DO THAT, BUT THE REALLY GREAT MAKE YOU FEEL THAT YOU TOO CAN BECOME GREAT.*          MARK TWAIN

# 6

# Events Which Move Stocks

The following is a list of events, somewhat in chronological order, which may have a positive or negative affect on the movement of stock. This list is by no means complete. A caution should be made: when trying to ascertain which way a stock is going to move, sometimes positive news can have a downward affect. Crazy as it may sound, it is still true. And remember there's news and then there is comments about the news.

1) The first noticeable event of the year will be the January effect. I have discussed this extensively elsewhere, but let it suffice to say here that as the new year begins, there are a lot of forces which start in late December into January, which cause certain types of stocks to have positive growth. (See page 63).

   Sometimes the move is short lived, but other times a move on a particular stock, or the stock market in general, because of January, can have an affect which could last throughout the year.

2) I have touched on this next point many times before. It is the "quarterly news cycle." Four times a year, stocks go through a news cycle. It first starts with the anticipation of news—mainly manifested in companies making earnings forecasts. The event moves into the actual earnings season, which is at the end of the fiscal quarter for any particular company. Most companies are on a calendar quarter, therefore the moves in their stock coincide with their earnings announcements at the end of each quarter. Again, the news can be good or bad and the stock can move in the opposite direction. Many times there is more movement in the stock due to the *anticipation* of the news than when the news actually is announced. It is a classic adage of "buy on rumor, sell on fact." Another aspect to the earnings season is that as of late companies are adding to their earnings report statements about their next quarter's expectations or next year's earnings potential. Often times really positive earnings are couched behind a somewhat less than enthusiastic comment about their future. We can change the market maxim to "buy on anticipation, sell on news." The last element of this is that

earnings *END*. Sometimes so does the rest of the news about a company. Starved for news, the company's stock oftentimes retrace some or all of their latest upward movement. These stocks are like cars in that they need gas to make it from point A to point B or to the next gas station. In this case, news is the gasoline.

3) The Summer Rally. Often times in the summer, many stocks do fairly well. Most of this is aided and abetted by the fact that the end of June and July is a news-reporting season. Sometimes the news does not come out on some of these companies until the first or second week of August. Also, in late spring and on into early summer, many pharmaceutical companies receive approval from the FDA on their drugs. Maybe the FDA officers want to go on vacation. But, nevertheless, many things happen in May and June and then we head into the latter part of summer.

4) The August doldrums. Many people have commented on how particular stocks in the past have not done well in the month of August. Once again, to me this could be true because a lot of people go on vacation in the month of August, including a lot of stockbrokers. I think there is another overbearing market affect: it is the end of the quarterly news cycle stated in number two of the Red Light, Green Light "No News Period." Traditionally the end of August, and on into the first week of September have not been good months in the stock market. The market literally needs to move into September, into the anticipation news cycle, which then heads into October, the next earnings season.

5) October. October presents several unusual situations. They are unusual in that item A, listed below, has only happened a few times. But any time you talk about a "crash" or a serious market correction, there is a certain amount of reverence for it. October does present two separate phenomena that necessitate our efforts at understanding.

A) The two major market crashes people talk about are 1929 Black Monday, and the stock market crash of 1987. Both of these were very serious in nature. One took several years to overcome. The other one took a little over a year, but the downturn was so drastic, that it is etched in peoples' minds indelibly. Because the two major market crashes have been in October, it has become a very volatile month. If you look at a chart for the month of October in any year, you will see wide swings in many stocks and in the market place as a whole.

B) Under the tax code, mutual funds must sell losing stock positions in the month of October to be able to "book," or claim a loss on that particular stock come December

31ˢᵗ. I know this sounds unusual, but it is an event worth noting. If a mutual fund holds a stock, which it originally purchased for $90 and the stock is currently down to $9, and the fund wants to book the $81 loss, it must do so before the end of October. This means a great deal of stocks which have been seriously beaten up may even have a little more of a downtrend the last few days of the month. Most of the selling goes on before October 20ᵗʰ–25ᵗʰ, so at the very end of October and the first few days of November, there is some serious bargain hunting to be had. Again, the criteria would be a stock that is down and has a high volume of selling at the end of the month and then after October 31ˢᵗ the selling to a large degree would stop. The stock might have a possibility of moving back up. We can place our money in the way of that movement by studying which stocks were hammered earlier in the year, which stocks are held widely by mutual funds, and if those stocks are now finding favor in the market place—i.e., stock splits, and "turnaround prospects" or better earnings prospects.

6) December. I have also noticed two phenomena in the month of December. Here they are:

A) After the first few days of December, there seems to be a sell-off in the market place. Look at the charts below covering 1991 to 2001. You will see the market may be strong towards the end of November and possibly the first few days of December. Many stocks sell off for the period up until approximately the middle of December. This is especially important if you are playing options—recovery. You could fall short and not have your stock or option recover before the expiration date. Once again, stocks may be forgiving, but options are rarely forgiving. And in options, time works *against* you.

B) There usually is a rally towards the end of the year. Some people call this a "Christmas Rally." That may be so, but there is a lot more to it than Christmas. A lot of great companies' stock will start to see movement the last part of December as well as into the first part of January as a lot of major money—I am talking billions of dollars—tries to move itself back into the market. This is done in order to be invested before the huge money flows into the market, in January. Basically the front door to the January effect.

7) Other important news/market events:

Throughout the year there are many reports given by the government, by polling firms watching the market and government actions, and by quasi-government agencies that

## DECEMBER 1993

## DECEMBER 1994

## DECEMBER 1995

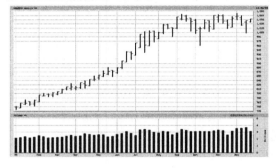

## DECEMBER 1996

## DECEMBER 1997

## DECEMBER 1998

## DECEMBER 1999

## DECEMBER 2000

## DECEMBER 2001

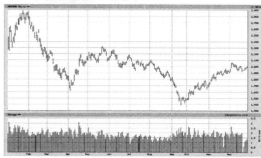

## DECEMBER 2002

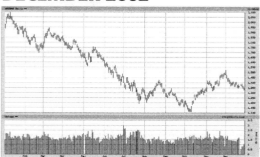

try to keep their finger on the pulse of the market place. Fed announcements have taken on a huge importance in the market place. The Federal Chairman announcement, or any news from the FOMC (Federal Open Market Committee), is heavily followed. People look for not only the specific announcement of a raising or lowering of interest rates, or discount rates by the Federal Reserve Bank, but also for the future. Is the FOMC biased towards raising rates? This announcement and commentary is one everyone should watch and use to try to get a handle on what is going on in the market place. I for one am going to pay a lot more attention to their every movement. Following is a list of other closely watched reports.

A) CPMR (Chicago Purchasing Managers' Report) is an indicator of the nationwide survey, formerly NAPM, now the Institute of Supply Management (ISM). If the rating is higher than 50, then this attests expansion.

B) ISM (Institute of Supply Management), formerly NAPM, is an index report of 450 purchasing managers' information which includes purchase orders and inventory.

C) CPI and PPI. The CPI (Consumer Price Index) measures inflation as a whole while the Core CPI occludes energy and food. This means less volatility, thereby making it more important to spectators watching inflation. The PPI (Purchaser Price Index) indicates whether producers are obtaining more or less for their products, which might signal inflation at the wholesale level. These are also widely watched monitors of the stock market and basically add to our viewpoint of the health of our economy.

D) Durable Goods Orders is an overall number on inventories, shipments and factory orders, which is "industrial demand." This report is revised monthly.

E) Gross Domestic Product (GDP). This is the total amount of goods and services the U.S. puts out. The growth rate number most economists believe to be an indication of future inflation is 2.5%.

F) Employment Report. This includes the employment rate as well as the unemployment rate, hours worked per week as well as hourly earnings on average. Reported monthly.

G) Employment Cost Index. This gauges the change in cost of labor, which is a major indicator. Reported four times a year.

H) Philadelphia Fed Survey. This survey asks individuals to critique current business activity levels as well as future levels for the next six months in the states of New Jersey, Philadelphia, and Delaware. Reported once a month.

I) Productivity and Costs. Illustrates the economy's efficiency through a ratio of output to input. Released four times a year and a revised report following a month after the final report.

J) Industrial Production. This report details the changes in capacity and utilization production of manufacturing, mining and utilities. This is reported monthly.

K) Many reports come from individual analysts about call option volume and put option volume. Basically this study shows which direction the market place is going to go. Many people refer to the technical analysis aspect of looking at the market, which is just one type of barometer. These announcements or reports can come at any time.

L) Brokerage firm analysts or other financial analysts report on certain stocks. This can obviously make or break a particular stock, but it also adds to the movement in a sector.

For example, the high-tech sector or oil sector, the pharmaceutical sector, transportation, industrial or any other sector.

M) Consumer Sentiment. This one also has become a very significant barometer of the market place. To me, any poll taken is only as good as the poll taker's questions. I am not certain that the questions being asked truly reflect the market place. However, my personal opinion doesn't matter, because whether they are the best questions and the most apt at that time is irrelevant. The market place looks to this number in a big way. For example, it could raise the DOW Jones average up 200 or 300 points in a few days with a good number, or with a number that is higher than expected. The reverse is also true.

N) Other important indicators, which move the market, but have a limited force on the market, are:

a. Business Inventories.

b. Housing Starts

c. Chain Store Sales

d. Consumer Confidence Index

e. Jobless Claims

f. Personal Income

g. Semiconductor Book-to-Bill Ratio

h. Help Wanted Index

i. Existing Home Sales

j. Wholesale Trade

*Publishers note:* Wade Cook comments on several of these reports on Liberty Network, Inc. MUST program. M.U.S.T. stands for Monthly Update Skills Training. Check this out on www.wadecook.org.

There are a host of other indicators, which include the crop report and news reports. We must now add war reports and terrorist activities to this list, as well as any corporate activities which support the war effort and the security effort.

*YOUR LIFE IS BUT ONE SMALL CORNER OF THE UNIVERSE, BUT IT IS A VERY IMPORTANT ONE.*

*WADE B. COOK*

# 7

# The January Effect

There are eight reasons why the Stock Market bounces every year. I hope this bounce will happen every year forever.

1.  The first reason is more personal to me, and I hope it will be personal to some of you. I like hanging around positive people. The optimists always seem to come back in January. The American Dream is alive and well. The glass is half-full people start to move. The big pile of manure with the kid jumping in means there has to be a pony in there somewhere. Those kinds of people seem to come out of the woodwork.

    Now, when I say that America is back, I also mean that this particular year is different as well. Patriotism is alive and well. Let's take a look at our holidays. The next three holidays we celebrate are basically secular: Martin Luther King Jr., Valentine's Day, and President's Day. The holiday after that is a religious one, the two big religious holidays of the year being Christmas and Easter.

    The three holidays after Easter, I think are going to be very, very patriotic. Memorial Day, July 4th and Labor Day. Those are our American holidays, all about America.

    You're going to see the American Dream, not just by Americans, but by American companies, come alive. American companies are going to continue to do well overseas, because the world still needs so much of what America has. If you look at the indicators, America is still leading in so many areas. You're going to see a big resurgence in American stocks.

    Here's an interesting example: not only is foreign money coming here, but a big European company announced that it is going public. The company is in London, Harrod's Department Stores. They not only went public, but they did so on the New York Stock Exchange. Is that strange? They left certain shares on the London Stock Exchange (good for them), but they went public in America. Does that tell you something?

2.  I think the number two reason why stocks go up in a bounce fashion in the first part of the year is because money starts moving back into Pension Plans and IRA's. Most Americans realize that they can put their money into their IRA on January 2nd, the first business day of the year. But how many Americans make their IRA deposits for the year on April 14th of the next year? They wait until the very last minute to put aside their contribution. If they really thought it through, isn't this kind of silly? If you have the money, would it be best to wait 15 months, or would it be best to put the money aside as soon as you possibly can? If you put it in this years contribution on January 2, you have another 12 to 15 months of tax-free earnings in the account.

    Now let's go the other way. There are a lot of people with 401K's and people with corporate pension plans. They can put aside $7,500, $15,000, sometimes even more into these plans. If you're one of the top earners in the country, you can put aside a lot of money into a defined benefit plan. But at some point in time, the amount of money you can put in for the year tops out. That is usually, even for high income earners, in June or July. The months of August and September have a big drought in the pension industry. Here's what happens. People will contribute a lot of money and donations out of their paychecks, but all of a sudden, in the middle of July it ends. That's it. That's their maximum allowable contribution for the year. So, what happens till the end of the year? Not much. No new money goes into these 401K's or into pension plans. They've capped out.

    Billions of dollars go into pension and IRA-type accounts through the first part of every year. That money starts pouring back into those accounts at the beginning of a new year. A lot of people want to invest in the Stock Market in their pension-type accounts with no tax ramifications. All of a sudden in January, they start contributing all kinds of money. You can even put money in on January 2nd, based on the *whole* contribution that you *think* you're going to make for the year.

    Billions and billions of dollars start pouring into pension accounts. Not all of it goes into the stock market as some of it ends up in Credit Unions or in bank accounts, but, a lot of it finds its way into the stock market. That addition of money, I think, is a significantly great reason why the market starts to turn around and go up.

## Dow Jones Industrials 2001

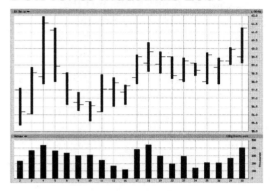

## NASDAQ 2001

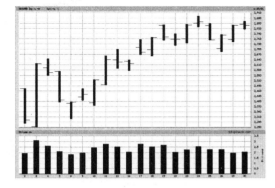

## Dow Jones Industrials 2002

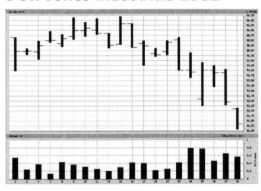

## NASDAQ 2002

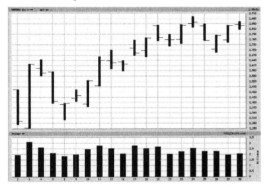

## Dow Jones Industrials 2003

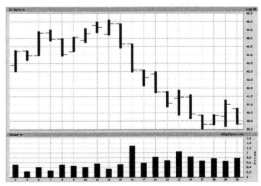

## NASDAQ 2003

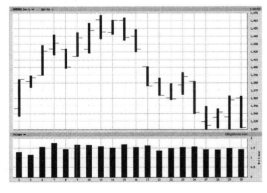

3. Bargains are everywhere. This is in regards to the tax-loss selling and to the fact that a lot of money *has been* sitting on the sidelines. Toward the end of the year, October, November, December, a lot of money doesn't move into these smaller companies from the big funds, even on some of these newer IPO companies. In fact, the price of these beat-up stocks goes down even further, with the year-end selling.

Here's another unique thing which has happened the past few years—there *have* been quite a few failed IPOs and a lot of companies that *could* have gone public but didn't. Do you know why? Because a lot of the firms that take companies public—the incubators, the venture capitalists—have lost their nerve. They have been beaten up so badly, yet they're sitting on top of the assets of 30 different companies. I have been reading a lot of reports, and right now there are a lot of *other* venture capitalist firms that are going through the rubble, like vultures, if you will, picking up these assets. What do you think they're going to do with them? They pick up this technology over here, and pick up another technology over there—they pick up a company's technology that *was* going to go public and changed its mind, but they sure still had good technology. They were going to go public at $200,000,000, but now others can pick up all the rights for their widget, their gadget, whatever it is, for $20,000,000. These bargain shoppers don't pay $200,000,000, they just pay a fraction of it.

If they're out there buying valuable assets for $20,000,000, what are they going to do? They're going to put them up for sale. What is the best way to do this? Pay $20,000,000 and sell for $25,000,000 or $30,000,000; or, take a $20,000,000 asset/business plan, get it out there, get it making money, and then take it public at 20 or 40 times projected earnings? Where do you think the money is? The money is in getting at this $20,000,000 worth of assets, reconfiguring it, and then selling it for $200,000,000 or $300,000,000, *not* $25,000,000. Now *we* can learn about these moves and tag along and try to make some money as some newly reconfigured company goes public. I like to buy stock in those incubators.

I can't go out and buy $20,000,000 in assets—I don't think too many people can. But, we *can* tag along with $25,000 or $50,000 here and there and latch on to some of these companies who are doing just that.

If you hear about a mutual fund or a grouping of investors who are doing this type of play, you have every right as an investor to call them and say, "Do you need any more investors?" "Yes, yes, we are looking for 300 investors to put up $25,000 each." You may get a prospectus from them and then *you* can determine whether you want to play along and be a part of it.

By the way, if I *had* a million dollars, I would rather put it into twenty $50,000 deals instead of *one* $1,000,000 deal. I would rather diversify my money. There are so many bargains out there—not just bargains in terms of companies, but bargains in terms of assets—that it is easier to diversify.

4.  A lot of companies, who had wanted to do their IPOs (Initial Public Offerings) earlier in the year, finally do them in November and December. Throughout any previous year, there always seem to be a lot of IPOs that hit the marketplace in the summertime and in the Fall. The irony is that a lot of these companies *wanted* to go public in January, February or March; but if you have ever studied the IPO process, whatever the absolute, last, lock-down, drop-dead date is, it's going to be six more months before anything happens. Any normal human being would think: We're going to get this IPO out on March 31$^{st}$, then the accountants and the attorney's take over and what happens to almost every deal? If it even stays alive at all, it is going to happen six to eight months down the road.

    Let me tell you a couple of other things. A few years ago, there were a couple of firms that raised money. They're what are called Venture Capitalists or Investment Bankers. Sometimes, with the acronym "VC" for Venture Capitalists, they call them "Vulture Capitalists", because they try to scoop in and take advantage of every deal they can. Just a few big VC firms raised over $100,000,000,000 (one hundred billion dollars) to put into new IPOs for new start-ups, and only $25,000,000,000 (25 billion dollars) of that money had been spent—or committed—at the year-end. Which means, they have $75,000,000,000 waiting to go into IPOs. *Then*, I read in the same report that there was more money just *sitting* and waiting, which had been raised in the previous year. This money is also waiting to go into deals. Seemingly, the IPO marketplace had dried up and there were not many IPOs. All of these people had cash to put into the IPOs and they did not do so. The future will be different. This money, at least much of it, will be put to work.

    Here is another aspect of IPOs that should be taken into consideration. We need to discuss the lock-up period and the twenty-five day rule. We'll go over them briefly here.

When a company goes public, there are 25 days when nothing can be said. From the day a company does its "new issue", the day it does its IPO offering to the public, nothing can be said for 25 *business* days, or 25 *trading* days. These companies enter what is called a "Quiet Period". The underwriters, the companies that took the company public, all of their analysts, their stock brokers, basically everyone, has to *hush up.* The IPO is definitely out there and on the first day there was a lot of fanfare, a lot of hype and hoopla, but then they enter…the "Quiet Period".

If your stockbroker were to call you about this company, they would be in violation of their company rules and probably some SEC regulations. They cannot hype the stock for 25 days. No one can PR the stock, they cannot put their President and CEO on CNBC—*nothing,* for at least 25 days.

If it's a big firm and they have good underwriting and a good PR department, they will blast out with all kinds of good information about the company at the end of this 25 days. Can you see them, after 25 days, coming out with a news report that says, "Oh, we messed up, we don't like this company anymore"—after they just raised $80,000,000 for this company? If they're going to do any PR at all, is it going to be good PR or bad PR? It's going to be good, of course, and they're going to support the stock for quite awhile.

Now, the lock-up period is this: When a company goes public, there are a lot of founders of the company—these are the people who started it–who can register their stock through the offering. Let's say you own stock in a company and it's registered in the IPO. You own a million shares. Would it be unfair to the investing public if, on the day the company goes public, you sell your stock right away? Could your million shares have a huge effect on the marketplace? Yes. So, they (the underwriters) might make you hold that stock for six months or more.

My point is, if a company went public in the middle of the year, those lock-up periods end in January or February. You might think that a lock-up period is negative. It's not. As I study lock-up periods, at the end of the six or nine or twelve months, the stocks usually go up. Do you know why? Because hardly anybody ever sells their stock at the end of the six months. Now think this one through. All of the anticipation, the thinking that the founders might sell, has been holding the stock back. It's gone from $18 to $30, and it's just kind of hanging around $30. Why? Because, there is a lock-up period, which has the stock of the nine original founders of the company on hold, and that period is going to end, let's say on January 12th.

Just because the lock-up period is over on January 12th, does it mean that you and all of your eight buddies are going to run out and sell your stock? No, it hardly ever happens. As soon as the lock-up period is over and the public realizes that all of the founders, the original people, are not going to sell their stock, the stock usually moves from that $30 to $35 to $40 very quickly.

I'll give you an example: Krispy Kreme®. Do you know Krispy Kreme has only been publicly traded for a few years and they've already done two stock splits? Their lock-up period was during the same time. There was so much fear that the stock was going to go down when they hit the end of their lock-up period. The stock had been right around $60, and this after two 2:1 stock splits. But, within three to five days after the lock-up period, people realized that all of the founders and the insiders were not selling their stock, and the stock went from $60 to $75, then up to $80 in a matter of days.

Below are two charts for Krispy Kreme Donuts (Ticker Symbol KKD). They both cover the same time periods—the initial trading day to the present. There were two 2:1 stock splits. See explanation (below) of why the charts look differently.

This first chart is rectified to adjust for the split. See the stock at $40 on the IPO date. A 2:1 split would put the starting price at $20. A second 2:1 stock split puts the starting price around $10. Your 100 shares would now be 400 shares.

The IPO was 4-4-00. The lock-up period was not six months, but one year. In fact, the lock-up period ended between the two stock splits. The stock continued to go up.

On the rectified chart, note where the two lines are down, about March 3rd and June 3rd.

## KKD Rectified

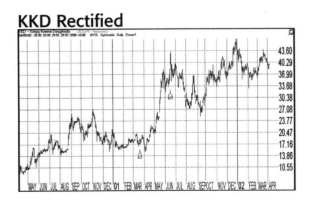

## KKD Unrectified

Once again, if you would have purchased 100 shares on the IPO, for $40 each, or $4,000, today you would have *400* shares at around $40 each, or $16,000.

The non-rectified chart allows you to see the stock split, climb back up, then another split and the upward trending stock throughout 2001. This company is still expanding. The lock-up period had no affect on this company's stock price.

I've studied a lot of these lock-up periods and you would be amazed. Not all of the time, but *most* of the time, the stock has a nice upward move *after* the lock-up period, which defies logic. You would think that if they *can* sell, they sell. I'm sure that some people do, but it doesn't happen all that often.

5. Picking up on the movement of big money in front of new money entering the market: as of late, this movement even starts in December. Caution: we're little guys. We wait until the end of the year to see how much cash we have available. We little guys hold

**KFT**

**SGEN**

**ACN**

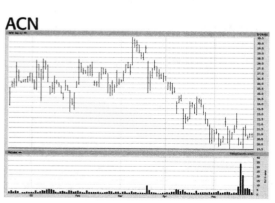

**USPI**

out whatever we're going to need for Christmas. But the mutual funds and the great big pension funds are sitting there with all this money. They know that January has historically been a really good month, so, about the middle of December—even if they have a lot of cash in their cash accounts—they start moving their money back into the Stock Market.

December has become a big month for money moving into the market and it continues into January. Why? Big money usually tries to get in the way of major movements. One of the things I have taught in my seminars is that we're always the last to know. We're buying into these stocks, the stocks have gone from $56 up to $70 and boy it looks like the momentum is just going to keep going. But what pushed that stock from $56 to $70? Was it all of the money that moved in the stock from the middle to the end of December? We then, as the last to come to the dinner table, start jumping in. The big money, the money that wants to play the January bounce, is already in there. This new money might now push the stock from $70 to $74 or $75, but the big movement has already happened.

Isn't that what you would do? If you think of the stock market like a surfboard, wouldn't you want your surfboard in position to be *in the way* of the next big wave that comes; not *after* the wave has already gone, and not *as* the wave is upon you, but in *advance* of the wave?

If you know historically that a new year has been a good time, and you're sitting there with $800,000,000 in a fund, what would you do with that money? You would get it in front of those stocks that have the highest likelihood of edging their way back up. You worry about February when February comes. Worry about the rest of the year when it comes. Right now, you want to get your money in the way of movement.

6.  People are willing to take more risk. Sometimes the only aspect of the new year mentality that people know about, is the movement *out* of these high-quality funds *into* stocks that carry a bigger risk, but have a greater potential. There are a lot of funds and people willing to take a risk in the first part of a year, who are not willing to take risks at other times of the year, especially at the end of the year. That is one of the most important points. The *willingness* to put their money into riskier, no-name stocks—high-potential stocks without much of a following—helps with the upward momentum of this bounce.

7.  We are past the year-end Window Dressing. I will explain this briefly, and then explain what it means as we move into the new year.

    A lot of mutual funds will start loading up on the bigger-name companies towards the end of the year, even though these bigger-name companies have already had their run. They're not expected to go up *that much* in the New Year. Fund managers know there are probably better prospects in other, smaller companies going up in the next year, but how do they want their books to look at the end of the year? Mutual funds are in the business of managing people's money. They want you to put your money with them. They want to show Disney, 3M and AT&T on their books, because these are familiar and easy-to-understand. They feel you will be more comfortable putting your money with them if you are familiar with the companies they own. When they produce their really nice big portfolio books, which show all of their holdings for the year, they do not want to list Acme Waste Management or any other small, no-name company.

The fund may have made all of their money in Acme, and it may have gone from $8 to $28, but it's a no-name company and they're going to get rid of it at the end of the year, even though they may turn right around and buy it (or other similar companies) again at the beginning of the next year. This creates an effect on a lot of these lower or no-name companies in December. Their stocks go *down* a bit, and the big companies' stocks go *up* towards the end of December.

Now, there's an interesting sidelight to this. Let's say this mutual fund has a stock which was at $8 and has gone to $28. Throughout the year, the stock has done very, very well. This mutual fund owns a million shares of the stock. When they unload the stock in December, for the sole purpose of *not* having it in their portfolio, this sale can have a dramatic impact on the stock's price, because a million shares being sold can be a huge determinant to an up stock movement. Now, this mutual fund company turns right around in December and buys a big-name $80 stock with the same money. How many shares can they buy now? Not nearly a million shares. Maybe a third of that. So you see, there's an impact; an upward movement in December in big stocks; a downward movement in small stocks.

Then the opposite happens in January. Mutual fund companies will sell, say, a million shares of an $80 stock, or $80 million and then have that money available for purchase of stocks with a greater near-term potential. To summarize, they'll *sell* a lot of the big-name companies in January, and *buy* a lot of the no-name companies.

8. The tax-loss selling in December is out of the way. At the end of the year there is a lot of tax-loss selling, because, even in really, really good years, there are still some company stocks which have gone down. If you have a stock that has gone from $90 down to $30, (even though you may want to keep it because you think it's going to

go back up) your tax accountant might say, "Unload it by the end of the year." Why? Because, then you can book a $60 loss against other profits. There is a lot of this type of selling, which happens at the end of the year.

These last few years have been so bad, though, that there has been *an excess* of tax-loss selling going on, even up to the last day of the year. It used to take five days for a transaction to clear your accounts. Now it takes three days, but with computers being so fast, your transactions are now reflected almost instantaneously. You will see selling right up to the Market close on New Year's Eve.

There you have the eight reasons. We are heading into a good uptrending market. If you look at the chart history, NASDAQ, the New York Stock Exchange, you would really have to look hard to find a down-January. They are there, you can look back several years and find them from time to time, but almost every time it happened, there were wars and rumors of wars, the depression, etc. January has been good, because it has all of these compelling reasons and market forces working to push the market up.

*Publishers note:* Wade Cook and other members are out and about giving seminars, workshops and forums sponsored by Liberty Network, Inc. Call 1-866-579-5900 or check out www.wadecook.org.

*WHAT IN LIFE INSPIRES DAILY NOBLE ACTIONS? WHAT IS IT THAT DELIGHTS THE HEART, STIRS THE SOUL, SWELLS THE BREAST AND SEEKS COMPANIONSHIP FOR SHARING? SIMPLY THIS, DISCOVERY.*

*WADE B. COOK*

# 8

# Investing in
# Quarterly News Cycles

Lately, I've spent a lot of time in my seminars talking about and showing people how to increase their powers of observation and apply that to increasing their profits. For example, if you see patterns, say a connection between a company's stock dipping or rising at certain times as the stock goes through a split, can you take advantage of this pattern? Can we make better trades? Can we get in at more opportune times and get out with more cash?

The obvious is not always so obvious. I demonstrate this in classes by getting everyone to sing "Twinkle, Twinkle, Little Star" as a group while I sing "Now I Know My ABCs." These songs have the same melody, as does "Baa Baa Black Sheep." The point is that these are two of the songs most widely sung by American children, who learned them from their parents, and rarely does anyone realize they are the same melody.

We need to get better at making connections. I look for connections in the stock market all the time and then try to figure out how to capitalize on those observations. I've recently discovered something so pervasive, so recognizable, that once you know and "get it," it will literally shake up a lot of things you do. It will help you avoid mistakes. It will help you trade better—better execution and more cash profits.

What I am about to explain is a price movement phenomenon based on the market's reaction to events on the corporate calendar. Many people have observed parts of this phenomenon. Others see one angle of it but don't see the connection. Still others see the same patterns and time periods but don't understand the "why" behind the stock movements. If you don't truly understand this cause and effect, it's hard to build faith in the process—to formulate your "law" and put that law to work for you.

> *"The man who knows how will always have a job. The man who knows why will always be his own boss."*
> *–Diane Ravitch*

Your stockbroker or financial planner may claim to have known about this concept. If so, chew that person out for not telling you. Anyway, I doubt they know the entirety of this process. I've not talked to one person yet who understands all of this before I explained it—no broker, surely no news writer or journalist, and no other author.

You are about to read probably the single most important thing about trading in the stock market you have ever read or ever will read. I call it "Red Light – Green Light." This pearl of business wisdom was found through years of struggle, and you minimize this process at your trading peril. Watch and be wise.

## Chronological Connections

In May of 1995 I took our company public. Our assets grew rapidly and we became a reporting company June 30, 1996, when the quarterly SEC reports are filed. The June 30 reports actually had to be filed within 45 days, or by August 15. This important point will come back into play later. Read on.

For years my accounting and legal departments have worked on our quarterly and annual reports. During this quarterly process, there are windows which open or close on what I as a CEO, Board member and insider can say. There are also specific time periods when I can and cannot sell my own company's stock.

Let's take our first "time out". I can pretty much *buy* stock whenever. It's in the selling of that stock or other stock holdings where restrictions exist. If I buy stock in a company wherein I am considered an insider (a person with information that the general public does not have access to), then I have to hold onto the stock for six months. If I do sell it before six months are up, say to recover my cash, I will have to give back to the company any profits I've made. This is called disgorgement. I'm not allowed to make a profit on the stock based on "inside" information. These rules are good. They protect the investing public.

After years of complying—being careful when to buy and sell, and being careful of what I say and when—I started observing things. Here it is plain and simple: News drives stock prices. Everyone knows this. But it is only one component, one piece of the puzzle.

Here's the question I asked myself. If I, as a CEO, am under all these restrictions—these open and closed window periods of time—then what about the 25,000 or so other CEOs, CFOs, COOs, CLOs, Boards of Directors and other insiders of all publicly traded companies in this wonderful country? Are they not under the same requirements?

## Important Dates

This is where the next piece of the puzzle falls into place. When can "insiders" talk? When do they have to go silent? And what effect does this quarterly phenomenon have on the rise and fall of their stock prices? We'll explain all of these as we move along, but first some important dates.

| | |
|---|---|
| December 31 | This is the year end for most companies. SEC filings |
| March 31 | must be submitted for the whole year, and this document must be audited by an outside firm. The filing deadline is 90 days later, or March 31. |

| | |
|---|---|
| June 30 | These are calendar quarter ends. Quarterly SEC |
| September 30 | filings may be unaudited. Filings are due 45 days later, on May 15, August 15 and November 15. Do you see an overlapping time period in the March 31 area? |
| December 31 | Filings for the previous year need to be made as a company is just finishing up its first quarter. |

Another point: Some companies may use months other than December as their year end. Most companies have a December 31 year end, but even if they don't, they usually choose a calendar quarter to be their year end. Why? The answer lies in this quick but powerful observation: Companies must file their 940s and 941s (and other Federal and State filing requirements). That's it. 940s and 941s. Now if you've been in business you've already thought, "Aha, I got it!" But some of you have never had to do quarterly employment filings. Our benevolent government makes everyone file at the same time—in this case on a calendar quarter. If you chose a different year end other than a calendar quarter, it will seem as if you have to have two sets of records—one for yourself and one for the government. Hence, for ease of paperwork most companies comply and have their year end on one of the four calendar quarters. This one fact alone will have dynamic effects as a vast majority of companies fall in line and march together, doing the same thing at the same time. You'll see the dramatic effects of this process as you learn more about "red light, green light" news periods.

So, to summarize, not all companies have the same calendar year end (December 31st), but almost all companies have the same calendar quarter ends. Some don't, like Dell. The patterns that follow quarterly reporting are somewhat predictable depending on the quality of the news. We'll get to that very soon.

## News—Changing Perceptions

Okay, let's start down the path. It's about June 15—a few weeks before the quarter ends. People start to talk. Analysts adjust and readjust their expected earnings numbers. The CEO of Big Company comes out in interviews or news releases and downplays the numbers, saying something like, "Sales have been good, but we have a charge off, so earnings will be $1.12 instead of $1.32." The stock drops $5, from $86 to $81. Now toward the end of June other news—mergers, share buy-backs, takeovers, stock splits, other sales figures, new product announcements, et cetera, et cetera—hits the streets. The stock wavers but heads back up.

Of all these newsy items, the type of announcement most followed is any announcement having to do with earnings. I've written about earnings, or P/E, in many other places. Many people base what they are willing to pay for a stock on the P/E, or price-to-earnings ratio. A typical NYSE company has a P/E of around 20—let's say 19.2. In short, this means that the stock will cost $19.20 for every $1.00 of earnings.

# 8-Investing in Quarterly News Cycles

The stock may be at $250 or $5 or 50¢, it matters not. Now a static or isolated P/E is not the only factor in price determination even for those who only follow P/Es. Other important considerations include these questions: Are earnings growing or contracting? How does this company's earnings compare to those of other companies? Are earnings even a viable measurement in certain sectors? Internet stocks are a scary diversion from sound rational practice in stock choices. Many have no "E" in their P/E.

Back to the point: Earnings is the most widely watched measurement of stock values. Because of this, all CEOs must be very careful of what they say about earnings.

Let's move down to the first week of July. The quarter is over, but the actual filing (10Q) has not yet been done. That will happen in a few weeks—at least by August 15, the filing deadline. Now, think this through. If the CEO, CFO or other corporate bigwigs comment about actual numbers before the proper documents are filed, it is assumed that he or she knows what the numbers should be. Do you see? Even if the accountants aren't through with the complete consolidated numbers, it would be determined that he or she should know. Because of this there is a complete news shutdown (shh! no talking, no talking!). No one will talk until the 10Qs are filed and the news release is out. Funny thing—the stock gets back to $86 and even up to $88. How does this happen? There is something happening here. Paranoia strikes deep. It is as if a whole group of people know something we don't know. In fact, we're the last to know.

Here's the pathetic, yet comical irony. Now the news is out—it's official. The interviews or press releases start up with something like this: "Earnings are ahead of expectations by about 10%. They are $1.22 per share." As the report goes on, you'll see an interesting twist. "We're pleased with the numbers and growth, but we contemplate a slowdown in sales next quarter (or year) and may not be able to maintain these high numbers."

Is this crazy or what? They good-mouth and bad-mouth their numbers in the same breath. Why? You must understand the fear these CEOs and others live under. They do not want to be seen hyping their stock. They couch the truth behind caveats. They pad everything. This is the way it is.

Now another unusual thing happens. Many times the stock goes down in spite of good news. It is a strange phenomenon. I'm still perplexed when it happens. It's part of the "buy on rumors, sell on facts (news)" syndrome. Sometimes it has to do with what has happened to the stock in the few weeks or months before the report. It has a lot to do with sentiment—expectations and the like. There are too many variables to mention in this chapter. It's a mystery wrapped in a conundrum engulfed by an enigma.

Based on many other news developments, so goes the stock. One event is particularly important: the Board of Directors meeting. The date of this event can be checked out, and nothing happens until they meet. This is significant. They discuss profits, available cash for dividends, mergers, share buy backs, stock splits, business plans, et cetera.

Do you see how important these topics are? Think of all the guesswork going on by people following the company. Rumor fires are easily kindled. Sometimes they get out of control. However they start, whatever they are, it all ends when the actual numbers and news hit the street.

All of this is very important, but then what? Where's the sequel? Where's the new news? It's now the end of July or first week of August. (The same could be applied to the end of the October/November or January/February or April/May periods.) The news is out. We don't have to wait as long as we did for Episode I—The Phantom Menace to come out in the Star Wars series, but wait we must. In short, in the absence of news, "this stock ain't going nowhere." The balloon isn't going up without hot air. The car isn't leaving the garage without gas. Superman isn't flying without his cape.

Here's a problem. What if we purchase stock at the height of this incredible (pre) news time? The stock has risen to $92. A big firm puts out a buy rating. Others follow. The company has even announced a stock split for August 20, a Friday. It just looks peachy—how can you lose?

Oh, and what if you like options? Those funny little derivatives which rise and fall as the stock does—and erode as the time moves on toward the expiration date.

Options present an awesome opportunity to make money as long as the stock moves exactly like you want it to. If you buy a call option, the right to buy stock, you want the stock to go up. If it goes down or stays the same, you lose. Now ask yourself: Why am I buying this option when all the news has played out? At least ask, why did I buy the option with a near term expiration date? Maybe I should have bought the option with an expiration date at least into the next news reporting period.

Now all in all, observing this "news—no news" period should help us make wiser decisions. Decisions when to get in, decisions when to sell. Here is an important question: "What compelling reason does this stock have to go up?" More importantly, what compelling reason does this option have to go up in value? The answer is simple, but far-reaching. If there is nothing to drive it up—no news, no rumors, no nothing—then watch out.

Do you see where I now come up with "Red Light, Green Light?" A time to buy; a time *not* to buy. Now, notice I didn't say a time to sell. There are times when we should not be buying options. This goes back to a premise I've taught for years: the way to win at the stock market is to not lose! We need to avoid making mistakes. Buying a call option when a stock has nothing going on to help drive up the price is likely to be one of those mistakes.

## A Look at the Calendar

By now you should have picked up on the important quarterly news periods. It helps sometimes to lay out a timeline or picture of the process. Before I do so, let's look again at a few things.

## 8-Investing in Quarterly News Cycles

1.  There are no set dates on which all companies start announcing newsy things. The dates vary. They are different because the board may meet at odd times. After the board meets the company may still make no announcement for several days or even weeks.

2.  Many companies make very few pre-announcements, if any at all. Some make a lot. These announcements start about two weeks before the quarter end. Often you'll hear, "Well, we're entering the earnings season," meaning that news is about to come out. Some people "get it" on this part of the whole process. What you'll never hear from TV and newspaper reporters is this: "Well, we're leaving the earnings reporting season."

Before I go on to (3), let me tell an interesting story: We were having our speaker training two-day session in March, actually the Ides of March (March 15) and the day after. It was in Seattle. We were discussing Microsoft. It's on everyone's mind in Seattle, as it's a Northwest company. There are news reports on it almost daily in our region.

The stock had been floundering from the middle of February through that time. I was explaining this whole new "news–no news" concept to our instructors. After awhile, the subject of Microsoft came up. It was about 9 or 10 A.M. on Monday. I pointed out that the stock was down and had been stagnant for a few weeks. I said, "Microsoft needs March 15th. Oh, it is March 15th! So the news announcements should start soon."

Shortly, news came out over the wire about the company laying a foundation to break up into five divisions in anticipation of a lawsuit settlement with the Feds. The stock went up a couple of dollars. A little while later there was more news. This time they announced that they might enter an agreement, or that they were in talks to possibly end the lawsuit. Up another dollar or so.

The next morning, March 16th, the word on the street was that they were going to blow away their numbers—meaning they were making more money than expected. All in all the stock was up something like $7 to $8 in those two days. I looked at my great instructors and said, "Seeeeeeeeeeee?"

It doesn't take a genius to figure out that if there's bad news, especially about earnings, or no news, that the stock will go down. Anticipation and expectation of news reports play a big part of this game. If there's good news or rumors of good news, the stock reacts accordingly. The old expression, "No news is good news" is out the window here. It's the opposite now: "No news is bad news" is more like it.

This leads up to number (3).

3.  A lot of stock movement depends on the quality of the news. At the time of this writing our economy is picking up. Many companies are earning a lot of money. A few are struggling. My guess is that 30% of today's news is bad and about 70% is good. This will change.

    So with a lot of good news hitting the streets, why do some stocks go down? One answer is that many investors think they can't keep up this level of profits. Dell, for example, went up (had positive earnings announcements) many quarters in a row. One quarter—the winter of 1999—they just hit their earnings estimates and the stock got tanked. They're still a great company, earning millions, but some anticipate future sluggishness and the stock reacts. The marketplace is a giant auction. A stock goes for what someone will pay for it. Built into this are many factors, and one of the most important is anticipation of future earnings growth.

    Check the quality of the news. Watch for news on one company and how it affects others in the same field. Observing this will let you see many buying and selling opportunities.

4.  Not all companies follow the same exact time schedule. Many space out their announcements over a few days. Many make all of the news announcements at one time.

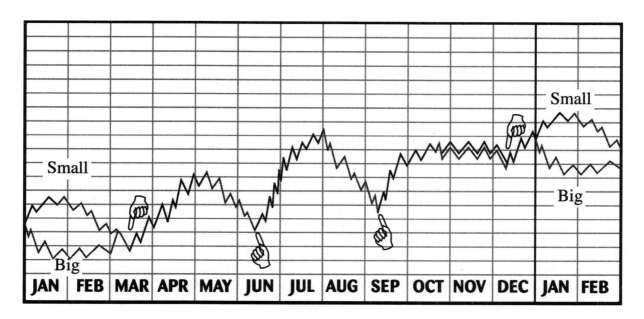

97

Often these announcements are known "on the street" way before the press conference. Ask your broker about the "whisper numbers." See what other companies have done. Try to get a handle on the direction of the stock. Most importantly, be careful of buying call options or stocks going into or in the middle of a "red light" no news period. Look for compelling reasons for a stock to increase. If you find none, watch out. Back off. Consider selling your calls or stocks in the midst of the newsy "green light" period—wait through the "red light" period, and buy again on dips on the other side of the red light time when the new news starts up again.

If the news is negative or the "red light" period has started, consider buying puts or doing Bear Call Spreads (see *Safety 1st Investing*). In short, time your entrance and exit points better.

Read the following information on a 1999 Microsoft announcement. See the nature of the news. See the "good mouthing" and "bad mouthing" that goes on.

This years ups and downs:

Look at the 14-month graph on the preceeding page. Note, this is a generality. *Any particular* stock's movement is based on many things—certainly not just a chart in a book.

## Observe:

1.  The serious dips are in Feb, May, August, a neutral November and bad first two weeks of December.

2.  October is a strange month with many erratic stocks.

3.  Look at the arrows. These represent the start of the news talk, the "green light" period.

4.  The months following the year end are erratic because of the quality of the news, plus share buy-backs and stock splits.

## Summary

This chapter is about making better decisions, timing our entrance and exit points for more enhanced cash flow. The more dots we connect, the better for this process and the better for our bottom line. We also discussed the quantity and quality of news—how even the company's "anticipation of news" period drives a stock up or down. Option trades need movement in the right direction to be profitable. Before buying calls or puts, ask the all-important question: What compelling reason does the stock have to go up (or down for puts)? If you don't have a good answer, then refraining from trading may be the best trade.

# 9

# Sailing the Seven "C's"

*"What in life inspires daily noble actions? What is it that delights the heart, stirs the soul, swells the breast and seeks companionship for sharing? Simply this, DISCOVERY." -Wade B. Cook*

I have found seven prominent characteristics of a company, especially their management team, which are crucial to succes. I love the water, so I've put them in a sailing metaphor.

## Character

The character of the company is often dictated by the management in place. Sometimes it is passed down from the original founders of a company-people who could have started the company many generations before when things were truly different. The character of a company is more than just a mission or theme; it is the very makeup of the company from the management down to the humblest employee. It speaks of the company's honesty in all of its dealings; it reflects the character it has in its advertising and marketing efforts. Contained in character, at its very core is how well the company takes care of its existing customers.

A good example of the all-encompassing aspect of character, would be the character that is depicted in the movie *"We Were Soldiers"*, based on a true story and starring Mel Gibson. It is a very intense movie; the "R" rating is due to the violent content. However, the character of the Colonel put in charge of these soldiers fighting in Vietnam speaks volume about not only his quality but the quality of his troops. This movie made me very proud to be an American. I see these similar characteristics exhibited in many American businesses today. Just the names of some companies depict so much. They were able to create a concept in peoples' minds of the quality, concern, and the overall mission of their company. Many people are proud to be associated with these types of companies; for example, Mercedes, Cadillac and other fine automobiles; some of the high-end stereo and high-fi equipment; and even certain hospitals in your area. There are just some companies that make you feel good to do business with.

## Charisma

Every company needs a certain razzamatazz. They need a product so exciting that their existing customers cannot wait to tell others about their product, service or pricing.

Many companies fight the battle for success in the pricing arena. I feel this is a problem. Customer service is tantamount to success. Wal-Mart, for example, has great pricing, but they are also one of the friendliest stores to visit. Their customer service is really good. The employees genuinely enjoy working there and like taking care of their customers. You truly do feel like you are part of the family when you are in their store.

Think about how difficult it would be if you constantly have to sell the product you have. Let me give you an example. In our company, we have taken a different tactic in marketing. Sometimes we bill ourselves out as "the company that has nothing for sale." We get people excited with knowledge. We're in the publishing and seminar business. We send out seminars on CD, cassettes and videos and even, coming soon, a DVD. People listen to the seminar, possibly share it with their stockbrokers or their friends, and if they like what we teach, they call us-they contact us in order to purchase the things they want. We do not have to constantly call and nag people.

Another example: I once was involved (from a marketing standpoint), with a company which sold lotions, potions and other items for skin care. The employees of this company we're so excited about a couple of their products, they would literally stand in line at a grocery store in order to put this lotion on the customers waiting in line, people they didn't even know! The product was so exciting they could not wait to share it with other people; and they did so by rubbing it on the hands and arms of total strangers. When you have a product that works so well and is that exciting, then you know you have a winner. The issue then is to continue with great marketing efforts and/or come up with products that will be "back end products" for future growth.

## Customer Care

Does the company have enough resources to stay viable? I read a book many years ago, which stated the purpose of being in business is to "get and keep customers." Many people say the purpose of being in business is to make a profit. That is true, but if a company doesn't earn and keep customers, eventually it will go out of business.

This speaks to seeking out new customers. Is the company seeking out new customers and is it maintaining existing customers? Further on in the same chapter in the book in business is to get and keep solvent customers.

## Capital (Money)

> *"A rising tide raises all ships."*          *--Anonymous Wall Street Adage*

I think anyone who has ever started up a business on their own understands how much capital is required. It is always way more than what anyone originally thinks it will be. Many companies raise money in the public arena, so they have enough to last until the company gets profitable. This money is used for research and development; for advertising and marketing; and for the operations of the company.

One of the problems I have seen over the last few years is the huge number of companies which have gone public and which have also raised hundreds of millions of dollars. Many of them have blown through this money so rapidly that before they turn profitable, the money is gone. A new name was even developed for this rapid use of cash. It is called: "Burn Rate." One major financial magazine even had a gravestone section on a certain page that listed all the companies which had gone out of business that previous month.

Many companies are able to get by on a shoestring. Many fortunes today were started in a garage or someone's back bedroom with hardly any cash at all. They were able to build their business out of operational cash flow, rather than from equity or debt financing. If a company is not able to receive debt financing, they often go to the equity markets and give up a piece of ownership in the company. Debt financing-the raising of sufficient capital to get by-has an additional burden. The debt must be repaid.

## Coach and Captain

> *"Kites rise against, not with the wind. No man ever worked his passage anywhere in the dead calm"*          *--John Neal*

As I have said so many times before, a company's management team is sine qua non to their success. Nothing will happen without a great board of directors and a great management team operating the day to day operations. This is relatively tough to check out, because management is always changing. However, since most companies have a web site, you can utilize it to check on their latest filings and find out about their management team. You can also see how well the management operates on a day-to-day basis. This would include taking care of current and past problems; dealing with new products and marketing; and how well they have articulated their company's vision for the future. It all comes down to experience, knowledge and abilities.

    a)   Cryning (sic)and Whining (No)

       This expression comes from my eight-year-old grandson when he was four-years old.

My daughter (His mother) has taught him well. She wanted to emphasize in most day-to-day situations that there is no crying and whining, basically trying to teach this young boy a lesson. He could not quite say the words right, so it came out of his mouth as "No Cryning, No Whining." He would go around the house and say that repeatedly.

I agree. There is no room for "cryning" and whining in the business sector-you take what you've been given and make the best of it. B.C. Forbes put it this way: *"Optimism is a (medicine). Pessimism is a poison. Admittedly, every businessman must be realistic. He must gather facts, analyze them candidly and strive to draw logical conclusions, whether favorable or unfavorable. He must not view everything through rose-colored glasses. Granting this, the incontestable is that America has been built up by optimists. Not by pessimists, but by men willing to adventure, to shoulder risks terrifying to the timid."*

*"Sour grapes do make fine wine."*                                              -Wade B. Cook

b)   Creativity

If the Coach and Captain of the ship are not all that creative, have they surrounded themselves with a creative team? Do they come up with new and innovative ideas in advertising and marketing? Do they have constant renewal of products? Are they constantly improving and trying to make things better? Which of the following sentences would best express how the company operates?

Statement #1: "If it ain't broke, don't fix it." OR

Statement #2: If it ain't broke, fix it anyway."

Again, which statement reflects the attitude of the company? Are they constantly improving? Tinkering? Using available resources to make improvements? Or, are they stuck in the past-thinking their product will stand the test of time without any improvements at all. Very few companies have products that stand the test of time and do not need any improvements. I can think of one: Ivory Soap. Almost all other companies products need to be in a constant creative mode to make them ready for the challenge of the future.

## Communication

How well does a company articulate its product or its mission in the business world? Do you clearly understand what its product or service is, or are you left bewildered and constantly wondering, "What is it that they do to make money?"

The ability to communicate-not only in the corporate culture from leadership and management to the employees, but also from the company to the outside world is paramount to business success. Simple skills, such as the use of the English language, are necessary to build rapport all along the corporate line.

One way you can check this is quite simple: do you like the information put out by the company to the public? If you're a shareholder, do you like the shareholder report? Does it articulate the mission and goals of the company? Do the company's advertisements on TV or radio adequately tell what the company is all about? Let me give a negative example by the following: In fact, this example incorporates almost of the 7 C's.

A few years ago, advertising during the Superbowl reached $2 to $3 million per one minute spot. Most of the advertisements were 30 seconds. A lot of companies took pride in their new TV spots, and they had their premier advertisement released during the back and advertised the next year. Many of them reported that they did not even have enough of an increase in orders, sales or interest to even justify the cost of the advertisement.

It was a no-brainer to me. I watched these advertisements, because I like the advertising business. In many cases, I could not even tell what company was being advertised. I did not know what they wanted me to do as a potential customer. Some of the ads were so far out, so esoteric, that I could not even understand the company or the product being advertised.

Many of these companies were of the new "dot-com" type. They had so much money to burn-in that the amount of money they raised for advertising was so high that they were sold a bill of goods and horrible advertising was produced for them. If they were on a tight budget, or if the founders had started the company on a shoestring and had very limited resources, maybe they would have learned to advertise better.

There are really two types of advertising: one is informational advertising, and they other is "call-to-action" type advertising. Informational advertising has never been my cup of tea. I want a direct response: for example, the phone to ring, or Internet site to be hit so we can measure the effectiveness of our advertising, gain a new customer and move them through our nurturing process.

Much of this was totally circumvented in those Superbowl commercials. It seemed that the companies only wanted these advertisements. This speaks to the character of the company, the capital that was expended, whether the company was centered on the core, the gaining of a customer and the charisma of the advertisement. In fact, most of these companies failed in all of these departments and the results spoke for themselves.

All in all, communication-a company's ability to correctly reflect its mission and products-is vitally important to the continued health of the company.

## Centered on the Core

Many people shoot short of the mark, and many people shoot beyond the mark. A company needs to have its central core business and stay true to that business. There are always distractions and new products and services being invented. A company should not change its focus until it proves itsself out. Far too often the conglomerates get so big and unwieldy that the company forgets why it was founded in the first place and what its current mission is.

Because many companies overextend themselves, oftentimes you will see them sell many subsidiaries and divisions in order to return to their central, or core business. This could take a two-or-three-year-re-adjustment, literally a re-awakening before the core business can resume and produce much good.

I personally have experienced this in our business; I wanted to diversify, so that if there were a down-turn in any one area, we would be covered by having business enterprises in other areas. To a certain extent this can be a big mistake-often one central management team cannot manage disparate businesses. Each business requires its own level of expertise, management and oversight. When I am looking for good companies today, I want to find a business which is centered on its core, and on making that core enterprise all it can be.

*"The man who strives to educate himself-and no one else can educate him-must win a certain victory over his own nature. He must learn to smile at his dear idols, analyze his every prejudice, scrap if necessary his fondest and most consoling belief, question his presuppositions, and take his chances with the truth.*

*- Everett Dean Martin*

# 10

# A P/E Ratio Update on Finding Value

## Three Ways To Measure Stock Values And Movements

One key to the wealth accumulation process is to find, buy and invest in value. Another is to position yourself and your money in the way of progress. In the stock market there are measuring sticks, or value determinators which can be used to ascertain good prices, and help you make better entrance and exit points. Actually, there are three.

### A) Fundamentals

The first is a stock viewed from a "fundamental" analysis angle. The "fundamentals" concentrate on more traditional stock evaluation methods. A stock is worth $X because of its earnings and/or earnings growth. A contributing factor is its debt ratio. Some people look at the book value (or break up value): what the company is worth if its components were sold. Some look at sales-to-book value, while others look at yield (the dividend amount divided by the stock price). Look at these three side by side comparisons. Paying those prices for high flyer, low- or no-profit Internet stocks was ridiculous beyond comprehension. Yet for a long time they seemed to go up. I thought then and I think now that high P/E stocks should be avoided.

### B) Technicals

A whole different viewpoint comes from "technical" analysis. This measuring tool helps ascertain stock and option movements. Analysts' computers look at lines on graphs to find moving averages, gaps (up or down) volume inflows or outflows of money, call and put volume. Their goal in life is to catch changes in market direction and capitalize on the change.

### C) O.M.F.s

My style uses both of these, with an added viewpoint. It is the OMF angle. OMF means <u>O</u>ther <u>M</u>otivating <u>F</u>actors: newsy items, or even the anticipation of news events, which move a stock. This could be earnings reports, dividend announcements, share buy-backs, stock splits, lawsuits or the settlement of lawsuits, management changes and many et ceteras.

Simply put, the fundamentals tell us <u>what</u> to buy or sell. The technicals tell us <u>when</u> to buy or sell. The OMFs tell us <u>why</u> now. Why buy or sell now. The OMFs give us specific event-directed entrance and exit points. It is how well we understand and work this combination which will determine our success.

## P/E Ratio Study

In late September 2001, we collected a list of stocks for companies with low Price to Earnings (P/E) Ratios. We were trying to show that many large, well known and well run companies had reached very low valuations just after the events of September 11th. We updated that list on October 9, 2001. After the market run-up of the last few months of 2001, we went through the list again at the end of January 2002. We found that several stocks had healthy increases in both stock price and P/E Ratio. Some, however, stayed at about the same level as October. Some P/E Ratios changed because the company increased earnings in the last quarter of the year. You might make a case that those stocks that did not increase may not have attractive fundamentals, but do your own research on that idea. One stock, Ford, actually had no P/E Ratio at all after reporting a large loss in the last quarter of the year, wiping out the previous 3 quarters of profit. Here is the list of stocks with side-by-side numbers from October 9, 2001, January 18, 2002, & April 15,2002.

| List of P/E Ratios | 10/09/01 | | 1/18/02 | | 4/15/02 | |
| COMPANY | P/E | CLOSE | P/E | CLOSE | P/E | CLOSE |
|---|---|---|---|---|---|---|
| Alcoa (AA) | 18 | $31.61 | 32 | $33.70 | 31 | $36.71 |
| Adobe Systems (ADBE) | 22 | $28.83 | 42 | $34.58 | 18 | $39.38 |
| American Express (AXP) | 18 | $29.00 | 29 | $37.02 | 31 | $40.16 |
| Bank of America (BAC) | 12 | $52.15 | 14 | $60.80 | 13 | $69.20 |
| Bank One (ONE) | 14 | $29.36 | 15 | $38.14 | 16 | $41.21 |
| Boeing Co. (BA) | 10 | $36.00 | 15 | $38.14 | 12 | $47.65 |
| Citigroup ( C ) | 15 | $42.70 | 10 | $39.15 | 16 | $45.92 |
| Disney (DIS) | 21 | $18.92 | 19 | $49.96 | 41 | $23.64 |
| Du Pont (DD) | 20 | $38.04 | 63 | $40.68 | 39 | $46.86 |
| Exxon Mobile (XOM) | 15 | $41.06 | 16 | $38.40 | 18 | $41.60 |
| Ford f) | 12 | $17.55 | n/a | $14.50 | n/a | $15.06 |
| General Motors (GM) | 9 | $40.81 | 26 | $49.77 | 16 | $61.10 |
| Intel (INTC) | 20 | $21.45 | 64 | $33.48 | 58 | $28.11 |
| IBM (IBM) | 20 | $97.14 | 25 | $114.25 | 21 | $85.35 |

| | | | | | | |
|---|---|---|---|---|---|---|
| Minn. Mining (MMM) | 21 | $98.44 | 29 | $106.80 | 28 | $121.55 |
| Sears (S) | 9 | $37.14 | 23 | $52.63 | 11 | $53.24 |
| World Com (WCOM) | 11 | $13.53 | n/a | $12.7 | 88 | $ 5.07 |

Now let's revisit some of these stock prices and look at a $50,000 investment spread out evenly among these companies.

| | 10/09/01 | | | 1/18/02 | | |
|---|---|---|---|---|---|---|
| Company | Price | Shares | (Value) Cost | Price | Value at Close | Gain/Loss |
| Alcoa (AA) | 31.61 | 88 | 2,777.78 | 33.77 | 2,967.59 | 6.8% |
| Adobe Systems (ADBE) | 28.83 | 96 | 2,777.78 | 35.95 | 3,463.79 | 24.7% |
| American Exp. (AXP) | 29.00 | 96 | 2,777.78 | 37.16 | 3,559.39 | 28.1% |
| Bank of America (BAC) | 52.15 | 53 | 2,777.78 | 61.12 | 3,255.57 | 17.2% |
| Bank One (ONE) | 29.36 | 95 | 2,777.78 | 38.62 | 3,653.88 | 31.5% |
| Boeing Co. (BA) | 36.00 | 77 | 2,777.78 | 38.33 | 2,957.56 | 6.5% |
| Citigroup ( C ) | 42.70 | 65 | 2,777.78 | 49.90 | 3,246.16 | 16.9% |
| Disney (DIS) | 18.92 | 147 | 2,777.78 | 21.24 | 3,118.40 | 12.3% |
| Du Pont (DD) | 38.04 | 73 | 2,777.78 | 40.51 | 2,958.15 | 6.5% |
| Exxon Mobile (XOM) | 41.06 | 68 | 2,777.78 | 38.64 | 2,614.06 | -5.9% |
| Ford f) | 17.55 | 158 | 2,777.78 | 14.70 | 2,326.69 | -16.2% |
| General Motors (GM) | 40.81 | 68 | 2,777.78 | 49.77 | 3,387.65 | 22.0% |
| Hewlitt Packard (HWP) | 16.72 | 166 | 2,777.78 | 22.61 | 3,756.32 | 35.2% |
| Intel (INTC) | 21.45 | 130 | 2,777.78 | 33.48 | 4,335.67 | 56.1% |
| IBM (IBM) | 97.14 | 29 | 2,777.78 | 114.25 | 3,267.05 | 17.6% |
| Minn. Mining (MMM) | 98.44 | 28 | 2,777.78 | 106.80 | 3,013.68 | 8.5% |
| Sears (S) | 37.14 | 75 | 2,777.78 | 52.63 | 3,936.31 | 41.7% |
| World Com (WCOM) | 13.53 | 205 | 2,777.78 | 12.78 | 2,623.80 | -5.5% |
| | | | **$50,000.04** | | **$58,441.73** | **16.9%** |

Interesting results, are they not? Is it over? Not by a long shot. Recently, in several classes, I gave the students, split up into teams, an assignment to find three companies with P/Es below ten. It was amazing. Within 30 minutes, each team (there were six of them) had 5 to 10. Some had found companies with P/Es anywhere from one to five. You can find these in the newspaper, online, through your broker and in many financial publications. It's quite easy.

# 10-A P/E Ratio Update on Finding Value

Now remember, P/Es are part of the "health" indications of the Company. Debt, dividends (yields), book value and sales (to book) are other measuring sticks. P/Es are just one component, but I think they are the most important one.

As you read the past several sections of this chapter, I hope you realize, not only how important earnings are to the health of a company, but how the *anticipation* of earnings affects how the company is viewed.

Recently, I've noticed from the many comments on News TV and News Radio, that the emphasis is not on the actual numbers, but on people's comments *about* the numbers. Some of this has to do with the anticipation of future earnings, but more of it has to do with their comments about the current state of the company.

As these comments make reference to the future and pertain to future earnings, they drive the price of the stock up or down. Let me give a few examples:

Example #1: When, AOL made its earnings report. It had lower-than-expected revenues, but the actual earnings, or the bottom line, beat the estimates of many analysts. The stock was up, even though the company said the near future did not look too bright. That was an unusual occurrence. Yes, they beat their numbers by only a slight margin, but their comments about the future were not seen in a positive light and yet the stock was up about 50¢. One of the other things affecting this stock was that they took a charge-off of part of their purchase (or the blue-sky amount) of the Time Warner merger. This one-time charge-off seriously affected their current earnings. People who are in-the-know would view this as a good thing, in that the company *is* earning money and will have a tendency to grow for the future.

You, as the reader of this chapter, will be able to view in hindsight what has happened to AOL's stock at the time you read this chapter. Before this chapter was written, AOL had quotes around $19.60 and opened up inclined slightly above $20. You can look back now and check out the charts from the time you're reading it to the end of April and notice the incline or decline of the stock. AOL has become a large, diversified company with the purchase of Time Warner. Yes, it took this one-time charge-off, or a one-time expense item, and that showed up poorly against the earnings. But again, people who really understand these financial reports and can read between the lines, would see this one-time charge then look at the long-term stability of the company.  AOL's ticker symbol is now TWX

AOL has now moved from a single-product type—that of being an Internet service provider and search engine—to a huge diversified company. The purchase of Time Warner assets substantially changes the nature of this company. This means, instead of being in a single sector that might have a lot of emphasis (note that much of this emphasis in the Internet sector is past-tense), it is now a huge multi-billion dollar company with many different assets and business ventures. *This* means the stock will not have rapid rises or rapid decreases—it will be a more stable incline or decline—again, based on the anticipation of how well the company will do in the earnings department in the future.

Example #2: VeriSign (VRSN). The morning I was dictating part of this chapter, VeriSign was getting hammered and was down about $5. This is a stock which was at $40 just months ago. Ironically, the company is still earning money, though not quite as much as it was before. It's revenues and its earnings are down, and now everyone needs to readjust their forecast for future earnings.

In the next paragraph you will see the actual news release on the morning of April 25, 2002 about VeriSign. I noted that with the stock down about $4.90, this is right in line with where the stock should be, based on a twenty-times Price/Earnings ratio.

## Bloomberg Press

> VeriSign said first-quarter sales rose 54 percent to $327.8 million from $213.4 million, boosted by its acquisitions of Illuminet Holdings Inc. And H.O. Systems Inc. The revenue was less than the $342.6 million average expected by analysts surveyed by Thompson Financial/First Call.

> "We had a very challenging quarter," Stratton Sclovos, the company's chairman and chief executive, said during a conference call.

> Sclavos said profit will be 18 cents to 20 cents a share in the current quarter, excluding amortization of intangible assets and other costs, on revenue of $320 million to $330 million. On that basis, which isn't in accordance with generally accepted accounting principles, it was expected to earn 23 cents on revenue of $361 million, the average forecasts of analysts surveyed by First Call.

Let me explain: in all of my books and seminars, I talk about a norm for P/E ratios of twenty. Again, this is just a standard number I use to judge many companies' P/E ratios. Historically, the average P/E ratio had been 15.5, but on the New York Stock Exchange right now, average P/E ratios are slightly under 20, so I just use 20 as a convenient number.

What VeriSign said is that, instead of having 23¢ per share earnings, they were going to have 18¢. The earnings are going to be down 5¢. Again, this is 5¢ for one quarter. Hardly ever does a company have the same earnings per quarter; but just for fun, let's extrapolate the 5¢ and multiply it by four, for four pre-penned quarters. That would be 20¢. If you then take twenty times 20¢, you would get $4. When the company says its earnings are going to be down a nickel for the quarter and then you see the stock fall over $4, it is right in line with what the market expects.

I give you this example as a clear way of seeing how important the earnings actual numbers are and how important the forecasts about those earnings are. It could easily be down the other 90¢ and fall even further in the next few days; not so much based on the actual numbers, but on the "guidance," or the earnings forecast for the future.

When I shout from the rooftops, "Follow earnings, follow earnings, follow earnings," this information about VeriSign will be an ample example for the stock to get trampled.

As of today, after we typed up that last bit of information about VeriSign, there was another news release that addressed the issue of one of their key people leaving. Could a key person leaving one company and moving to another company affect earnings? The answer is "Yes, to both companies." Obviously this is seen as a negative to VeriSign as the stock continues to show signs of weakness.

Example #3: On April 8, 2002 International Business Machines (IBM) announced that they would not make the current earnings estimates for the quarter. The earnings report for that quarter was due about 10 days from then. Specifically, they expected earnings per share would be in a range from 66 to 70 cents with revenues in the range of $18.4-$18.6 Billion. The consensus estimates at the time were for 85 cents per share with revenues of $19.7 Billion. The stock had closed at $97.25 the day before and moved down to $87.41 after this announcement. When the actual earnings came out on April 17, the company reported 68 cents per share with revenue of $18.6 Billion. With the earnings the company said much of their business has stabilized and that the 2nd quarter could turn out to be quite good. The company also said it has strong cash flow and earnings growth should increasingly come from operations, supported by cash flow. The stock closed after the earnings announcement at $88.95.

Example #4: On April 18, 2002 KLA-Tencor (KLAC) reported earnings per share of 17 cents, 2 cents above the estimates. The stock had closed the day before at $68.66. During the conference call on the earnings report, the company said that gross margins had decreased slightly. They also said that they only expected 2nd quarter orders to increase by 10%. The estimates from Wall Street analysis had been somewhere around 20-30%. The stock went down about $3 that day, closing at $65.61. The stock continued it's downward trend over the next several days.

We started this chapter with a thought in mind that I could help you learn how to choose stocks in a more wise manner. Remember, our simple reason for investing is to make money. We do not make money by going backwards. We should avoid bad investments at all costs. A famous basketball coach one time said that the way to win basketball games is to not lose. The way to win at the stock market is to *not lose.*

If a dedication and an extensive study of the process of determining the value of companies and their stock price, based on their current and future earnings and other fundamental factors does not cause us to choose really great stocks that will race forward, it should at least stop us from making mistakes—those of choosing stocks which go down in value.

Remember also to put in your stop-losses. You may have a stock that shows all kinds of reasons for going up. Maybe it's currently at $18 and every indication is that this stock will go to $23 or $24. You either decide to own the stock outright, wait for the increase and then sell it, or you decide to use the stock to write covered calls and generate cash. It matters not. Put in your stop-loss at around $15. You do not know what is going to happen in the marketplace in general, or in that particular sector. You do not have any control over people's comments about the stock, or over the industry in which the stock is located. Because you have no crystal ball for the future and no control over news events, you should protect your downside.

When we purchase a stock, we should know our exit point. In fact, we should have two exit points: one if the stock goes up and the other if the stock goes down. Simply put, we need to manage our downside as well as our upside.

## Cautions As You Move Ahead

1.  To make sure you're not overpaying for a stock, watch the P/E in changing markets. In a bull market the P/E can be higher. In a bear market you would expect a lower P/E.

2.  Certain industries have different P/Es. Banks have low P/Es—say in the 5 to 12 range. High-tech companies have higher P/Es-say around 35 to 60. Check the sector to see what you're paying.

3.  If your bank P/E is at 15 and the average is 18, you are paying a premium for the stock. It's okay if you expect higher earnings. If your food sector P/E is 16 and the company you're considering has a P/E of 12, then you're getting it at a discount.

4.  A low P/E is not a pure indication of value. You need to consider its price volatility, its range, its direction, and any news you think worthy.

5.  You may want to check the historical level (P/E) of the stock. If the current P/E is above the 5 or 15 year historical P/E, the movement of the stock may be about to drop back into line.

*Important:* The activities or news of a company—that which has driven the P/E to its current level—does you no good prior to your stock purchase. This is why you also need to look at, consider, and take into account the future earnings estimates. Yes, be careful, but remember, you make your money after you buy the stock, so it is the future that will pay you—in dividends and in growth.

*OUR THOUGHTS BECOME OUR ACTIONS; OUR ACTIONS BECOME OUR HABITS; OUR HABITS CONTROL OUR DESTINY.*

*WADE B. COOK*

# 11

# Stock Repair Kit—
# How to Fix Sick Stocks

Let's do an example. Say we buy 1,000 shares of a stock on a dip at $18. We wait for it to go up a little, then write a covered call on it, selling a $20 call for $2 a share, or $2,000. What happens if we don't get called out on or before the expiration date? To get called out means to sell. What if right after the expiration date the stock heads into one of those "no news" times—a red light period—and the stock tanks? Now we're sitting there with stock we bought at $18, expecting it would go to $21 or $22 in the short term. Not only did it not go to $22, it went *down* to $16. Does that sound like a breakdown to you?

I'm going to show you what to do to help repair this situation. We did this purchase cautiously but wisely on margin, because this stock had every indication it was going back up. 1,000 shares at $18 is $18,000. At 50% margin, we have $9,000 of our own money tied up.

Now if the stock dips we have two problems. First of all, we could get a margin call and have to bring in more cash because the brokers need more collateral in the account. The second problem is common when we write covered calls: we wind up selling the winners and keeping the losers. By selling a covered call, we're selling the upside—in this case, the upside sell didn't pan out, and we now hold a losing stock. When we took in the $2 or $2,000 we committed to letting someone buy this stock from us. If the stock went to $25, that additional profit would be theirs.

Let's take care of the margin requirement. When we purchased this stock for $18 and later sold the $20 calls for $2, we took in $2,000 of premium. That $2,000 premium is in our account, and can be used to cover the extra margin requirement. Our covered call became a kind of preventative strategy in this situation.

Now let's address the issue of owning a losing stock. You really have *seven choices:*

1. Continue to hold the stock.
2. Sell the bugger. Use your money elsewhere.
3. If you really like the stock, buy more.

4. Write covered calls against the stock to bring in more cash.

5. Do a LOCC—covered calls with a twist.

6. Rolling Covered Calls

7. Sell two—buy one

## Seven Choices—Explored

**CHOICE #1—HOLD ON** Whether you wrote a covered call or not, or whether you purchased the stock for $17.50 or $18, its still now at $16. Choice #1 to me is a victim's strategy. It's good for talk at parties, but is that all?

If you still think the stock can go back up, holding is one choice. If you think it can go down further, then maybe choice #2 would be better. You don't need me to do this. You also do not need a lazy, inept stockbroker, however.

One way to mitigate losses is to put in measures so you won't lose any more than you're comfortable with losing. I've repeatedly said to "know your exit before you ever enter a trade." Now, I'm saying, you need two exits. One if it works. This is, sell at the exit point to the upside. The other is an exit point to the downside.

There are two methods:

1) Put in a stop-loss order. It costs nothing to place this order, until you actually sell the stock. Let's say you think the stock will go up from this $16, and while you don't want to lose any more, you could stand another $2 loss. Put in a stop-loss order at $14. If the stock tanks to $8, you'll be glad you did. Oh, don't you wish you had put in a stop-loss of $70 when you bought the stock for $78? $78,000 to $70,000 is bad enough, but not as bad as the basement price of $16,000.

2) Buy a put. The $15 put out two months is $2. The $12.50 put is $1. As the stock goes down, your put will go up in value. Sell the put for a profit, and now with the stock at $14, start through this list again.

**Choice #2—SELL.** If you're trying to make up lost ground, as in get your assets back, then you have a choice in this. Sell now and deploy your money into better positions. Problem? The same decision making process that got you into this mess is probably still with you. What have you learned? Can experience teach you something? Is your broker going to sell you their latest "pump and dump" stock du jour?

You still have $16,000 left. Can you work it better with more of a tilt toward monthly cash flow to add to your asset base?

**Choice #3—BUY MORE.** Maybe the $16 range is a better support level. Check the technicals for support or moving averages. I'm not big on "dollar-cost averaging." I refer to it as dollar-dumbing down. I'm not talking about this. $16 just might be the launch (support spring) that you need. Buy more, or buy call options to capture the upside move.

These additional shares can be kept or used for covered call writing. Don't forget your protective measures.

**Choice #4—WRITE COVERED CALLS.** This is a favorite of mine. It gives you a chance to fight back. It lets you add cash to your account for whatever purpose you choose. Please remember the rules for covered call writing as outlined in my *Wall Street Money Machine.*

This is a perfect strategy for those who think owning call options is too risky. By buying calls we have a one in three chance of making money. Sometimes $1/_2$ in three chance as the stock must rise and rise quickly or we'll lose. Selling calls stacks the deck in our favor—we gain a $2 1/_2$ out of 3 chance of making money.

The stock has dipped to $16. Let's say for this example that we start fresh. We have not previously written covered calls. This time we just own the stock and it is down. We don't want to sell for a loss and even though we think the stock will go up, it probably won't have a big upward move in the near future.

The next month out $20 calls are going for $1. The $17.50 calls are $2.50. The choice has to be based on this all-important question: Do I want to sell the stock or not? We cannot choose a strike price or a month for expiration until we know the answer. If you want to sell the stock, sell the $17.50 or even the $15 for $3.50. If you don't want to sell the stock, say you want to keep it to fight another day, then sell the $20 call. It probably won't go above $20 in one month.

Let's do the $17.50 call. In one day we have $2,500 in our account. We're fighting back and we're just getting started. The stock goes to $17.25. We don't get called out. We still own 1000 shares and we get to keep the $2,500.

More decisions. Check the list again. #1 (keep), #2 (buy more) #3 (sell), or hey, let's do it again. #4, the stock is at $17.25, which puts the 17.50 calls at $3, the $20 calls at $2. It seems to be having a tough time with $17.50 so let's do those again. $3,000 is much better than $2,000, even though you would gain $2.75, or $2,750 to the upside with the $20 calls.

$3,000 in the account. That's $5,500 so far. The stock goes to $16.25, but in one week it's at $18.25. It finally broke above $17.50. And it's on its way to $19. Time has expired, and the $17.50 calls are going for $2. Aren't you glad you didn't buy those $17.50 calls? Yes, the stock is up, but time is deteriorating and the implied volatility is going out of the premium.

More choices:

A) Leave it alone. You'll probably get called out at $17.50. Take your profits and run.

B) Buy back the call. Yes, purchase ten contracts of the $17.50 calls for $2. End the position. On this trade alone you've made $1,000 because you sold that option for $3,000.

C) Now what?

1) Sell the stock and be done with it.

2) Sell the $20 calls for $1, or $1,000. You take in the $1,000, but you've also moved up $2.50 on the strike price. If you get called out you'll make another $2,500.

3) Sell the $20 call options for the next month out (five weeks from now). They're going for $3,000. That's more cash and you're still in the game.

D) Repeat: Lather, rinse—do it again.

Selling covered calls puts you out of control of the upside gain of your stock. You take in cash now but give up everything over the strike price. The "buy back" strategy is easy to do and puts you back in control of the upside and gives you more choices—again, ask the question: "Do I want to sell this stock or not?"

*Also note: you can do everything I just listed in an IRA account.*

**Choice #5—COVERED CALL WITH A TWIST** The stock is at $16. You want extra cash, but don't have the time to baby sit the position. Consider a LOCC, Or Large Option Covered Call. Its May, the $20 call option for November is going for $8. You would have a position, in place for five months, but you're okay with this. $8,000 cash now and you give up everything above $20. Remember that it's at $16. You would get the gain up to $20, keep the call premiums sold so far, plus keep this $8,000. Yes, and you can buy back that $20 call on dips, or as you get closer to the November expiration date. You're in the money and you're in the driver's seat.

**Choice #6—ROLLING COVERED CALLS** You've sold the $17.50 call. On a dip, buy it back. Close the position. On the next rise in the stock, sell it again. I've only done this twice in one month, but I hear some of my students have done this 3 and 4 times. They're more dedicated than I am. This takes a lot of monitoring, but is well worth it as you master the support and resistance level. In fact, many of them call it, "ROLLING COVERED CALLS."

**Choice #7—BUY ONE—SELL TWO.** Here is a way of capturing some upside profits and mitigating your losses. Remember that the stock dipped to $16 and we had to use our $2,000 in premium to cover the margin, so we might be breaking even right now. Here's how we recoup some of our losses and sell double the amount of contracts that we originally sold. Buy the number of option contracts to match the amount of the stock we currently own. In this case, sell twenty and buy ten contracts. Sell two, buy one.

Let me explain what I mean. With 1,000 shares of stock at $16, we're going to sell twenty contracts of the $20 calls—double the amount of contracts we originally sold. We'll set the strike price out about three months; since this is May, we'll sell contracts that expire in July. With the stock on a dip, these go for about $4 each. Selling twenty contracts brings in $8,000 cash.

For the same month, we'll buy ten contracts of the July $17.50 calls at $6 each. We own 1,000 shares, so we're going to buy ten contracts to cover the rest of the twenty calls we sold. That will cost us $6,000. We sold two, bought one. We are "covered," but with 1,000 shares of stock and ten contracts to buy another 1,000 shares at $17.50

Let's explore what we have accomplished by doing this. First, our hope here is to break even. Even if we spend $8,000 to buy the lower strike price calls, that would be all right. In this case, we netted a small profit, about $2,000 minus commissions. We've generated some cash by selling the same strike price out a little bit further. What else have we done? If you look, we have now created a ten contract Bull Call Spread. We own the $17.50 calls and we've sold the $20 calls.

We took in $8,000 to sell twenty contracts, and we could spend $6,000 to buy ten contracts. What do we get out of this deal? The answer, an immediate $2,000 but there is more. We are still in the game. Look at what we've done: we have created a $17.50-$20 Bull Call Spread. This type of a spread is created when we own a call option at a low strike price and sell a call at a higher strike price. We substitute the options for the stock.

Okay, pretend that this transaction is done with stock. Then we'll substitute the option and see that we'll make about the same amount of money. We purchase a thousand shares of the stock for $17,500 and sell it for $20,000. Our profit would be $2,500. A typical Bull Call Spread is a debit spread. It costs us a net debit to put it in place. We would spend money to put it in place and take in money when we sold the option.

Let's break away for a while and look at a typical Bull Call Spread. The same stock, at $18 will be our example. The cost of the $17.50 Call, out one month, is $3. It is .50 cents in-the-money. We sell the $20 call for $1.75, or $1,750. We net $1,250. It costs us a net out-of-pocket amount of $1,250, and if everything works okay, we'll net profit $1,250, minus commissions. That's nice but to do this trade we would really have to be bullish.

Let's try it again. Let's buy the $15 call for $4 or $4,000 and sell the $17.50 call for $2 or $2,000. There is a net debit (cost) of $2,000. Now the stock only needs to stay above $17.50 and we make $500. To see this, let's move away from the options and use the stock. If we owned 1000 shares of the stock at

$15, that would be $15,000. Now, if we sell the stock for $17.50 we would take in $17,500. That's $2,500 more than we spent.

A ten contract $2.50 spread represents 1000 shares. Substitute the option for the stock. We have the right to buy 1000 shares at $15 and someone has the right to buy 1000 shares from us at $17.50. If the stock is above $17.50 on the expiration date, we'll get exercised on, and in turn exercise the $15 calls. We make $2,500.

Hold it. We bought and sold options, not the stock. It cost us $2,000 to put this spread in place. Yes we gross profit $2,500, but we have the option cost of $2,000, so our net is $500. Doesn't seem like much, but $500 profit on a $2,000 expense is not bad for four weeks. When the trade is over we have back in our account $2,500—our original $2,000, plus our profits of $500.

Note: commission will eat up $100 to $200 of the profits, so I usually do 20 contracts at a time—$4,000 to make $1,000, and I really try to have a $1,500, or $1,750 cost in my $2,500 spread. Then I could net $1,000 before commissions.

## Back To The Repair Job

The above explanation, while tough to get through the first time, presents a spread that is learnable and achievable. It requires a fair amount of study, a few months of paper trades and a skilled broker. Most stockbrokers do not know how to do this type of trade. There is much more information in *Safety First Investing* regarding Bull Call Spreads and my favorite spread, the Bull Put Spread. Let's do another set of trades.

Our purchase of the 1000 shares of stock, even though on a dip, allows the "sell-two, buy-one" possibility. We own 1000 shares of stock at $18. It's dipped to $16, but remember we took in a $2 option premium for selling the $20 call. So far, we're about break even. Now, by selling 20 more contracts of the $20 call, and moving out a few months to pick up a larger premium, we've created a cover call situation with our 1000 shares. Ten contracts did that. We also purchased ten contracts of the $17.50 calls, and by doing so have created a ten contract $2.50 spread. We're long the $17.50's and we're short the $20's.

For our example in the last section, you'll see that most Bull Call Spreads cost money. They're debit spreads. But look at this transaction. We sold twenty contracts of the $20 calls at $4 each or $8,000. We purchased ten contracts of the $17.50 calls for $6, or $6,000. We pocket $2,000. We're ahead already.

Let's see what happens. First, the stock. If the stock goes back up to or above $20, we get called out. With the original purchase at $18, then a $2,000 option premium from the sell of the original covered call and a new $2,000 for selling the new $20 calls and the purchase of the $17.50 calls, we're at a $6,000 profit.

We're not finished. Let's look at the Bull Call Spread we put in place. If the stock stays below $20, we won't get called out. The $20 call will expire. However, we'll be able to sell the $17.50 for whatever we can get—maybe $1,000, maybe $2,000—maybe nothing if the stock goes below $17.50.

But, if the stock goes above $20, and remember we have 2 months for the stock to inch back up above $20, the spread works and we make an additional $2.50, or $2,500. That puts our profit at $8,500 (minus commissions) on a 2 to 3 month hold on the stock.

The play is over. Time to find another deal. Question, what if you had listened to your stockbroker?

Good: The stock finally went back up to $20 and you sold it for a $2,000 capital gain.

Bad: The stock went down to $16 and you sold it—a $2,000 loss.

This Sell-two, Buy-one strategy lets you recover your losses in several ways. You're in the game—this time making $8,500.

So there is your repair kit for covered calls. Buy the stock, sell the call, and if it doesn't work, double up. Sell twice as many of the original strike price calls, and buy the same amount of calls as the amount of stock you own. Try to break even on that transaction to create a Bull Call Spread, and pull in extra profits when the stock turns around and starts working for you. You may never need your "stock repair" kit, but keep it handy just in case!

*I LIKE PLAYERS WHO MAKE THE TEAM GREAT, RATHER THAN GREAT PLAYERS*

JOHN WOODEN

# How to Trade in the Stock Market

# Book 2

# 12

# Chocolate Blue Chip Cookies—
# Build a Great Portfolio

This recipe is about baking a delicious batch of cookies, which can be eaten now or stored for the future. The type and size of these cookies will be determined by the need of the baker (investor). In short, this recipe is about building a portfolio that will stand the test of time.

I have written extensively on finding good stocks, ones that will go up in value. Therefore, I will refer you to those other sections. One part of this baking or investing process is to choose investments you know will be either short-term trades and also some for your retirement. There is a great deal of information on this topic in Book 1, Chapter 5. It would be easy to say this recipe is for everyone, but it is not. It is only for those people who are willing to deal with the normal vicissitude of the stock market. Some people's temperament will not even allow them to do any sort of stock market investing. For them, real estate or gold, or owning their own business would be a better arena of engagement. No matter what type of investments a person likes to own, or trade, some of the following baking directions are applicable in most investment endeavors.

## Ingredients:

Look for stocks that have one or more of the following reasons for going up in price. Take note that all of these ingredients start with the same words, "compelling reason" for making an investment.

Ingredient: compelling reason #1: the company is making good money, as exemplified in its P/E ratio. The company's history of earnings looks good and the earnings appear to be increasing. Earnings have a lot of influence in regards to the potential upward movement of the stock.

Ingredient: compelling reason #2: We look for stocks that are in certain sectors of the market which have a great potential for going up. Even if your stock is not "blue chip" but is in a good sector, it can tag along with the rest of the stocks.

Ingredient: compelling reason #3: The stock has been beaten up. It is seriously down in value. You need to be careful because the stock could continue to go down, but you look for stocks that are of a turnaround nature. This could be from new product approval, new management, the winding down of a lawsuit, merger with another company and a turnaround in their earning prospects.

Ingredient: compelling reason #4: Similar to ingredient #3, you might have a stock that has gone down for no apparent reason. Maybe it was caught in a down draft by one or two other stocks in the same time period. By itself, it should have not gone down, but it did and therefore could have the highest likelihood of bouncing back up.

Ingredient: compelling reason #5: The whole market place is on an upward trend. Your stock is going to participate in that movement.

## Mixing Instructions:

Taking into account one or two ingredients listed above you are going to determine what type of cake you want, simply meaning—what you want the cake to do for you. This will determine how you mix these ingredients together. Again, one of the advantages of the stock market is that you can mix multiple ingredients at one time. You literally can create your own "mutual fund" by proper homework and by wise choices. You need to ask yourself a series of questions:

1) Do I want to own this stock and tuck it away somewhere in my portfolio and leave it alone while it does its thing?

2) Am I buying this stock for short-term trades? Is it, a quick turnaround, a bounce, or a rolling stock?

3) Do I want to use this stock as collateral, as in a "margin account," for the basis of purchasing other stocks?

4) Do I want to use this stock as the foundation for selling options against the position to generate cash income into my accounts? This cash income can be used for other stock purchases, for purchasing more of this same stock, or for with drawl from the account for use elsewhere.

## Baking Time:

I have given many reasons why I think holding stock in the market for a 20 and 30 year period is way too long. We are simply not long-term people. The products and services of a company might become obsolete; a large company can have competitors from seemingly small companies which could devastate it's earnings potential. The large fund managers do not keep their stock positions for very long; and many financial professionals are conducting what I consider a "pump and dump" scenario wherein they are trying to drive up the price of the stock to enable them to sell out of their positions for a profit. We usually get left holding a stock with dubious characteristics.

It is important to realize that ownership of a stock should have a beginning, a middle and an end. Even if you own stocks for the long term, might I recommend that your long-term horizons be considered two to four years? Keep revisiting the story line of the company. Does the stock continue to have an upward bias? Has the compelling reason changed?

Let me give you one way to determine this. At any point along the time line of stock ownership, ask yourself the question, would I buy this stock at the current price? If you previously purchased the stock for $40, and happily have seen it go to $60, then ask the question, would I buy this stock at $60? If the answer is yes—the company still looks good, it is still making money and has every likelihood that the stock will continue to rise—then continue to own it. However if you answer the question, no—you see that the company has had its run, it will take a long time for earnings to catch up with the current stock price, and there is no compelling reason for this stock to go much above $60—then sell it. I would not *buy* it at $60, so I should consider *selling* it at $60.

## Eating The Cookies:

**<u>A REMINDER</u>**—There are other things that can be done with any stock for cash flow purposes. This cash flow aspect is my bias. Therefore I look at each stock, or investment, as to what I am going to earn from this investment in the near term and what I am going to earn from this investment in long term, including selling the investment to generate immediate cash for additional investments.

Ask the question, what else could I be doing with my money? Perhaps take the $60 and look for other $40 stocks with the highest likelihood for price advances. Use the stock for writing covered calls. Use my research to buy more. Unload part of my position—maybe reclaim my invested dollar and let the rest of the position run its course. Go to a movie.

> *"Sometimes when learning comes before experience it doesn't make sense right away."*
> *~Richard David Bach*

Once in awhile, it is good to review the basics of good and wise stock selection. Here is a brief list of seven items you can use, either as checkpoints or as rock-solid criteria for choosing stocks that will beat the averages. Remember, that's the key. It's not that any one stock will make you wealthy, it's that your stocks will be better than normal. The simple way to do this, is to stack the deck in your favor—only purchase stocks with the highest likelihood of near-term increases.

You will notice the first three items in this list of seven have to do with earnings:

1. Follow Earnings: compare the stock to itself. What is this stocks personal earnings history? Remember, in the overall market, the Price/Earnings ration is historically 15.5—so you could check the stock historically against itself and historically against the market in general.

2. Earnings: compare this stock to other stocks in the same sector or industry. This comparison will be a story in and of itself. Determine if the stock you are considering purchasing is overlooked by Wall Street. Has it gone down in sympathy with other stocks, yet has a lower P/E ratio than other, similar stocks?

   One way to check this, would be to check the P/E ratio of the index. For example: there is an Internet index (Ticker: DOT), a high-tech index (Ticker: MSH), a Pharmaceutical index (Ticker: DRG), transportation (Ticker: TRAN), media (Ticker: GIP), defense (Ticker: DFI), banks (Ticker: BKX) and a host of others.

   As I have so often said, everything returns to the norm. You could look at sectors, and your particular stock may be at a better Price/Earnings ratio than the sector in general, but the sector itself may be on a serious downtrend. So, why do you have a position in a roller-coaster that's going downhill. We should be looking for uptrending stocks and stocks in sectors that have very little serious downside adjustment potential.

3. Earnings: check the growth of earnings. Yes, it's good that Americans are getting back to lower expectations in the 5-7% growth area, as compared to growth of 15-50%, as it was a few years ago. However, is the company you are considering buying stock in growing its revenues and growing its bottom line. Check the last three years and see if you can distinguish a pattern of growth.

   If you want to be more detailed, you can check patterns of growth of other stocks in the same sector, as mentioned in number two above.

   Another aspect to look for in a company's earnings potential, is a company that will benefit from the current economic conditions. You can read the newspaper every day and see trends in certain sectors. For example, the housing sector is above average right now. There is growth in the manufacturing arena, the consumer sales businesses like Wal-Mart and JCPenney's seem to be doing well. Travel is another area that could see some growth, because it was so seriously curtailed after the September 11th terrorist attack. Security, especially security in regards to travel security, will probably do well in the next few decades. Obviously, defense and all defense related stock will do well as America builds up its arsenal again.

4.  Good Management: does the management clearly reflect the mission of the company? Have they been through good times and bad times. Has management moved from one company to another, and how well did they do with the last company.

    Remember, an "A" Team can take a "C" product or service and either make it better, or find another product or service for the company. The adage, "bet on the jockey, not on the horse," is a very true statement.

5.  The Market Niche: is the product or service of this company easily identifiable? You can check this by how well you can explain to other people what it is that the company does. Confusion usually means "No." Confusion and anxiety in the stock market mean that the stock is going to have a hard time, simply because people do not know what the company does.

6.  Low-Debt. Remember the debt of a company should not be much more than 30% of the market cap of the company. This is an easy figure to calculate. Debt is a killer of businesses. Even if a company has good revenues, the high cost of servicing large debt can be devastating. With interest rates low, many companies are refinancing their debt, and the profits should be translated to the bottom line in the next few quarters and over the next few years.

7.  Book Value: this is also considered the break-up value, or what the company's assets are worth if sold on the open market, minus their debt. Remember that the book value contains the assets as of their last SEC filing. According to GAAP (Generally Accepted Accounting Principles), an asset is carried on the books at the market value or cost basis, whichever is less. This cost basis is the depreciated cost basis. In short, the company could carry assets on its books which are worth substantially more in the real world, as opposed to how they're characterized on their books.

    A typical stock will trade at two to three times the book value of a company. For example, if the book value is at ten, it is not uncommon for the stock to trade between $20 to $30. For some companies, the stock price could be much higher even than two to three times book value. For example, Microsoft, at the time of this writing, had a book value of $8.75 and the stock was trading at $30. Microsoft does not have a lot of assets (note that it has a lot of cash), but it is such an incredible profit-machine.

Here are some companies that have a reversed ratio. Indeed, you will see that the stock price is substantially under the book value. That does not mean they are necessarily good deals, but it *could* mean they are takeover candidates, and could also mean the stock should grow substantially and still be within the realm of normalcy.

| Stock | BV | Stock Price | |
|-------|-----|-------------|---|
| HLSH | $10.03 | $2.79 | (*potential fraud–be careful) |
| ACF | $12.31 | $13.09 | (Pretty Close) |
| DYN | $9.20 | $4.23 | ($2.15 in cash per share) |
| EP | $11.33 | $7.35 | |
| ILA | $8.00 | $4.05 | |
| SFE | $2.21 | $3.92 | (close, but watch this one as IPO's pick up) |
| CPN | $10.48 | $4.90 | |

Note: Many of these are energy stocks, which have been beaten up lately

Summary: There are bargains everywhere. In this type of economic marketplace, it behooves all of us to do better homework. This simply means we need to be stock-specific. Each stock needs to have its own story-line. Each stock has to have a compelling reason for going up—and the more reasons for going up, the better. If you could find a stock with good numbers and all of the seven above, you'll probably have a winner.

# 13

# Rolling Stocks—
# Refrigerator Cookies

Rolling stock to me is like a cookie tray full of delicious cookies. It is not a whole meal, but a delectable source of continuous cash flow. Any baker in the kitchen is going to choose this recipe when he doesn't have the inclination to work more complex recipes. Other strategies could produce more profit, but at a higher price, and a higher risk.

## Ingredients:

I particularly like low cost stocks. By this I do not mean penny stocks, but stocks between .75 cents and up to $7 or $8. There are many stocks that form roll patterns in the higher ranges like $60 to $66, or $105 to $112, but they are such expensive ingredients that many small-time bakers cannot afford them. What we look for, so that these cookies come out exactly like we planned, are stocks that have formed a roll pattern. Stocks are going up, down, or sideways. In this particular recipe; we want stocks that are moving side ways—stocks that move repeatedly between two price points. The price point at the low end of the range is called the support level, and the price point at the top end of the range is called the resistance level. Look at an example of these types of cookies in the following charts.

You will notice that these stocks are moving in a sideways pattern. Most of these companies are not fully-grown. This simply means you are not basing the entire decision to trade or not to trade the stock on the fundamentals-or the health-of the company. The technical analysis of looking at stocks will come into play here. These stocks move on news, and sometimes the lack of news. These stocks do not move on fundamentals. They are news driven. Sometimes the real risk is finding stocks that are not heavily traded. Again, for the ingredients to be mixed together properly, we look for stocks that move in these repeated rolling patterns. Some stockbrokers call the cookies on this cookie tray "channeling."

Many recipes have ingredients that are hard to find. This one is no different. The stocks that form rolling patterns usually cannot be found by looking at the prices of stocks in the newspaper. You would literally need to watch the newspaper everyday to pick out one stock for up to two months, or more likely up to six months before you would find any roll patterns. They would be very difficult to spot this way.

# 13-Rolling Stocks–Refrigerator Cookies

Let me give you a few suggestions.

1) I look at CNBC from time to time, or the Bloomberg station on TV. As the ticker symbols scroll across the bottom of the screen, if I am in the mood to do rolling stocks, I will look for 10 or 15 stocks that are trading in the pennies all the way up to $2.00 or $3.00. I will then get a chart on each company for the last six months, or year, and look to see if it has had a roll pattern. Again, I must stress that just because it has rolled between a certain range for the last six months, there is no guarantee that it will do so in the future. The stock could be coming up on good news or bad news, the company could be merged or purchased by another company, or the stock could even quit trading.

2) Many years ago I stated that I like to find rolling stocks in companies that were in some stage of the bankruptcy process. This can still work to a certain extent. I must add some very strenuous cautions here. When a stock goes into bankruptcy, and when a stock is coming out of bankruptcy, it is a very dangerous time to use it as a rolling stock. Sometimes in the middle range, say a few weeks or months after the bankruptcy notification the stock can form roll patterns. Remember most of these stocks roll because of news. Sometimes for bankrupt companies, the news is all they have going for them. You would play the news or the anticipation of the news, associated with your particular rolling stock. I have oftentimes seen the ownership in a company's stock completely dissolved because of a bankruptcy judgement. Usually the creditors end up owning the company. Therefore when a company is coming out of bankruptcy as a new company is formed, and rumors are flying around about how it is going to be restructured, more than likely you are going to be left holding the bag if you own the stock at that time.

3) On our Monthly Update Skills Training at www.wadecook.org we are constantly updating a list of potential rolling stocks. Even though we try to keep this updated, you still should do your homework, check out the roll pattern, and see if the stock is still rolling, and rolling to your liking.

4) I have an advantage, because our company does seminars all over the country. We have many students who tell us about stocks they are rolling. We have become a clearinghouse for this kind of information. One advantage you will receive if you tie into our company seminar system is not just receiving good instruction, but tapping into the brainpower of tens of thousands of people.

5)  Lately I have noticed commercials advertising services with recommended lists of stocks. I will not vouch for any of these companies, as I am not a subscriber.

## Mixing Instructions:

One of the decisions you will have to make after choosing a rolling stock is how many shares you want to buy. Many beginning investors and new investors choose the rolling stock recipe because it is not a complicated recipe and it doesn't require a lot of money to get started. However if you use a very small amount of money, sometimes the profits are so small that the commissions eat them up. To make repetitive profits with these rolling stocks, do the following:

1)  Do as much research as you can on any potential candidate.

2)  Study the rolling pattern and determine if there is enough profit in the rolling range. I have found in the past the stock has to roll at least .50 cents or the trade is usually not worth it. Let me give you an example. A stock goes from on $1.50 to $2.25, and once in a while pops up to $2.50. That sounds like a nice profit— .75 cents. If you were to do 1000 shares, it would cost $1500 plus commissions to enter the trade. When you sell the stock at $2.25 you would take in $2,250, generating a profit of $750. After commissions this could leave you $650 to $700. I think you can quickly see how important it is to ask for low commissions on these types of trades—especially trades <u>you</u> have initiated with your stockbroker. The $750 of profit is really nice for this small trade. If the stock went from $1.50 to $1.90 and you think this .40 cents is a nice profit, but then realize you have to pay commissions of $70 to $90 per transaction, you can see how the profits would be pretty much eliminated. The stock went from $1.50 to $1.90, your $1500 went to $1900. It looks like a $400 profit, but after $180 for the round trip commissions on the trade, you would be left with just a little over $200. That is substantially different than $650. This is problem number one.

Problem number two doesn't meet the eye to the new investor, but it is very important. Each one of these trades is done at the "bid" or the "ask." When you buy, you are *buying* at the ASK, and when you sell you are *selling* at the BID. Let me give an example. When the stock was around $1.50 the *bid* and the *ask* were actually $1.30 (bid) by $1.50 (ask). When it reached its resistance level, around $2.25, it was actually $2.25 x $2.40. You might easily look at a chart, and even though you might be happy with the lower profit of $400, if the *bid* and the *ask* were slightly askew, say the $1.50 stock was really $1.50 x $1.60 and the *bid* and *ask* when you sell the stock was really $1.70 x $1.90, then you could see how this trade would not work very well.

The point is the chart could be deceiving. You buy the stock this time at $1.60. It doesn't sound like much of a difference between $1.50 and $1.60, but on a small trade it is a substantially different amount of money. Then when you sell the stock, you actually do not sell it at $1.90 even though that is what it looked like on the chart, or whatever tracking mechanism you use. You would sell it for $1.70. You see now what looks like a $400 profitable trade turns into only $100 profit, and the commissions could easily cost $100 or more.

It is very important when you look at these trades (based on a stock's chart) that you do not let your eyes deceive you. Make sure you have good contacts or glasses on so you can see the upper limits of the trade. Many times when stockbrokers give you a price, or when you see a price on your own computer screen, that is the price of the last trade. That price could be the bid or the ask on either side of the trade, but it is the "last trade." That last trade could be above the bid or the ask, in-between the bid or the ask, or below the bid and the ask price. There are a lot of strange pricings that go on with a rapidly moving market. The only thing you want to watch for as you mix these ingredients together is if the stock truly has the potential of allowing you to buy it right so you can sell it right.

3) This next instruction is one of the basic rules of rolling stocks. In fact, it has become a basic rule of virtually every one of my cash flow recipes: Don't leave the cookies in the oven too long. I call this instruction "know your exit before you go in the entrance." This is a strategy that I found which worked when I was doing my real estate deals. I was into quick turning real estate, but at first I wanted to sell the property for every penny I could get out of it. One day I was listening to some Bible cassettes and I heard the following scripture; Leviticus 19:10. "Thou shalt not glean the field..." This scripture weighed heavily on me. I started selling houses for under the full value and started selling many more houses per month. In fact I must say that it is the one scriptural thought that led to my success in real estate. When I played the stock market, at first I tried to sell the option (or the stock) for the maximum price, but later I found that if I was willing to leave a little profit on the table, I could sell my position much quicker and make multiple plays.

For example: I had one stock that was rolling between $2.50 and $3.50. I did this trade many times. Once in a while it would dip down to $2.25 and even $2.00 and sometimes it made it as high as $4.00. If I would have tried to sell the stock at $4.00, I would have missed out on numerous trades with a profit of .75 cents to $1.00. The point is that when you look at a chart and see a roll range, you don't necessarily have to buy at the lowest price, and sell at the very top. You need to be able to find a mid-point range and still be happy with the trade. One of the beauties of this recipe is that you can bake many cookies at one time. Hardly any baker in real life would bake some chocolate chip cookies with cinnamon cookies and have three sugar cookies at the end of the cookie sheet. But in the stock market we can do this. We can do two or three rolling stocks at one time. Each one will have its own characteristics, its own baking time and its own profit structure.

Now we have all the ingredients in the bowl, we have mixed them, and we are now ready to put the cookie sheet in the oven.

## Baking Instructions:

We have two choices in determining how long our cookies are going to be in the oven. We can look at the chart and determine the roll range, and continue to watch this stock very closely and get out at the optimal price. If one of the bakers in the kitchen has a lot of time, he can watch through the oven door window to determine if the cookies are done or not, just by looking at them. These types of bakers (or traders) can make a lot more money than I can, or than most of my students can. The second choice you have in timing is this, to know your exit before you go in the entrance. By setting the timer on the oven, you have pre-ascertained what your selling price is going to be. When the timer goes off, the cookies are done, and you can get them out of the oven at the precise time. This means you would place a "GTC" order, or Good 'Til Canceled. This can be for any amount of time, but functionally it is for 60 days.

From my experience, most of my stocks have rolled for around 5 weeks. Some roll up to their high point in about three weeks and then back down, but it is usually five weeks or a little bit longer. I have had some of my students do more rolls than this. Look at the following:

*"Since Sept. 2001 I've consistently made 20% on rolling stock. My portfolio has grown from $9,000 to over $16,000."*
*-Bill G., MN*

*"I just wanted to let you know, that I was able to play one (rolling) stock over a three week period, seven times, and was able to realize a $7,000 profit from a $500 investment."*
*-Thom A., TX*

The second way to bake the cookies is to know your exit and pre-set the price point when you are going to get out. I don't want anyone to think this is the normal baking time. It is not. In fact I have never made this much with so little money at one time. Here are three more testimonials from some of our students; I offer them here so that you can see it has been done.

*"Quick turn rolling stocks – less than $5.00 stocks looking for .60 turns. In the past 5 trading days I have made a little over $1,100 on account of $6,600 that is approx. 17% return."*

*-Sam Y., UT*

*"Since Jan 2002 we have made over 40% in two accounts and 35% in two others using rolling stock."*

*-Doug B., CA*

*"Rolling stock HLTH got in with 5,000 shares at 6.80 got out at 8.00 with a profit of $6,000. This took about a week."*

*-Bruce H., IL*

Obviously, the trades listed above are past tense, they were a snapshot in time and you will not make those same trades. I offer them here to show you that it can be done. To summarize the baking time: watch the transaction very close. This might allow you to get in and out numerous times. By placing an order GTC, you could be in Hawaii on a vacation, if and when the stock hits the sell point, the stockbroker's computer will trigger the sale. Once again, you have another advantage in the stock market, because while you are on our vacation, the functionaries in the stock market will not only know when the cookies are done, but they will take them out of the oven for us.

## Mixing the Ingredients:

I have written extensively on rolling stocks in my first book Wall Street Money Machine, and a newer book entitled "Red Light Green Light." I do want to put a brief excerpt from some of those books here. It is the three patterns of rolling stock.

Log on to the Monthly Update Skills Training (M.U.S.T.) at wadecook.org. Subscribers can see lists of potential rolling stocks. Call 1-866-579-5900 for more information.

# 14

# Options—
# Cream Puffs

This next recipe involves a lot of yeast. As you know from other recipes, yeast is a leavening agent. It literally makes the dough come alive and grow, before it goes into the oven. Yeast also gives bread its succinct flavor. Many of you have left small amounts of dough out for hours in a baking pan. This allows the yeast to rise, causing the dough to fluff up into nice large dinner rolls, ready to be baked.

Options can do this too, in an investment account. They can add a lot of power and strength. Or just like bread dough, one small punch to the dough, or even someone walking by with enough force, can cause the bread to deflate. Options can be wonderful, they taste very good, but they require a certain skill level and have an added element of risk. Therefore they are not for everyone.

A call option gives an investor or trader the right to buy a stock at a certain price. A put option gives the investor or trader the right to sell a stock at a certain price. If you think a stock is going to go up, you would buy a call option. If you think a stock is going to go down, you would buy a put option. For this discussion we will deal with just call options.

An option is usually substantially less than the stock. For example, XYZ stock is at $52. The right to buy the stock at $50, say out two months, is $5. Now watch. A little yeast goes a long way. One contract (100 shares) would cost $500. If the stock goes to $54 right away, the option could go to $6, or $600. If the stock goes to $56, the option could go to $7.50, or $750. When there is a small movement in the stock, there is usually a corresponding movement magnified in the option. But remember, yeast gets old. It loses its ability to work. With options, time works against you. If the above stock stays at $56, the $7.50 option value will shrink to $6 (the in-the-money portion) as time deteriorates—as it gets closer to the expiration date.

This is why I keep saying a stock has to go up, and go up in a timely manner, for the option to work.

Options go in three month cycles, but as you get close to the actual expiration month there are always options out the next one or two months. We could buy an option to buy a stock for up to 9 months in advance and even longer with LEAPS®. LEAPS® are the right to purchase out one to two years. An option is not a down payment, as it does not apply towards the purchase price. An option is a derivative of the underlying stock. Because of the expiration date, there is a certain added risk factor. This risk is simply that time works against you. It is almost like the baking process, only you have a negative baking time. That would be ideal, but as you buy an option out two or three months, the stock needs to go up, and go up very quickly for you to make money.

Because of this time element, we need to understand what goes into an option so we can determine if we want to be a trader of options.

## Ingredient #1:

We need to determine what makes up the option price. This price is also referred to as the premium. There are three and possibly four elements in determining an option price. Without getting cliché, an option will sell for what someone is willing to pay for it. For example, if you have a steady moving, yet very slow climbing stock, the option price will be very small. If you have a very wild moving stock, one that is very erratic, the option will be much more expensive.

1) In determining a price, option market makers use a computer model. In any modeling situation you need to have a constant. Most mathematical formulas have a constant of one. The constant used in option pricing is a "risk-free rate of return" factor. This computer model uses the United States T-Bill rate. It does move, but very slowly, therefore it is almost a constant.

2) The time left to expiration. This almost becomes intuitive if you think about it. You will pay more money for an option that expires in six months, than for an option that expires in one month with the same strike price. For example, to buy a option one month out on an $80 stock may be $2. To buy the same option (strike price) six months out on the same $80 stock would be $6.50.

3) Here is where the fun begins. This is the yeast of this recipe that can almost not be controlled. It is referred to as "implied volatility." One way of looking at this is the speculative value, or the speculative nature of the underlying stock. Implied volatility simply is someone's best guess at what they can sell the option for, based on the underlying stock. If the stock is a slow mover, the implied volatility will be low. If the stock is fast moving, going up and down frequently, it will be a higher priced option. If the stock is in a very speculative arena, i.e., the pharmaceutical industry, or the internet/high tech industry, it will have a higher price. The implied volatility is represented as

a number. It refers to a percentage. If it has an implied volatility of 30, it means 30%, which means the stock could go up or down 30% within the next year. There have been stocks with implied volatility of 80 and 90, that would mean $100 stock could go down to $10 or up to $190. Obviously that is someone's opinion. I have even see some implied volatility numbers as high at 110. Again that is 110%. Somebody thinks this is a stock that could move to the upside or the downside in a big way.

Implied volatility makes up most of the option purchase price, therefore it should be looked at and studied carefully. Sometimes options seem very expensive because the implied volatility is very high. Sometimes people back away from certain options just because they are so expensive, yet sometimes that is where the money is made.

4) The "in-the-money" portion of the stock price would also be added into the option price. For example, if the stock is at $84 and you were to buy the $80 call option for $7, $4 of the $7 is "in-the-money." The $3 is the out-of-the-money, or what is called the "time value" portion of the option premium.

Quick note: the more the option premium is "in-the-money" the less time value is in the option. Let's use the same example of the $84 stock. The $7 call option premium on the $80 strike price could look like this in the future: if the stock moves up to $86, the same $80 call option could still be $7. This would signify that some of the time value in the option has expired—meaning the premium has deteriorated even though the stock has moved from $84 to $86. The value of the option has not gone up correspondingly. Once again this should give you cause for concern with options. The stock can move in the direction you thought it was going to move, but it does not necessarily mean the option will move comparably.

When we play options, we have an expression called "tick for tick." This means if the stock goes up one dollar the option goes up one dollar. This is very rare. But keeping with our example: if the $86 stock, at the $80 strike price has a $7 call premium, the stock moves to $88, the option moves to $9, then you can see that as the stock moved up $2, the option also moved up $2. Also in option trading, we look at the "delta" of a stock. This refers to the correlation between an option price and the stock price. A delta of 100 (100%), would be tick-for-tick. A delta of 60 would be 60%. This means that as the stock goes up one dollar, the option goes up .60 cents. Obviously in option trading we are looking for a high delta. The higher the better. However, the higher the delta, the more you will pay for the option.

Many people bake their cake and/or dinner rolls with high delta options. I agree—there is a certain level of safety—but many people find they gain a bigger bang for their buck by buying slightly out of the money call options, or slightly out of the money put options. In this case with the stock at $84 you would buy the $85 call, if you think it is going to go up. This call option might be $3. If you remember the $80 call was $7, but by buying the $85 call you have only $3 tied up. If this were 10 contracts it would be $3000, instead of $7000. Now the stock moves to $85 or $86, the $3 could become $4. It doesn't sound like much, only $1,000 profit. But $1,000 in two or three days or two or three weeks is not bad on a $3,000 investment. The $3,000 is also obviously a smaller amount to lose.

Options obviously give you a type of leverage, just not the same type of leverage as investing in real estate. What it does allow you to do is tie up only a small amount of money and position yourself for a better rate of return—more cash back on each dollar invested.

Now to the down side. If you own the stock, and it tanks, you realize very soon that you have a very risky investment, because there is such a large potential downside. In some ways I think stocks are riskier than options. For an option, the only downside would be just the amount of cash you have tied up in the purchase of the option. Remember you are not signing a contract to *buy* the stock at a certain price—you have the right, but *not* the obligation. If the stock does go down, you could lose all or part of your $3,000, but you have nowhere near the downside risk, compared to owning the stock. This is why we call options a "low-cost, limited-risk" investment. And again, where do you find investments with limited risk, but unlimited upside potential? In fact, the limit is not really unlimited in actual day-to-day investing. Time works against you and a stock movement has natural boundaries—moving lines in the sand though they may be. In short, the stock will only move so much. Let me share a testimonial.

> "I started trading on 10-19-95 with $2,900… I recently took an account from $16,000 to $330,000 in two weeks, and $35,000 to $2,484,000 in six weeks. I made $1.25 million in one day."
> - Glenn M., IL

Even for my students this is a rare occurrence. Yes, I taught this man and yes, I gave him a fighting chance, but he made this money on a rolling stock with a $2 swing. I'll explain, but I can't remember his actual numbers so I'll use fictitious numbers. The point made will be the same:

In a Stock Market Workshop, our regional two-day "experiential learning" event, he learned about rolling stock and about options. Company X (I think it was IDCC) originally rolled between $5 and $7. It moved up to $10 to $12.

One day, when the stock was around $10, he purchased the $12.50 call options. I think they were going for 25¢. One contract was $25. He bought hundreds of contracts and was hoping for a double—sell the option for 50¢. Surprise. The stock shot up to over $70 in a matter of days. Wow, and Double Wow!

Think about this. Let's look at just one contract—the right to buy 100 shares of the stock. The stock is at $72.50 and he had the right to buy it at $12.50. That's $60 in-the-money. We won't even mention the time-value here. $60 times 100 is $6,000. Not bad for $25. Lucky? Yes. In the right place at the right time? Yes. And remember, he had hundreds of contracts. Ten contracts would net $60,000. One hundred contracts (purchase price $2,500) would net $600,000.

Then, when the stock shot to $80 plus and backed off to around $70, he bought the $80 calls for January (at dirt cheap prices) and sold them two days later (December 29th) for a $1,200,000 profit.

And just think: He did all this after coming to my Stock Market Workshop. Whoa! Okay, okay, I'll only take partial credit. By the way, all I do is sell recipes, or education. I have no investments for sale—only knowledge and finally, I received nada, zip, zilch from his trades. He ate the whole cream puff himself.

Now this recipe is not for everyone. It is available for those who are willing to study out the process, understand the risk and the reward, be willing to move quickly (especially at the exit point), and be willing to shoulder this added element of risk—the expiration of time.

## Ingredient #2:

Because options are a derivative of an underlying stock, it is absolutely paramount for you to know and understand the behavior of the underlying stock. If you think it has an upward bias, then you could buy a call option, or sell a put option. (Look to another recipe for selling puts). If you think the stock is weak and will have a tendency to go down then you may not want to buy a call option. I cannot stress enough how important it is for you to do adequate homework on the underlying investment when you are mixing up the ingredients of this recipe.

## Ingredient #3:

There has to be a compelling reason for the stock to move. This is so much more important with options than with stocks. Stocks can be forgiving over a period of time, options are unforgiving. Time expires; the high premium you pay for an option can go away. Again, even if the stock does what you want it to do but not in a timely manner, your option could go down in value and you could loose some or all of your money. The deterioration of an option premium should be studied intensely. Simply, it will be like the yeast in a cake mix where it can lose its potency. To a lesser extent, an option's potency is the implied volatility. Another aspect is stability of the T-Bill rate. This will only be a small part of the yeast's potency.

## Ingredient #4:

With options you have the potential of a) risking a little and gaining a lot, b) you could also spend a bit more money on the stock, risk a lot and yet as the stock moves, gain only a little, or c) You could also risk a fair amount and gain a fair amount. One of these scenarios is where I think all investors and traders will be at different times. You need to find yourself in one of the three previous sentences. This will help you determine what kind of chef you want to be.

## Ingredient #5:

Options give you the opportunity of both buying (long) and selling (short). We can buy options; both calls and puts, and play a long position directly on the stock. We can also sell calls, which means we are agreeing to let somebody buy stock from us at a certain price. Or we can sell puts, which means we are taking on the obligation to let someone sell us the stock, at a particular price. At first blush, selling puts seems pretty tough, but it is still one of my favorite strategies, especially when you add in it's cousin the bull put spread.

## Ingredient #6:

YOU. I know you are not going to jump straight into the bread dough recipe, but you need to stay very close to this process. You are part of the recipe. If you are going to be successful, you will find that you must be a big part of the equation. This recipe will not work without you.

## Ingredient #7:

I will add, that the recipe could work if you have a very good stockbroker who is adept at option trading. He/she should be a technician of the process. They should know how to get in and out, how to set their orders, and purchase options at a better price as well as sell them at a better sell price—meaning "in-the-spread". If your stockbroker is not extremely adept at options, you should probably consider not using him/her for options. An inept broker could cause you to loose just like a bad mechanic fixing your car. I think you know this in real life and you are doing yourself a disservice if you think every stockbroker has the technical expertise to conduct quick in-and-out trades.

## Mixing Instructions:

To determine how you are going to use the mix of options, you need to determine your own risk reward desires. I know this is cliché, I also get tired of reading it in other peoples' books. But you cannot determine what kind of options you are going to play, either buying or selling, if you do not know what you want from the trade. Review the three sentences in ingredient four, and determine where you want to be. I have virtually gone through this process in every one of my *Wall Street Money Machine, Stock Market Miracles, Bulls and Bears, Safety 1st Investing, Free Stocks: How to Get Your Stocks for Free, and Red Light Green Light, books* . I hope all this information helps you find who you are—meaning what you want out of these deals.

1) Just like in rolling stock, you must know your exit before you go in the entrance. What is the compelling reason?

2) You must determine if you are going to be there to monitor this stock/option on a-day to-day, or even hour-to-hour basis. You can place your order-to-close position right when you are filled on your buy (or sell) to-open order. In other words, as soon as you get filled on your first order, you can immediately place your next order, which is to close. Good alert systems are necessary because when a stock reaches a certain price or the option gets to a certain price, you are out. Let me state this again in point #3.

3) You have a couple of choices on clearing out of an option. One would be that the option would hit a certain price. For example, you buy a call option at $3 and tell your broker you want to sell it for $4.50. Again, I will add you should have an exit strategy on the downside. For example if the option goes down to $1.50, you are out. You have an upside exit point and a downside exit point. Another way to do this is to look at the stock price and a recent chart, for a month or two and determine the high point, or the price to which you think the stock is capable of going.

Let's go back to the $84 stock. You determine the stock will have a tough time with $86. That would be a major resistance level. With the stock at $84 you would tell your broker that when the stock gets to $86 you are out of the option no matter what the price. Your $7 option could be at $6.50 with a .50 cent loss. If you own the $80 call option and the stock moves to $86, this could move the option to $8.50. You purchased it at $7,000 and you are now selling it at $8,500. This means you would get out at a $1,500 profit if you traded ten contracts.

4) When to get out. Once again the question is not *when* but *why*. When you ask yourself the question "why did I get in? " you should know what your exit point is. Remember do not enter a trade without the exit point. Another quick question would be to ask yourself "would I buy the call option at this price?" If no, then consider selling.

5) Just like any baking process in the kitchen, you need to be an expert. You need to learn the precision it takes to conduct proper trades. I have been a chef for many years, and I know that just because I cook a soufflé one day perfectly does not mean it will be done perfectly the next time. It takes months, and sometimes years of cooking in the kitchen to become a true expert. It takes a decade or so to gain the precision to be a most excellent race car driver. It takes years for CPAs and attorneys to develop their skills where they are truly helpful to other people. Why would anybody think that

he could enter a kitchen and bake a soufflé perfectly the first time? This holds true for options. For example, if a person did get lucky, and made a lot of money on the first one or two option trades, why would he think the next trade is also going to be done perfectly? Again you have to practice trade. Develop your skills; develop your expertise: not only your *competence* level but your *confidence* level.

## Baking Time:

Again this comes back to the issue of knowing your exit. Yes I do a lot of one-day trades, but they are rare. Option trading to me is "position trading." Instead of taking a large amount of money, by purchasing the stock, I can take a smaller amount of money and purchase a *position* on the underlying stock. But whether I use the fundamentals, and news items related to the fundamentals, as in an upcoming earnings release, or whether I use the technical viewpoint, which could be a support level or a bounce, or a break out, I know my exit before I enter the trade. I know how long it is going to stay in the oven.

Most option trading is one of short-term horizons. Each option rises and falls very quickly. Many people are not willing to move this quickly and therefore should avoid option trading. Many people do not understand how much of an enemy time can become to this option process. The option market place will humble even the most experienced trader if they do not pay attention to the ingredients listed above. Yeast can do funny things. Option trading, as I have stated so many times before, is very rewarding, once you have learned to deal with all the risk factors.

# 15

# Stock Splits— Muffins

It's Springtime and the weather just doesn't quite know what it wants to do yet. It's a bit cool this morning, but the day ahead looks to be hot—full of meetings, attorneys and a stock market that just doesn't want to cooperate with all my good intentions.

Aaaaahh…But from the kitchen the smell of morning muffins comes wafting down the hallway. About five minutes to go. I don't know why I can't wait for them to cool down. My favorite way of eating them, I should say "devouring," is to slice the muffin in half, and smear on the butter. Margarine won't do and just a little won't do—I mean *smear*.

Oh, I know how many calories are in a typical muffin. I've read that no matter what diet you're on, even one muffin will turn it upside down. And the butter. A cholesterol counter would need a calculator in this kitchen. But…well, no buts, it's just so darn good and I've found no better way to start the day.

One such day many years ago when I was writing real estate books, packing to travel and giving seminars, I noticed something in one of my stock brokerage statements that not only caught my eye, but got me very excited.

Now to put this in perspective, I did not own a lot of stocks. In fact, I was so busy with real estate, I sometimes went months without even looking at my brokerage statements. I just threw them in a drawer.

There must be a mistake, I thought. There were 400 shares of Novell (NOVL) in my account at $59 a share. Drat. I bought the stock earlier at $60. Another one went down. But 400. That was odd. I called my broker, "Hey, what's Novell at?" "$59.50," he answered. "Didn't I buy 200 shares last Fall?" "Let me check. Yes. Wade, where have you been? You bought 200 shares, but they did a two for one stock split. You now have 400 shares."

I continued, "Are you sure? Why aren't they at $30 then?" He informed me, "Wade, they've gone back up. And do you know what? Last week they announced another two for one split. It will happen on August 30th."

That experience was my tip-off that the stock split game was afoot. It would be like taking a duplex, making it a four-plex, nine months later making it an eight-plex and so on. You can compound profits in real estate, but not this way.

Stock splits are obviously unique to the stock market. I went hunting for more information. I checked books, went online, checked magazines and news articles and, you know what? There was very little information available.

Some research pointed out how well most stocks did after a stock split. Much higher rises than stocks in companies which did not split. Sometimes a stock splits; sometimes new stocks are issued as dividends: it's called stock for dividends. The tax consequences to the company (how it's characterized on their books) may be different, but to the investor the net affect is the same. You had 100 shares, but after a three for one stock split, you have 300 shares. You were given two shares for each one you owned, so wherein you had one, you now have three. The company had 120,000,000 shares issued and outstanding, now it has 360,000,000.

As I explored the process, I noticed trends. I discovered many unique things along the timeline of the split. I realized you could play the split many times, and a most important discovery was that a trader could use options for quick in-and-out plays. The muffin is split in half, smear on the butter and enjoy.

Now, let's move on. I noticed many years ago that stock in companies which split their stock had a tendency to perform better than stock in companies which did not split their stock.

With many companies, you'll see that the splitting of the stock has created almost an endless supply of opportunities. There are many ways to play stock splits, so we'll go through the basics at first and then get down to some of the variations, and include a discussion in the baking instructions.

## Ingredients:

Not all companies do stock splits. Some execute them very infrequently, perhaps every five to ten years. Still other companies split their stocks on a regular basis.

The ingredients for baking this type of muffin is simply a stock that is splitting. It's not difficult to find companies doing stock splits, as most of these are mentioned in the highlights of the financial news channels and usually on the front page of the business sections of most newspapers. Note: just because a company is doing a stock split, it does not mean you should play that particular company's stock.

The ingredients for this recipe are better found in the types of plays that can be made. We'll go through some of these here. Please note that I have written extensively on stock splits in other books of the *Wall Street Money Machine* Series. You can find much more detail there.

Before we put these muffins in the oven, we definitely must know when to take them out. In the following Ingredients / Timing section, I will give five times to get involved in stock splits. I hope by now, and as you get to know me, you'll read more into that statement than is written. When I talk about getting involved and consistently repeat the theme throughout this and other books to *know your exit before you go in the entrance,* I hope you now instinctively assume, "Therefore, there must be five times to get _un_involved."

You don't necessarily have to get uninvolved on every one of these strategies to make a profit, but for maximum profit on each particular short-term play, you must figure out where you're going to get uninvolved—where the trade works and where it does not work—and choose your exit point.

## Baking Time/Instructions:

1.  One place you can get involved in stock splits is before the company makes the announcement. I know this sounds odd, but it really is not that difficult to find stocks getting ready to do a stock split.

    I have noticed in the past that the two to three weeks, yet sometimes the month or so before the stock split announcement, there is a tendency for the stock to spike up. If you were to look at a chart, it may show almost a 90° angle.

    Obviously, someone knows something we do not know. Maybe people who study this company in detail would be able to ascertain, or might even hear rumors, that a stock split is imminent.

    We can find these stocks before the announcement in one of several ways. One of the tell-tale signs that a company is getting ready to do a split is when they announce that they are going to have the shareholders vote on the new authorization of more shares of stock at the upcoming shareholder meeting. The Board of Directors does not need shareholder permission to split a stock, but they do need shareholder authorization to issue more shares.

    For example: if a company has 100,000,000 shares of authorized stock, with 80,000,000 shares issued and outstanding, and they want to do a 2:1 stock split, they would need at least 160,000,000 shares to do so. It is not uncommon for the company then to have a shareholder meeting and have the shareholders vote for even 200,000,000 more shares of stock. This could signal a 3:1 stock split, or just the simple fact that they want to have more shares on hand.

Granted, they could be authorizing more stock for acquisitions of other companies, for doing an IPO in order to raise more money, or for selling to the public in a secondary offering to raise money. However, it is often the case that more shares are authorized so they can do a stock split and have enough shares available.

I have also noted in the past that many of these stock splits run in groups. For example, many of the oil stocks, within a one- or two-week period of time, will announce 2:1, 3:1 and 4:1 stock splits. Almost as soon as the heat dies down from those stocks, the hi-tech stocks all announce stock splits en masse. The week after this the bank stocks and the week after that the pharmaceuticals.

Another way to get involved in pre-announcements is to track the history of the company and note that they either A) split the stock when it reached a certain price in the past or B) split the stock at timely intervals—say every 15 months or every 18 months.

There are other ways to find pre-announcement stock splits, but one of particular note would be rumors on the street, and what analysts are saying about a particular stock. The way to find these is simply to keep your ear to the ground.

2.  The second time to bake these stock split muffins is on the announcement. This is on the company's news release about the stock split. The news release is usually accompanied with other information. For example, as I have taught elsewhere, stock splits, along with many other types of company news, do not happen until the Board of Directors meet. Once they meet, they may come out with many different types of information, ie: earnings, dividends, a share buyback, other newsy-type items and lastly, that they're going to do a 3:1 stock split.

    Of importance is *when* they make this announcement. They could announce it after the market closes, from 4:00 PM Eastern Time, or on throughout the evening. They could make the announcement a half hour to an hour before the market opens in the morning; *and* they could make the announcement intra-day. <u>This is not a good time to get involved</u>. It's like the muffins are already burnt before you put them in the oven. (See Baking Instructions number 2)

3.  Many unusual things happen between the time of the announcement and the actual stock split. From the time the company makes the announcement, until the actual split, there is usually a four- to eight-week period of time. It seems the larger the company, the longer the time between the announcement and the split.

For example, General Electric and Johnson & Johnson and some of the other big companies took two-and-a-half to four months to complete their stock splits, but the norm is about four to six weeks. This could take a company through a Red Light period into a Green Light period, or vice-a-versa. This passage of time will come to play when we get to Ingredient / Timing numbers four and five.

Between the announcement and the actual split, the stock will go up and down based on other news announcements, what the market is doing in general and what is happening in its particular sector. I have noticed that these stocks often form slight rolling patterns. These rolling patterns usually have an upward or a downward bias. There are many other things which will determine the price of the stock, other than the fact it is doing a stock split.

The stock split, for example, may draw attention to the company. That attention means many people will be scrutinizing the stock. The occurrence of a stock split in-and-of itself is probably not a good enough reason to buy the stock. Other factors need to be weighed in.

If you're buying the stock from a fundamental point of view, you would check on many of the other items which measure the health of the company. If you're buying from a technical point of view and are just trying to find support levels or other times the stock price has reversed itself, then you would look at the charts to see where the stock has been. If you have a lot of time and can track the movement of the stock, you will find many opportunities to get involved between the announcement and the split.

4.  a) For those who like quick-turn trades, there is a possibility of just such a trade in what I call "the rally into the split." There is a special formula which needs to be adhered to. This can become a trade you practice and get good at, and even stack the deck in your favor.

Many stocks have a nice surge, or what I call a rally into the actual split date. This often occurs even when there is no news—a red-light period. Here's the scenario: the split is scheduled four weeks from now. It's a 2:1. The split date, sometimes called the "pay date," is set for Friday. Friday is very common. The ex-dividend date will be the next trading day, or Monday. If you have 200 shares on Friday, you'll have 400 shares on Monday.

The stock was at $70 when the announcement was made. It spiked to $76, then backed off to $64. It has climbed its way back up to near $80. It briefly went over $80, to $84.

This is important. It's now the Wednesday before the pay date. The stock is at $76. I buy the $75 call for $3. I hope to make $1,000 profit on my ten contract, $3,000 trade. I also bought the $80 calls for next month. They were also $3,000. I'm hoping for a $2,000 profit on my ten contracts. This $80 strike price call, out another five to six weeks, is also my back up policy.

Before I go on, let's look at what I would not have done. If the stock had not been up to $80 or above, I would not have purchased the $80 calls. I might not have purchased the $75 calls either. Maybe I would have purchased the $75 calls if the stock had been up to $78 or $79, but only maybe. For this rally to work, we need a compelling reason for the stock to go up, and *go up in a timely manner.*

Remember, time works against you with options. The stock needs a quick one to two day move. If the stock is fighting resistance at the $75 to $80 range, the deck is stacked against me. The fact that it's been above $80, and hopefully more than once, means it can get there again.

The stock rallies on Thursday to $78, the call option goes to $4, then $4.50. I'm out. My $3,000 is now $4,500. It works or it doesn't work. I don't want to hold this option over the weekend. Why? Time now works against me. The price may stall or dip on Monday and hey, I'm happy with my profit. This was designed to be a two to three day trade. I positioned myself in front of the split rally, and now I'm out.

What about the $80 call? I hold on till Monday, Friday, this option spiked to $4.50 also. On Monday, right after the market opens, the stock is now at $39 ($78 / 2 = $39), backed off to $38.50. My ten contracts became twenty contracts, and the $80 calls became $40 calls. Some time elapsed and they were going for $1.75. I sold the twenty contracts for $3,500, a small profit of $500. I wished I had gotten out on Friday for $4,500. I must read *Wall Street Money Machine*, AGAIN.

5.  b) The muffin goes flat. There is an occurrence after the stock split that is so pervasive it bears mentioning. Actually, it's a caution. Almost invariably, the stock price will back off right after the split or within a few days. Sometimes it takes weeks.

Here's the scenario. The stock did rally. It was at $82 on Friday. It opens Monday at $41 and rises to $42. We got out of our position on Friday. We chose to "fold' em." Drat! We could have made a little more, but...by Thursday the stock is at $38. Look at these six charts. Notice the downturn right after the split.

Okay. If we own the stock, it's a temporary dip—hopefully. But even then, wouldn't we have done better to sell the stock at $82 (or 2 x $41), and buy it next Friday at $38?

But, what if we're playing the options? Time goes away. A dip in the stock could take all the profits out of our options and they probably won't recover sufficiently before the expiration date. You could buy the puts and play the downturn, but it's tougher to make money this way than you think.

I don't like old, stale muffins. I don't think holding the stock or the options through the split is a prudent move. So far, all of these trades have been short (two to three days, or two to three weeks) position trades. Get the muffins while they're hot.

6. <u>After the Split</u>: If you want a longer-term trade, or an investment, consider the stock a few weeks after the split, when it hits $36. That's $72 pre-split, or about the price the stock was at when it made the stock split announcement.

Many of these stocks do very well. Here's one reason. Rarely does a company announce a split if they're not doing well. Oftentimes an earnings announcement is imminent. We've tracked hundreds of these and almost always the company comes in with good numbers. This could be a stock or option trade; it could be for a few weeks (in and out) or for longer-term hods.

## Summary

There are five times to get in—throw the muffins in the oven—and five times to get out. Each of the five can be practiced. Each of the five has a beginning and an end. And you can become an expert chef at this process with study, practice and connecting the dots.

Excuse me. I've got to run to the store for some more butter. Honey, can you watch the oven for me?

*"Stock split #2, I bought QCOM call option for $40, 1 contract the day they announce 4:1 stock split. It gapped up past my $60 GTC and filled me at $90 = $5000 play."*
                                                                                    *-Anthony P., OH*

*"Using stock splits…. I took $5K to almost 22K and 58K to 102K in about 10 months."*
                                                                                    *-Brenda W., AL*

*SUCESS COMES FROM YOU, NOT TO YOU.*

*WADE B. COOK*

# 16

# Covered Calls—
# Icing on the Cake

Most people like frosting, obviously some more than others, as we can tell by looking at the waistlines of Americans. The following recipe is not about the cake but about the *icing on the cake*. You know from your life experiences that many cakes have really good frosting. Sometimes it is almost as thick as the cake underneath. Other times frosting is very skimpy, barely covering the cake.

When a cake is in the process of being served, it's interesting to watch how some people say they want a corner piece so they can get more frosting, and others want a center piece with frosting only on the top of the cake and not on the sides.

This recipe is about adding power to an existing strategy. It is a wonderful strategy, which, once mastered, will actually bring cash into your account. It is called Writing Covered Calls. It is designed to add money to your asset base. It is a perfect strategy for bailing yourself out of a bad stock situation. It can be done monthly or longer term. It can be adjusted to fit your lifestyle and your trading style. You can be as busy as you want, or as passive as you want.

## Cooking Utensils:

There are three components for making this frosting.

1) We need to add "open position" to our trading utensils; in this case, it's a selling strategy. Anytime the word "write" is utilized in the stock market, it means to "sell." To write a call means to *sell* a call option. To write a put means to *sell* a put option. In this case we are going to sell a call option, thereby generating cash into our account against the stock position we own. By selling, we open a position.

   Option contacts are in 100 share increments, so in the future you should buy stock in 100 share lots. You should also avoid DRIP programs: Dividend Re-Investment Programs on stocks which you want to use for covered call writing, because you could end up with an odd amount of shares. If your underlying stock is in a company paying dividends, you probably should choose to receive your dividend in the form of cash instead of shares of stock.

If we own 600 shares of a stock we have the right to sell six call option contracts against that position. In short, this would give a purchaser of these call options the right to buy our stock away from us at a set price. We use the word "covered" because we actually own the stock. We agree to sell our 600 shares at a certain price. We will sell them, or get "called out" if the stock is at or above the strike price on the expiration date—the third Friday of the specified month. We could get called out early, but this rarely happens. Boo Hoo…Usually, we write covered calls to actually sell our stock; by getting called out before the expiration date, we have rushed our profits to the "now" position and we have cash to do other deals.

2) In most situations we need an underlying stock. We could do this in a "naked" position—meaning that we do not own the stock, but we'll cover that strategy another time. You could also do a variation of this strategy with another call option as the underlying investment and create something called a bull call spread; we'll save that for another lesson as well. (See *Safety First Investing*)

We should not forget any of the components of our discussion on buying and owning good stocks. We should check the fundamentals, the technicals and the OMFs (Other Motivating Factors) such as news, to see that our underlying investment is solid. We want the company to have a good story line—meaning, every likelihood the stock will continue to move up. If you own stocks and you think they are going to move down, you should use some of the repair kit strategies, as in stop loss orders and buying puts to protect the downside. In short, you write covered calls when you are happy to own the underlying stock investment.

As I have mentioned in other chapters of other books on Writing Covered Calls, the most important underlying question—the foundation of this process—is to ask a question upon which all decisions will be based. That question is this: "Do I want to get called out?" ("Called out" means to sell the stock.) Look at the underlying stock. If the stock is weak and not showing signs of recovery, you may want to go ahead and sell the stock outright and not write a covered call. If the stock is weak but showing signs of recovery you may want to sell a slightly in-the-money call or slightly out-of-the-money call—again, depending on the answer to the above question.

If you want to keep the stock for writing covered calls for several months then you would sell an out-of-the-money call. For example if we own a $28 stock, we would sell the $30 call, or even the $35 call. If you don't care whether you sell the stock or not then you could write a slightly in-the-money or slightly out-of-the-money call option and let it ride until expiration, then wait and see if you are called out or not. That final resolution will be determined by where the stock is compared to the strike price on the expiration date. I bring this up again because you will not be able to choose which of these ingredients you are going to put into this frosting until you know whether you want to keep owning the stock or not. All of your decisions rely upon the answer to this question.

3) Call option. We should have a good working knowledge of what makes up the pricing model of a call option. When we are in the business of selling, we should try to sell for the highest price possible. In writing an option we are probably going to sell it for the price at the "BID." Even though it is the market price for that snapshot in time, we do not have to sell it at exactly that price. We can put in an order to sell the call option for any price we think we can get.

When we sell a call option, we are basically taking on an obligation. We should be paid well for taking on that obligation, which is to deliver the stock or sell the stock at a set price. Like all options, these positions have an expiration date. Our position will be considered "open" until the stock is either called away from us early, which means we have sold it, or until we arrive at the expiration date. All options expire (have no time value) on their expiration date.

When we own stock, we own the future of the stock—regardless of what earnings and other factors may do to the price of the stock. By selling the call option against the stock, (the option premium), we have given away the "upside" potential of the stock. We have sold away everything above the strike price.

If we own a $28 stock, and sell the $30 call option for .75¢, we will take in $75 for each contract. Let's once again say we have 600 shares of the stock, which, at six contracts at $75 each, will generate $450. The $450 will hit our account in one day, but the position could remain open until the expiration date. If the stock goes up to $31 or $32, and if we have not closed out the position, we will not participate in anything above $30. But, we will participate in anything *up to* $30. If the stock is at $28 and it goes to $32, then on the expiration date we will get called out at $30. This means we also make another $2 per share. Multiplied by our 600 shares, we wind up with another $1,200, in addition to our $450 for selling the calls.

# 16-Covered Calls–Icing on the Cake

Before the expiration date, we can always buy back the call option. For example, the stock has risen to $29.75, time has elapsed, and the expiration date is imminent. There is virtually little time value left in the premium as the option is worth .35¢ cents. We have a couple of choices: 1) we can just leave it alone. The stock will either stay below $30 or go above $30. We are willing to keep the stock or have it purchased away from us: 2) we could buy back the call position which would neutralize, or end, the open position.

Let's say the $30 call option is now worth .35¢—remember it is only a quarter out-of-the-money. You must ask yourself "Why?" We might be able to sell the $30 call option for the next month out for $2.50. This would generate $1,500 cash into our account. We have kept the same strike price (purchasing back the original option), but we have moved the expiration date one month into the future by selling the next month out.

Another scenario would be the $35 call option. It's going for .75¢. We take in .75¢, multiplied by 6 contracts (600 shares), and we generate another $450. It seems almost like extra busy work, but just think: we have spent $210 (.35¢ x 6 contracts) and we have generated another $450 cash into our account. One good thing is that we have moved up $5 on the strike price. If the stock were to continue to rise and we were to get called out at $35 that could generate another $5 multiplied by 600 shares, or $3,000 into the account. Plus, the $1200 from $28 to $30 as mentioned before.

One of the reasons I like writing covered calls is because of the "buy back" feature, which always allows us to regain control of our money. You can sell away the upside of a stock, and then buy it back. Many of my students do this two or three times a month. In short, they sell the call option on a rise, buy it back on a dip, and then on the next rise in the stock they sell the call option again. They keep the same stock and try to use it multiple times for generating income into their accounts. The most I have ever done this has been two times in one month. It is simply because I am too busy to monitor my accounts in such an extreme manner. Many of my students do better than me as they have more time to do this extra homework.

## Ingredients For Cake:

The main point is that these ingredients are going to be blended with the utensils. This frosting is going to become the cake, and the cake is going to become the frosting to a certain extent. The covered call we are going to write to generate income is going to be married to the stock position. Therefore the quality of the "derivative" is going to be based on the quality of the underlying investment. If you have a high quality investment, one that you have purchased after doing much homework, then your ability to make money in writing covered calls will be effectively enhanced. Don't try to get a really great tasting cake from really bad ingredients.

We need a good market place to operate in. If the kitchen is all messy and dirty and causes an inability to properly use the ingredients, we may want to sit it out until the kitchen is cleaned up. The stock market can also become very sloppy. It can be in a downtrending mode, and nothing we do seems to work. I have had experiences like this over the years, and it is hard to make quality trades in a less than quality market place.

## Baking Instructions:

As in all option positions, the baking instructions and time constraints will be in accordance with the underlying stock.

## Timing:

1) Usually we write a covered call for around three to four weeks out. This means that at the end of each expiration date, the week after the third Friday of the month, we will write the next month out covered call. We try to pick up (sell) as much time as we can.

2) We may not want to sell the call at that time if the stock is on a dip. A Wade Cook Market Maxim that will make this strategy work is this: "buy the stock on a dip (weakness) and sell the option on strength." If we think the stock is going to rise in the near term we may want to wait to sell the call option. Please note: you can put in an order to sell an option that is currently at a dollar for $2 by placing a GTC order, or "Good Till Canceled."

3) You can also do a buy/write and get one trade a little cheaper. A buy/write happens when you buy the stock and sell the calls simultaneously.

4) If we find that we have more time to monitor the position, we may be able to rapidly sell the call, and buy the call back on the next dip in the stock, a week or ten days later, and then sell the call option once again on the next rise. I alluded to this before. It is similar to doing a rolling stock but doing it as a rolling covered call. This could be done multiple times—again, based on your dedication and the amount of time you have to monitor the position.

5) We could also do a *L.O.C.C.* (Large Option Covered Call). In this type of transaction we would sell the call option for 5 or 7 months into the future. We hope to get called out, and by doing so, generate a huge premium—sometimes 80% to 100% of margin

amount we use to purchase the stock. I have written extensively on this topic in *"Free Stocks: How to Get the Stock Market to Pay for Your Stocks."* I think this book is especially applicable to people who are very busy with their businesses or careers.

If we own a downtrending stock, or are trading in a weak or downtrending market, the following strategy may help. We have a stock we do not want to sell. We want to wait for it to turn around. One way to trade is to sell an "in-the-money" call. Let's go back to our $28 stock. It has dipped from $35 but we don't necessarily want to sell it. It has not shown signs of recovery. In fact it could continue to go down. We could "pre-capture" the profits right now. We could sell the $25 call. The stock is at $28 and the $25 call is going for $5.50. Now if the stock dips down to $26 we would have pre-captured the larger premium generating more cash into the account than by selling the $30 call option. In this case we would get called out at $25. Again we can still buy back the $25 call as we near the expiration date, end the position, and then sell the $25 call for a further out month. If the stock drops to $24 we would not get called out. We would still own the stock. But look at this: the stock has dropped from $28 to $24, a four-dollar drop. We have picked up $5.50. We still gained $1.50, in spite of a drop in the stock. This speaks to the fact that there are "stock repair kit" methods to recover from a downtrending stock.

Now with the stock at $24, we can make a host of new decisions. We can sell the $25 calls, or the $22.50 calls for the next month. Do we take in a bigger premium now on a lower strike price or a lower premium on a higher strike price, hoping that the stock will go up? The point is that we are back in control of the decision-making process.

## How To Eat:

This whole section has not been so much about market timing but about length of timing for writing a covered call. Once you get a good understanding of how call option premiums work, and specifically how the option price deteriorates with the passage of time, you will be able to make many wise decisions. This strategy is designed to work on a variety of cakes. For example, you might have some of the following:

1) You have a rolling stock going between $6 and $8. While it is moving towards $8 you may find it advantageous to sell the $7.50 call and put some extra cash into your account right now.

2) You may have purchased a "slammed" stock which has gone from $18 down to $12 and you are waiting for it to bounce, but it hasn't quite bounced in the time period you wanted it to. You can sell the $10 calls or the $12.50 calls and generate cash while you are waiting for the stock to bounce higher.

3) You could have your semester investor type stock, that you are holding for 2 or 3 years, but from time to time you could use those right term hold stocks for writing covered calls for generating extra income.

4) Rolling options. Many people have found higher priced stocks around $40 to $90 that are rolling three to five dollars in a given period of time. They can play rolling options by buying a call and selling a put or by buying a put and selling a call either at the high end or the low end. If you have a stock that is of a higher price and in a rolling pattern, you may, by studying the pattern, decide to use the same stock for writing options against it.

The point is that many stocks serve many purposes. One of my suggestions at many of my seminars has been to pick your top 10 or 20 stocks. Just like the top 20 in a rock-n-roll, List of songs, you have your top 20 in stock-n-roll. You can get good at 20 stocks. You can understand the basic mission of the company: you can learn important dates of the company, like earnings reports and other news types events: you can notice patterns and chart certain stocks. You can even memorize support and resistance levels. Most human minds cannot do this with hundreds or thousands of stocks. I know a lot of people try to do this with their computers and I wish them well. I have found that in my busy life I do most of my trades on the phone to and from basketball and while I am out running errands. I cannot look at a computer screen, or even printed out charts. I have to do my investing through the eyes and ears of other people. This has caused me to limit the volume of stocks I am trading; again, I limit the amount so I can become an expert on a few stocks. I do not want to be guilty of "jack of all trades and master of none." I suggest you consider the same. Get to be an expert on a few stocks——stocks you like, and not burden your mind with so much clutter that you have a hard time keeping track of the stocks in your portfolio or stocks you want to trade.

Covered calls are a workhorse, the frosting that will make everything taste better. You will not use it all of the time, but once you get good at it, I will suggest to you now that it will become a strategy that will work for you in good times and bad times and one that will help you generate more cash and build up your assets in your stock market portfolio.

## Writing Covered Calls

*"I wrote a covered call on RMFD, stock went down just after I sold the call. I bought my position back that same day, the stock went up the next day. I sold the stock and made approximately $1,000 on the option and sale of the stock—this was a two day deal."*     -Allen R., NC

*"Cash in was $2,000, profit was $1,750 that is a 87.5% return in 10 days."*     -Alton C., FL

*"I purchased SCIO stock 2 weeks ago at 19.50. I sold the calls for 4.75 or $1,425. I had 150 shares on margin. If I get called out at 20.00 I have a $1,575 return on a $3,000 investment for a 50% return in 1 month."*                                                      -Benjamin C., UT

*"Covered call CPWR 9.60 bought on dip. Wait to sell calls at 1.45 on 40 contracts made $5,800 on $23,600."*                                                                                -Bill B., MI

*"November 29, 2001 I bought 2 contracts of the Jan 30 calls on ISSX on news that it was being added to S & P mid-days. It was at 29.06 on November 30. I got out with a $1.50 profit, which was a 17% return overnight! Very exciting trade."*                    -Christa K., B.C.

## L.O.C.C.

*"I sold L.O.C.C. on KLAC and CCMP and did very well…, I have cleared over $1,000 many times."*  -Marvin W., MI

*"L.O.C.C. system on BRCM bought stock at $38.00 3 contracts Nov. 30 each at $12.60. Bought them back at 3.80."*                                                              -Anthony P., NJ

*"Aug. 30 I did a call on 1 of 2 C with RFMD. L.O.C.C. sold 1 C of RFMD Feb 40 for $14 1/2 or $1,450 into account. In Oct. the stock went down so I bought back the contract at 75/share to close out the position."*                                                            -Chuck P., TX

# 17

# The Fisherman's Smorgasbord—
# Bottom Fishing

We are always looking for bargains—sometimes what I refer to as "Bottom Fishing." I have a few favorite seafood restaurants here in the Northwest. One thing my very favorite restaurants have in common is a combination seafood bucket. At a few of the restaurants they dump a bucket of seafood on a piece of butcher paper right in front of you. They put a bib on you, leave you with a chopping board and a wooden mallet, and then let you go to town. In the bucket there are clams crabs, lobster, shrimp and various kinds of fish. I discovered the "Crustacean Investment Principal" in my real estate days. My fellow author Ken Otterman came up with this concept after doing many real estate deals after my style. It was simply this; we would go into neighborhoods and find really shoddy properties, buy them, use a small amount of money to "fix-up and clean-up." We then could turn around and sell them as a fixer-upper. Other people would buy these same types of properties and fix them up to the maximum highest price. We learned early on that people like to buy fixer uppers. We would buy them, do a minimal amount of fix-up work, and sell them right away. The Crustacean Investment Principal means we buy those little creatures that crawl on the ocean floor and eat all the garbage—like shrimp or lobster—then turn them into very expensive delicacies. The same works in the stock market.

The following recipe will reveal many secrets that big time investors use to capture huge potential profits. These will all be pure stock plays, except for "turn-arounds," which could be done with options. The purpose here is to put the right kinds of ingredients together and then watch them grow. The point is that sometimes you will never know what is going to turn out.

## Ingredient #1: IPOs

One type of crustacean we are looking for is an IPO, or Initial Public Offering. We try to find pre-IPOs, those we can purchase private stock in, before they go public. I find some of these at BottomFishing.com. Note: I own stock in many companies listed on this site. Another type of IPO trading opportunity would be to invest in the company right as it is going public. These are hard to get into and easy to lose money on. The last of type of IPO is a company after it has gone public. One such time to get involved with these

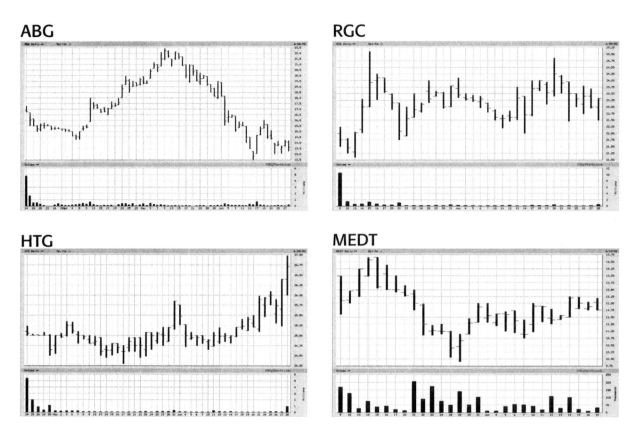

post IPOs is after the 25 Day Quiet Period. You see, when a company goes public, the underwriters and any of their analysts or stockbrokers and company leaders cannot PR the stock. They can't say anything. But usually, a few days after the 25 Day Quiet Period, they come out and support the stock. Look at these four charts. Notice you would have to trade the stock as there are no options available for six months. Check out BottomFishing.com for examples.

## Ingredient #2: Out of Favor Stocks

Today there are many stocks trading between $1 and $5 that used to be over $100. If these companies have found their legs gain, they may be good candidates to rise again. Note: today there are $2.50 call and put options. There are so many formerly high-flying stocks which are now under ten dollars. Shop carefully.

## Ingredient #3: Bulletin Board or Pink Sheets

Another type of bottom fishing we can do is to find companies that are on the pink sheets, or electronic bulletin board (OTCBB). These are very risky and yet could be profitable.

## Ingredient #4: Turn Around Candidates

Remember there are certain types of crustaceans that can grow back a leg if they lose one. We can look for this same ability in companies. Find companies with regeneration ability. One way is to look for high book values (BV) compared to the stock price. These companies become take-over candidates.

## Ingredient #5: Spin-offs

Many large companies "spin off" divisions, or subsidiaries. This might be a good place to find value. Remember when Pepsi spun off Taco Bell, Pizza Hut and KFC. It's now called Yum Brands, Inc., and trades under Ticker Symbol YUM.

## Mixing Instructions:

I have written extensively on each one of the six ingredients in other books. Please check all of the *Wall Street Money Machine* series for more information. Let's look right now for bridges of commonality among the above ingredients to see if we can find a way to use a small amount of money for putting this smorgasbord together. First of all, just like any smorgasbord, each one offers a selection of our own favorite foods. There may be 90 items from the salad bar to the dessert bar, but most of us only pick 7 to 10 of these items. Take this example into account when it comes to choosing from the ingredients above. Even though there are six ingredients, we should probably work on becoming an expert at one of these styles. My personal favorite is the IPO market place. I love watching small companies go from the private sector into the public sector. A lot of my students really like spin-offs. The only problem with spin-offs is that they do not happen frequently enough in order to help us develop an expertise. There are many companies that have gone down in value, but it does not necessarily mean that a cheap price means a good bargain, or a great value. You really have to do your homework on these. Picking up on that, let's go through several things you can do to build a good-looking plate.

#1. Do your homework. These really need to be studied out. You should be projecting trend lines. See if they even have earnings. Check their price/earnings ratio. You should be looking at the book value as well—basically check on the fundamental health of the company.

#2 These types are not that easy to practice trade. They take a while to develop out. (Refer to baking time #1). You need a lot of patience for these types of trades. Sometimes they take four months to a year to pan out. Therefore, they are difficult to paper trade. One way to paper trade is to "retro trade," or to go back a year or so on the history of the company. Look at companies who's stock was down in the basement and follow the progression of the stock. For example, make note of how difficult it has been for the stock to regenerate or move upward. Answer these questions: What will make it grow? What is holding it back?

## Baking Instructions:

1. You need to follow a common theme throughout many of my recipes, which is to find strong management. It is so very important for this type of trade. In many regards the management behind the product or service will drive the stock in one direction or another.

2. You do not want to put a lot of your money into any one trade. This is the classic type of trading style where you need to diversify. If I had $100,000 available for this type of trading, I would try to find 10 such deals with $10,000 into each trade. If I had only $10,000 for this type of investing, I would put approximately $2,000 into five different trades.

3. These trades are not the best suited for placing your sell point at the very beginning when you purchase the stock. In these stocks, you might buy one at $2, and hope it goes up to $100. It usually takes time to develop. It also takes a lot of patience.

## Supplemental Material: Stock Valuation

Any type of negative news, even the anticipation of news, can impact a stock. Rarely will a good investment a company makes be treated with equal time as its mistakes. In fact, there's no real place to report this type of good news. You won't see: "Company A's investment of $5,000,000 in Company B is now worth $60,000,000 after Company B's IPO." You'd have to be an expert financial report reader to find it out.

Bad news gets a lot of press. But remember, press reports are fleeting. They are on to tomorrow's story. You still own the stock in this company, with all the bad news. Do you hold, sell, or generate income, say by writing covered calls? Well, first, check the real story. Is it making money, or not? Are earnings growing or contracting? Again, was it truly a one-time charge, or is there more bad news around the corner? Listen carefully to what the company's leaders are saying. Are they bullish or not?

This next part is most difficult for us armchair investors. We need to kick the tires. We need to find out what the company is made of. Okay, it's had some bad investments, but has it had any good ones? How are they carrying assets on the books?

You see, assets are carried on the books as of the last Quarter's SEC filing. Some of these assets could be worth a substantial value more than how they are listed. However, it would be rare to see assets carried at less than their value. Remember, (GAAP)—"cost or market—whichever is lower."

Picture American Airlines with its land, gates, airplanes, etc. It could have billions of dollars carried as millions. Weyerhauser has millions of acres of land—with trees and other resources. Some of this land was purchased around the turn of the century—NO, the last one. Companies have invested in other companies with the thought of it going public. They're still waiting.

Book Value is a determination of a company's value based on the break-up and sale of the components. The Book Value is easy to find out—just call your broker, or most good computer programs (stock search) will list this value. It is not uncommon for a company's stock to be trading at two to three times Book. Many are at eight and ten times Book Value.

Let's look at this a little more closely. I can't stress enough, though, that the listed Book Value is how the assets are being carried, according to GAAP, and according to those values as of their last Quarterly Filing. Take a look at how many banks have been buying up regional banks. Granted, banks have odd reporting requirements. They carry loans on their books a certain way. These loans, plus assets, make up their Book Value. Their stock is at $20, but the Book Value is at $24. Their stock is at a discount to Book Value. They are a target for a takeover. Conversely, another bank's stock is at $14 and the Book Value is $10—AND it's still a target. Maybe even more so. Why? Because the true value of its assets are larger in real life than how they're being characterized on their books.

Now, away from banks, but let's still explore a takeover, or merger. Often, these transactions are done with stock, with little or no new cash. Sometimes, the assumption of debt is involved. It doesn't matter. There still is a valuation placed on the deal. It is carried on the books at that price. Do you see how the valuation of the stock in one company can be almost instantaneously affected by the rise or fall of a sister stock?

## Restricted Trading To Free Trading

Many companies have invested in private companies with the hope that this new company would go public. This private stock, once the company nears the going public process, is often called Rule 144 stock, or restricted stock. There are other names, but these will suffice. If the new company goes public, the investing company is under serious restrictions as to when and how fast it can sell the new stock.

The holding time is now just one year. So, Company B goes public. Either the stock Company A owns is registered in the IPO (unlikely and it still has selling restrictions) or Company A submits Form 144 and registers an appropriate amount of stock for sale. This registration is good for 90 days. If selling volume increases, a new registration can be done, even before the previous 90 days have expired. However, even though the company has registered this stock, it doesn't necessarily mean it has to sell this stock. Maybe the price drops, or news comes out that something good is about to happen with the thought that the stock might go up. They wait to sell. For this discussion on valuations, the important point is this: this registered, now free-trading stock, can be listed on the books at the current stock market price. For years, all of this stock still had to be carried on the asset portion of the ledger at the original cost. Do you see how our $1 stock, now worth $14 or $114 could be carried at the original lower value?

This is important. Once again, it is possible that a million dollar investment, now worth billions, is carried at the original cost until it goes public and is registered.

## Incubators

This discussion will take on added meaning when we explore a few incubator-type companies. Incubators in this regard are companies which have as their business plan that of investing in or helping companies to go public. There are simply not many publicly traded companies that do this. Here are a few: Safeguard Scientific (SFE); CMGI (Ticker the same); and Internet Capital Group (ICGE). You might recognize one or two of these. They had stocks in the $100 to $200 range. What happened? Many of their holdings, and most of their work, was in the high-tech companies—some primarily in Internet companies. The bottom fell out on this arena and, while hundreds of companies were set to do IPO's and go public, the last few years have seen this IPO business, once a fire hydrant of activity, come to a trickle.

Okay, the "take public company" is almost dead, but as Billy Crystal said as Max in *The Princess Bride*, "He's only *mostly* dead." These companies still have huge investments in companies which have gone public (SFE was 20% of Telelabs: TLAB), or are still private, but waiting to go public.

So, before I go on, I want to pose a question. Please ponder this and come up with an answer. One of these companies owns stock in say 30 different companies. Some of this stock has been owned for four to six years. Some of the little companies have totally gone out of business. This original list was 52, now 30. Some are making good money and most are just waiting for the IPO market to turn around, then they will go public.

Here's the question: how are these assets carried on their books? Cost or Market? More or less? Could the asset be worth less than their original investment? Yes, in the real world. But…but…even though the company is making money; and even though it's ready to go public at $30 a share, their $1 purchase priced stock is still on the books at $1. My point: Kick the tires. I'm not recommending these stocks, always look at their share price compared to their Book Value.

|  | As of 10/29/01 | |
|---|---|---|
| **Company** | **Stock Price** | **Book** |
| SFE | 1.32 | 2.72 |
| CMGI | .38 | 1.54 |
| UAL | 2.12 | 38.07 |
| ICGE | .18 | -.14 |

* Note the closeness of the stock price and Book Value. Remember, this is *Internet Capital Group, Inc.* All of its holdings are Internet related. Could this be the reason its Book Value is so low?

These value comparisons are from incubator-type companies, but lest you think these are the only companies trading at less than Book Value, look at the following. I've thrown in the Price/Earnings ratios for fun.

| **Company** | **Stock Price** | **Book** | **P/E** |
|---|---|---|---|
| ITWO | 5.13 | 16.67 | — |
| CNET | 5.15 | 14.50 | — |
| LENS | 4.28 | 5.63 | — |
| MIND | 4.95 | 6.04 | — |
| ITX | 4.87 | 11.64 | 10 |
| COLT | 7.71 | 10.91 | — |
| CREAF | 5.89 | 6.14 | 2 |
| SKS | 7.03 | 15.96 | 12 |
| OPTV | 7.90 | 29.23 | — |
| MTZ | 4.61 | 10.48 | 3 |

I want to reemphasize that these Book Values are out of each company's latest SEC Filings. It is possible, but highly unlikely, that the Book Values shown here could be less than what's listed. However, it is highly likely that any one of these companies' book values could have assets, valued in the real world, at substantially greater values than what is listed. We're told in life to accentuate the positive. The SEC tells us to accentuate the negative.

# 17-The Fisherman's Smorgasbord—Bottom Fishing

## Summary

This discussion has two punch lines, or two endings, if you will. Both of these insights are valuable. I come at this as part president of a publicly traded company. I lived this discussion every day. Simple things affect our stock. For example, when we register stock (Rule 144) which we own in a company which has gone public, it becomes a marketable security. Not only does its value increase to the street value, but it now shows up as a short-term asset. The ratio of short-term assets to short-term liabilities is important to some analysts, so we like restricted stock to become free trading stock. I could go on for hours, as we had investments in several companies which have went public.

## Okay, the two endings:

#1) One-time expenses seems to be a current epidemic. Hopefully the waterfall will be over soon, and we'll return to a more peaceful cascade of water. To me, this means opportunity. Stocks are low. P/E's are low, even from the historical 15% P/E averages. Stock prices today are as low as option prices a few years ago. Add the shedding of bad investments, with a tax cut, lower interest rates and an economy beaten down, but trying to recover, and I feel good.

*Please note: these charge-offs, one-time expenses and the immature way the media reports them are not over, but much of the bad news is past tense.*

#2) With Book Values written down—GAAP-wise—it's time to find real bargains. Once the economy revives, two things will happen: a) Companies will start doing IPO's (going public) and hence their stocks will reflect a truer value, and b) companies will start aggressively taking over other companies. They'll look for a relationship strategy first, then they'll look for value. And as far as I can tell, there is value everywhere.

So, for me, the glass is half full. I'm looking for value and opportunity. I want to get my money in the way of movement. A small part of that money will be in companies which own stock in a diversified slice of the American Pie.

Check out BottomFishing.com for information on some of these companies. Note: Wade Cook owns stock in some of the companies listed there.

# *JUST FOR FUN...*

Understanding Investments

STOCK: A magical piece of paper that is worth $33.75 until the moment you buy it. It will then be worth $8.50

BROKER: The person you trust to help you make major financial decisions. Please not the first five letters of this word spell "Broke".

BEAR: What your trade account and wallet will be when you take a flyer on that hot stock tip your friend gave you.

BULL: Statements and expressions your broker uses to explain why his recommended stocks and mutual funds tanked during the last quarter.

SHORT POSITION: A type of trade where, in theory, a person sells stocks he doesn't actually own. Since this also only ever works in theory, a short position is what a person usually ends up being in (i.e. "The rent? Well, I'm a little short this month.")

COMMISSION: The only reliable way to make money in the stock market, which is why your broker charges you one.

*A MANAGER IS A PERSON WHO DOES THINGS THE RIGHT WAY, A LEADER IS A PERSON WHO DOES THE RIGHT THINGS.*

*WADE B. COOK*

# 18

# Options 101

Even getting a basic understanding of stock options is a little bit difficult, but oh-so-valuable if you "get it." Let's say you're a teenager. A certain tennis shoe from Sketchers is hot. Your friend buys a pair for $100. The stores are sold out, but you put down a deposit and order your pair. The style you selected has been really popular, and just before the new ones arrive, the price has been raised to $150. You're glad you locked in the price at $100. But you've changed your mind. News is out that there is a new style coming.

You want the new style, even though they're $130. Your other friend, Bill, wants your place. You put down $20, and he's willing to give you $30 for your ticket, your receipt, your right to buy them, at $100. He gives you $30, and you profit $10. He pays the balance of $80 and his total price is $110, not the new price of $150.

Oh, and just after he buys the shoes for $110, several new styles come out and the pair he just bought is on sale for $75. Too bad.

Stock options and shoe deposits can only be compared to a certain point. Obviously, Bill has the same size shoe as you, or this trade would not have worked. Thousands of people own IBM or Disney. The basic common stock fits all.

Also, an option to buy stock is not a deposit. It does not act like a down payment. A stock option (calls) gives the owner the right to buy the stock, but there is not an obligation that the potential purchaser actually buy the stock. In short, he has the right but not the obligation. Likewise with shoes: if Bill forgets, or changes his mind, no one is going to come after him or you for the balance. Later, they'll just put the shoes back into inventory and sell them.

An option gives you the opportunity to lock down a price for a stock purchase. If the stock goes below this price, you would not exercise or use your option to buy the stock. If you still wanted to buy the stock, you would just do so on the open market. If the shoes were put on sale for $75, why would you use your deposit of $20 and pay $80. Throw the slip away, buy them for $75 and save $5.

The word "right," as in "right to buy," is an interesting word. On the freeway, you have the right to be in the fast lane, but maybe you shouldn't. You have the right to work hard at school and get A's and B's, but many people ignore this right and don't do the work necessary to get good grades. You have the right to mind mom and dad, and will be rewarded for doing so, and #@*% if you don't. Rights are not obligations.

Back to stocks. If you really like a stock and feel it has every inclination of going up-you've done your homework and you're ready to go—you could buy the stock to make money, or you could use low-cost, limited-risk stock options to do so.

XYZ stock is hot. It's earning money and the future looks good. The stock's around $65. It's been up to $70 and backed off the last few days when the whole market was down. Now's your chance. Ten shares would cost you $650. One hundred shares would be $6,500. One thousand shares would cost $65,000. That's a lot of money in anybody's book.

Your stockbroker suggests call options. It's May and the $65 call options for July are $4. That's right, you pay $4 and have locked down the *right* to buy this XYZ stock for $65. Wow, if the stock goes to $73, let's see what happens. You do not have an obligation. You only could lose this $4.

First of all, what are you buying? The answer in this case is nothing but time—two months, more or less. You're buying what time will do to the stock. Isn't it the same if you bought the stock? If the stock goes up or down, it's yours until you sell it. Not so with options. You own the option until you sell the option, use it to buy the stock at $65, or until it expires.

Options expire on the third Friday of the month, unless it's a holiday, then it would expire on the prior Thursday. Now, in truth, options expire at 11:59 AM (Eastern Time) on the Saturday after the third Friday. You can't say the third Saturday, as that Saturday just may be the fourth Saturday. It happens like that twice a year. Also, you wouldn't want to say Saturday anyway. The Stock Market closes at 4PM Eastern Time on the third Friday, and the option market closes a few minutes later. You can't trade after that, so functionally, the third Friday is the expiration date.

Something has to happen before that time for you to make money. With a call option the stock must move up a lot, and move up quickly for you to make money. Let's explore this. $4 has purchased for you the right to buy the stock at $65. The price is locked down. The day is set. In stock options (American Style) you can exercise the option anytime on or before the expiration date. You can also sell the option anytime you choose. Behind the scenes is the OCC, or Options Clearing Corporation, which makes sure trades are conducted properly. Options have market makers. Similar to stock specialists, or stock market makers, these people make a market in options. They buy and sell options.

Pricing is done by the bid and ask. The previous XYZ $65 call option was $3.80 x $4.00. Normally, we buy at the bid and sell at the ask. Options are also in one hundred share contracts. It's $4.00 per option, but we have to buy one hundred of them. One contract will cost $400 plus our broker will change a sales commission. If we were feeling wild and risky, we could buy ten contracts. That would be $4,000, but think, we have the right to buy 1,000 shares of XYZ stock.

I bring this up to show you how much money can be generated and also show you how tough it is to make consistent profits. Before I bring up the negative, let's dream a moment. If this stock goes to $90 before July, our one contract (100 shares at $400) would be worth at least $2,500. How so? $90 minus $65 is $25. If we have the right to buy a stock at $65 and the stock is at $90, that right could be sold for at least what is "in-the-money." That's $25 times our one hundred rights. $400 to $2,500. That's huge. The $65 call options on July 10th may be listed at a bid and ask of $25 x $25.50.

I'll put a few good testimonials here. Remember, these same people probably lost a lot of money on other, unluckier trades:

> *I turned $200,000 approximately into $1,200,000 in 6 months.*               *-Larry G., CA*

> *I've made $1,338,081.43 net profit in 11 1/2 months. I originally started with $36,000…*
> -
> *Myke L., WA*

> *I started trading with $2,900…I recently took an account from $16,000 to $330,000 in 2 weeks, and $35,000 to $2,484,000 in 6 weeks. I made $1.25 million in one day.*
> *-Glenn M., IL*

I like these testimonials which show huge gains, but I'm more into teaching how to build up *steady* monthly income.

Let's backtrack: why did I say $25, at least? We need to discuss what it is that makes up the price of options. This discussion will take awhile. We'll get back to our $4 shortly. First, let's look at June 30th. The stock is at $90 and the bid and ask for the $65 call is $27.50 x $28. "Hey," you ask, "a moment ago you said the bid and ask was $25 x $25.50. What gives?"

"Elementary, my dear Watson, elementary," said master detective Sherlock Holmes. The $25 bid was on July 10th, not June 30th. More time has elapsed. Remember, when we bought this option we were buying time—more importantly and more completely: Time Value. What makes up time value? Let's first look at a chart, and bring up an option rule with many exceptions: *when there is a small movement in the stock there usually is a magnified movement in the option*. Again, usually.

| Date | Stock | Strike | Option |
|---|---|---|---|
| 20-May | $65 | $65C | $4.00 |
| 25-May | $67 | $65C | $5.00 |
| 2-Jun | $70 | $65C | $7.00 |
| 6-Jun | $74 | $65C | $10.00 |

Look at the small movement. $65 to $67. Not much, but nice. If you used $6,500 to buy your one hundred shares, and it was at $6,700, you'd be happy. That's almost enough to cover commissions and make a little. If we did options, our $400 is now $500. Again, nice—but not much after commissions. When the stock hits $70, we could sell the stock for a $500 profit. $300 profit if we played options ($700 minus our cost of $400 = $300).

So you see, the cash return is better on stocks, BUT THE RATE OF RETURN IS BETTER ON OPTIONS—we have so much less money tied up. Let me interject my personal trading style here. I do not buy options to buy the stock. I buy options, planning for the option itself to grow in value. I sell at my exit point, go to a movie, and try again in a few days.

Now to the time value. Why did the stock go up $2 and the option only went up $1? Then, as the stock went up another $3, the option went up only $2. And the real question: how come the option went down a few paragraphs ago, even as the stock stayed at $90?

## Option Pricing

Option market makers are in the business to sell options. That's how they pay their bills. Literally, they have to get people to lose so they make money. I know that's harsh, but so goes the world. You will be their next victim, if you don't know what makes them tick. Maybe, we all need to emulate some of their business practices—though not the devious ones.

Option market makers put a price on an option based on what they think people will pay. Let's stay with our XYZ example. Towards the end of June, there are rumors that this company is going to have block buster numbers. There is also speculation that the company is a takeover candidate at $100 a share and lo and behold, there's expectation of a two for one stock split. The stock shoots up. You did your homework, but this is better than expected. You lucked out.

If the stock is above the strike price, in this case $65, at say $72, it is in-the-money by $7. It's $7 above the strike price. If the $65 call is going for $10, of the $10, $7 is actually paying for the stock down to the $65 price. $7 of our option is said to be in-the-money. We're buying, or we own, an in-the-money call. If the stock is at $72 and we buy the $75 call option, we're buying an out-of-the-money call. If the stock is at $65 and we buy the $65 strike price call option (for our $4) we're buying an at-the-money option.

Anything above the strike price that is not in-the-money is out-of-the-money. Out-of-the-money is the time or the time value. This is what the option market maker wants to sell us. This is also called the "speculative value," See #3 below.

## Modeling

Like most things in business, there are software programs and models to help out. Option market makers have a historical model in a software program, backed up by pricing software to adjust the price of options—both up and down—as the stock price changes, or as events, speculation and supply and demand manifest themselves. This model is to protect them, not us. Let's see how it works.

There are basically three components to the modeling program:

1) RISK FREE RATE OF RETURN: Every mathematical formula or relationship needs a base or a constant. Most formulas use "one" as the constant. Not here, however. This is an investment comparison so the constant used for risky investment would be a safe investment, but one with a rate of return. The U.S. T-Bill rate is used. It changes, but ever-so-slightly as time passes.

2) THE TIME TO EXPIRATION: I think you can see that the more time you buy, the more the option will cost. Our July expiration was $4. The October $65 call option is $7. Time goes away, but in a steady manner. Many options hold a high price until a few weeks before expiration. More later.

3) IMPLIED VOLATILITY: Here's where the fun begins. These are big words, so let me use a few other big words to help. SPECULATIVE VALUE. This speaks to how much the stock moves. It's also someone's best guess at what the stock or option might do. An example, the $4 we paid for the $65 call option on XYZ stock seems puny to the $65 call on MNO stock at $9. Yes, the stock is also currently at $65. Why $4? Why $9? In short, it's what someone will pay. MNO is supposed to have a new drug out that cures the misunderstandings between men and women. It's a billion dollar drug. The stock should go to $200. Now, think, if the stock could go that high (or to zero if the FDA doesn't approve the drug), the upside is huge. People are willing to pay $9 for the right to buy this stock at $65, and they're only buying the upside for two months, to July.

The implied volatility could make up 70% to 80% of the option price. It's speculation. It's someone's best guess. It's what we pay cash for when we buy options. I like to sell these expensive options, but that's for another discussion.

Let's stay with this $9 option on the drug stock (MNO). Nothing happens in May or June. The stock is still around $65, and the option has gone down to $5. Why? The time is going away. Only a few weeks are left to expiration. Rumors pick up. There is to be a company press conference on July 12th, five days before expiration. The stock goes to $70, the option barely moves. It's at $6.

On July 10th, the company announces that the drug has been approved, *but* only for women. The stock tanks, the option goes to zero. We lose. Why such a drastic downturn? Because this drug was primarily for men. Why would women use this drug, they've pretty much got men figured out anyway. With no large market for the drug, anticipated earnings are adjusted down and the stock price falls to $50. The right to buy the stock at $65 just became worthless.

4) WHAT ABOUT OUR $4 OPTION? Let's return to our good trade. The $65 stock has moved up to $90. The strike price is still $65. It's late June. The stock just hovers around $90. The time goes away. The $27 price goes to $25. You'll always be able to sell the option for its in-the-money amount, or $25. Nice profit.

It only takes twenty to thirty seconds to sell. We're out of the trade and have made money on one, lost on one—we're net ahead. Back to the books.

MORE ON IMPLIED VOLATILITY: Here are two important statements. These are out of the Bible of the option industry.

a) When stocks dip (or go down) implied volatility goes up; conversely, when stocks go up, implied volatility goes down.

Now, why? This is a tough one. The next sentence explains why, and it's very important that you understand the connection.

b) Fear is pure and potent, greed is always tempered with reality.

There we are again: fear and greed. The two opposing market forces. Everything happens in the market because of one of these two emotions.

Fear: The stock is down, it's on a dip, it has tanked—will it go up? It should. How much? Who knows? Option prices explode because the implied volatility goes up.

Greed: It can't go much higher. It's about peaked out. The run is over. It can't go much higher. The implied volatility, that which makes up most of the time value in the option price, goes down.

Fear is powerful, greed brings out the negative.

Another example: A stock has really been on a ride. It's near its all-time high. Good news was everywhere. It's gone from $60 to $90 in a short time. It looks like it will never end. The next month out $90 call options are only $3. They seem cheap. You buy ten contracts and spend $3,000.

| Date | Stock | Strike | Option |
|---|---|---|---|
| TODAY | $90 | $90 C | $3.00 |
| Later Today | $91 | $90 C | $3.50 |
| One week | $92 | $90 C | $4.00 |
| Two weeks | $92 | $90 C | $3.95 |
| Three weeks | $91 | $90 C | $2.00 |
| Expiration | $91 | $90 C | $1.00 |

This is an amazing study, if I do say so myself. Here we have a stock rising and the option barely budges. You see, the implied volatility is sucked out of the option premium. We have a case where the stock is up but we lose on the option.

One time I had a transaction going. It was a one-day trade as a big internet service company was to announce earnings after the market close. The stock was at $63. The $60 calls were $6. The stock went up to $64, almost $65, throughout the day, but then suddenly backed off to $64, then $63. I wanted out. A quick call and a sell order got me out at $7.50. The option was $7 when I called, but the stock was falling, implied volatility (remember fear is powerful) was going up and I sold out at a $1.50 profit, or $1,500. Go figure. It doesn't make sense, but it is real.

Now to you. You should paper trade options until you figure them out. Most stockbrokers do not know how to trade options, and so have them paper trade with you. Connect the dots. All of the components are important. You must learn what makes up the time value, how it changes and the market forces working for you and against you. With options, time becomes your enemy. With stocks, time is usually your friend—time forgives many mistakes. Options are a limited-time investment. This feature alone adds an element of risk only suitable for the bravest and most savvy of investors.

*THERE ARE NO SECRETS TO SUCCESS. IT IS THE RESULT OF PREPARATION, HARD WORK LEARNING FROM FAILURE.*

GENERAL COLIN POWELL

# 19

# Writing Covered Calls: The 20% Monthly Cash Flow Challenge

In this chapter we're going to explore Writing Covered Calls. Of all the topics we'll cover, this one is my favorite. My favorite used to be rolling stock—I've made a lot of money with that strategy; but, as you know, I keep looking for cash flow strategies. As a matter of fact, I keep asking the question in my seminars, "Why are we doing this? What are we after here?" A few people will answer and then I finally tell the whole audience, "Look, usually when I ask that question, the answer is, 'Cash Flow.' So whenever I ask that question, you answer 'Cash Flow.'" Then when I ask the question again, everybody shouts out "Cash Flow!" We're going to show you how to potentially generate some incredible cash flow and hopefully get your money working harder than you work.

In order to do so, we need to go back and define a few words and maybe even do a bit of a review. I want to make sure you're familiar with the basic terms, so I'm including a list of terms and a summary of how they apply to writing covered calls. For some of you, this is review. For those of you who haven't attended my Wall Street Trading Bootcamp™, one of my other courses, or read my books, this will be a new language. It's a language you need to understand and speak fluently in order to work the stock market.

## Talking The Talk

ASK: The current price for which a stock or option may be bought.

AT-THE-MONEY: A call option is said to be at the money if the current market value of the underlying stock is the same as the exercise price of the option.

BID: The current price at which you could sell your stock or option.

CALL, OR CALL OPTION: An option contract giving the owner the right (not the obligation) to buy shares of stock at a strike price on or before an expiration date.

CALLED OUT: The option to buy the stock is exercised. When your option is exercised, which can happen on or before the expiration date, it is done randomly and electronically. For example, if you own 1,000 shares you could <u>be called</u> out of a portion of your shares or all of your shares. If your stock is in the money on or around expiration, you will be called out. If you get called out, you will not know about it until the Monday following expiration. Check with your broker the following Monday after expiration Friday, just to be on the safe side.

CONTRACT: An option contract controls 100 shares of the underlying stock, so 10 contracts are the equivalent of 1,000 shares.

COVERED CALL WRITER: An investor who writes (to write means to sell) a call on a stock or some other underlying asset that he/she owns, guaranteeing the ability to perform if the call is exercised.

IN-THE-MONEY: A call option is said to be in-the-money if the current market value of the underlying stock is above the exercise price of the option.

INTRINSIC VALUE: The amount, if any, by which an option is in the money.

MARGIN: The additional equity loaned to you by your stockbroker, based upon a percentage of the equity of your underlying assets. The underlying asset is used as collateral for the loan. Put simply, if you have 50% margin capability in your trading account, your broker will loan you the money to purchase up to the same number of shares you are buying. If you were purchasing 1,000 shares of a particular marginable stock, you would only have to put up enough cash to pay for 500 shares.

MARGIN ACCOUNT: An account in a brokerage firm, that offers additional equity as a loan based upon a percentage of the equity of your underlying assets.

OPEN INTEREST: The total number of option contracts outstanding for that specific option strike price and expiration date.

OPTION: The right to buy or sell a specified amount of a security (stocks, bonds, futures, contracts, etc.) at a specified price on or before a specific date (American style options).

OPTION CYCLES: The sequence of months assigned to a company's options.

OUT-OF-THE-MONEY: If the exercise price (strike price) of a call is above the current market value of the underlying stock, the option is said to be out-of-the-money by that amount. If the exercise price (strike price) of a put is below the current market value of the underlying stock, the option is said to be out- of-the-money by that amount.

PREMIUM: The money you pay or the money you receive for buying or selling calls or puts.

RATE OF RETURN: The sum resulting from dividing the cash in (your cash taken in, or profits) by the cash out (your investment). Cash In (divided by) Cash out= %Yield.

*The yield figure that you get does not say whether it's a monthly, an annual, or a 10-year yield. This merely tells you your rate of return.*

STRIKE PRICE: The price at which the underlying security will be bought or sold if the option buyer exercises his/her rights in the contract.

TIME VALUE: The remainder of an option premium after subtracting its intrinsic value.

UNCOVERED CALL: A call option that is sold without ownership of the underlying stock. Selling an uncovered option is sometimes referred to as "going naked."

When we talk about writing a covered call, a call is an option—and remember, an option is the *right*, not the *obligation*, to buy or sell a particular stock at a set price (strike price) on or before a certain date. That date is effectively the third Friday of the month, because that's when the stock market closes. A covered call means you actually own the stock.

For those of you who own stock right now, I want you to think about your own stock portfolio. Let's say you bought some stock at $9 a share: it's gone down to $8, it's been up at $9.50 and once in awhile it bumped into $10. You were hoping this stock would go to $20 or $30, but you've had it for the last year or so and it just does not get up to those ranges. It keeps floundering around $9 or $10 a share. You would be willing to sell that stock, but you sure would like to sell it at $10 or even $12.50. Here's the question you need to ask yourself, "Would I be willing to sell this stock I bought at $9, for $10?"

If you think the stock is going to go to $20 or $30, then the answer to that question is probably, "No." Of course you would not be willing to sell it at $10 if you think it's going to go to $20 or $30. But, if you don't think it will go much higher and you're willing to sell it at $10 a share, then you have another opportunity—an interim-method of generating cash into your account.

Specifically, you're going to sell someone the right to buy the stock from you at $10 a share. You're going to "write"—and when I use the word "write," it is synonymous with the word "sell"—a covered call. Now you're saying, "Hold on a minute, what is this? A 'call' is the right to buy, so now you're telling me I can *sell* the right to *buy*?" The answer is "Yes!" You can sell someone the right to buy your stock from you.

Options are always in one hundred share increments. If you have 185 shares, you could only "write," or sell one contract. If you wanted to sell two contracts, you would have to buy another fifteen shares to make it two hundred.

# 19-Writing Covered Calls: The 20% Monthly Cash Flow Challenge

Writing covered calls is a phenomenal way to make money. Warren Buffett is one of the richest men in America. He has made hundreds of millions of dollars a year writing covered calls. He wrote a lot of covered calls on Coca-Cola® back in the late 80's and early 90's. Coca-Cola would roll between the low 40's and the low 50's and he would give someone the right to buy the stock from him at $50 a share. Whether or not they exercised their right to buy the stock, he got to keep the premium he received for giving someone that right.

The whole idea of an option is that you're taking the right to buy something and there are two potential plays. One is to actually buy the *stock* and the other is to buy and then sell the *option*. What we're talking about right now is *selling* a call, not *buying* a call.

Let me tell you where I learned this. Several years ago, I purchased a Novell computer. Novell is a company out of Provo, Utah who bought WordPerfect a few years back. Their stock actually went down quite a bit to around $16 a share. I had been following this company for many years and buying their stock. The stock would climb to around $60 and do a stock split down to around $30 and then repeat that pattern. At one time it got down to around $20, $22 a share and I bought some of it at that point. It even got down to $16 or $17 a share and then I started buying a whole bunch of it.

I sold some of the stock at $22 and $23, but for about a year and a half, every time it got down around $16 to $19 a share, I would buy some more. I was buying it in the hope that the stock would go back up to $30 a share, but it didn't do so for a long time. It would go up to $20 or $21, but then back down to $16 to $18 so I would buy a few more shares. I ended up owning a lot of this stock—I had 3,800 shares after that year and a half to two-year period of time. Even on margin, where you only have to put up half the money, that's a lot of cash to have tied up in one stock.

I was really tired of owning this stock, so I called my stockbroker and said, "The next time this stock reaches $20 a share, sell everything I own." He responded, "Well Wade, if you're willing to sell it at $20 a share, why don't you write a covered call on it?" I realized that was the second time I had heard about this "covered call" thing, so I asked him, "What is a covered call?" He took a couple hours of his time to explain this to me. I'm pretty dense when it comes to learning some of these strategies—but once I really grasp them, I can turn on the fire and really get some things going.

My broker explained to me that I could write a call for October (this was in September a few years back). In an option play, there is a bid and an ask, and if you're going to buy an option, you buy it at close to the ask number.

Let's go back to our Novell example for a minute. Let's say the stock is at $16.50 and you're hoping it goes to $20. Right now the bid is .75¢ and the ask is $1. If you were to buy the option you would buy it at $1 and if you were to sell that option, you would sell it at .75¢. Behind all the options deals is what is called the Options Clearing Corporation, which makes sure that all options are matched up at the end of every day and that nobody gets left in the lurch.

I asked, "How much could I get for selling my Novell stock?" My broker checked his computer, punched in a bunch of numbers and informed me, "Right now the bid is $1 and the ask is $1.25." I said, "Hold it! You're telling me that right now I could sell someone the option to buy this stock from me at $20 in October, and they would be willing to buy that right for $1.25? I could get $3,800 cash in my account tomorrow, in order to give someone the right to buy this stock from me at $20 a share in October and I'm willing to sell it at $20 a share anyway?!" He said, "Yes," and I said, "Boy, this is a no-brainer. Do that!"

He punched the numbers in his computer and five to ten minutes later I was the proud new owner of all this cash. I had $3,800 that hit my account the next day. All I had to do was sell an option giving someone the right to buy my stocks from me, at a price at which I was already willing to sell.

These stocks could be "called away" from me, or "exercised on." This means, if the stock goes up to $23 or so, I could get called out in October; and remember, I'm going to get called out at $20.

Mr. X over in Tallahassee, FL, has walked into his broker and said, "I really like this Novell Corporation—what are the options in October?" His broker looks it up on his computer and tells him, "Right now they're at $1.25." Mr. X says, "I want to buy a bunch of those." So he bought some calls. His risk is that the stock will go up. He wants to either buy the stock at the $20 price and lock in that price, or he wants to sell the option. If the stock goes up, the value of his option goes up from $1.25 to $2.50 and he makes money that way. He can either buy and hold the stock or buy and sell the stock, or he can sell the *option* once he has purchased it.

If the stock goes down to $18 or $19, rather than up to $20 or $21 by the expiration date, then he just loses his money. In this example, Mr. X is going to lose $3,800 if the stock does not go up.

Let's go over the difference between "covered" and "uncovered." The word "uncovered" means you do not own the stock. I know that sounds kind of weird, but you don't have to own the stock to sell the call option. You can sell someone the right to buy the stock from you when you don't even own the stock. You're probably thinking, "Well that's really risky." And it is very, very risky. Therefore, many of you will not be able to do this strategy in your accounts until you #1 have more money in there, or #2 have more experience. You may have to start small and do a few deals here and there before your brokers will even allow you to sell an uncovered call.

The other term for an "uncovered" call is "going naked." You don't own the stock and you sold someone the right to buy it, therefore you're naked on the call. The risk in this case is, if the stock goes up to $21 or $22 and you get called out at $20, you would have to purchase the stock at $21 or $22 to have the stock you have agreed to sell at $20.

# 19-Writing Covered Calls: The 20% Monthly Cash Flow Challenge

If the stock stays down around $19, you have no cash tied up, you sell the call, get the money in your account tomorrow and don't get called out—but you get to keep the premium. I make a lot of money selling uncovered or naked calls, but it is an extremely risky strategy.

As far as covered calls go, you could purchase stocks for the sole purpose of writing calls on them and using those stocks to generate income. With the covered call strategy, the longest I have ever held a stock and continued to write covered calls on it, was four months. I was able to sell the call premiums and generate lots of income into my account.

Now that we have covered some of the basics of covered call writing, let's move on to the challenge of creating monthly cash flow.

## The 20% Monthly Cash Flow Challenge

It seems our "rate of return" comments at our seminars come under continuous scrutiny. For example: recently, some government bureaucrat challenged the validity of a statement that twenty percent monthly returns could be made in Writing Covered Calls.

Let's put this in perspective. February 28th of 2001 was a major challenge in the life of our company. We had a 6.8 Richter Scale earthquake here in the Washington area, which shut down all of our building for a month or so, and then more than half of our building remained unusable for six months. This challenge on a statement made at one of our seminars will be nowhere near the challenge presented by the earthquake a year ago.

We realize that, to many people who are rutted in the "4% annual return on a savings account" mentality, thinking about getting a cash on cash return of fifteen to twenty percent a month seems almost heretical.

So, we went to the mat and dug up some information which I think is most interesting. This information is from February 28, 2002, around 10:00 AM. The reason I use the date in this instance, is because this is a snapshot in time. The marketplace is what it is today, and each of the stocks you will see on this list were at a certain price at 9:00 or 10:00 this morning. The call and put options on those stocks were also at a certain price, and that price changes from minute to minute. These examples are given to prove the point that such returns are possible if the proper homework is done, and *if* people are up to speed on how the actual formula works.

Just by way of introduction, I feel it necessary to explain a "covered call." A covered call, in most instances, would be a situation in which an investor owns a stock. They would then sell an option against their stock, and somebody, whom they will not know, will purchase the right to buy their stock away from them at a predetermined price. For example: if you own a stock at $18 and have one thousand shares, you could write a thousand options against it. Options are in one-hundred share contracts, so one thousand shares would be ten contracts.

Let's say that the call option is going for $1, out for the next month. Options expire on the third Friday of every month. You could write a call position against your stock, and give someone the right to buy your stock away from you at $20. If you do not want to sell your stock at $20, then you should not have sold this call. Now that you have sold the call, you have generated $1,000 cash into your account in one day, which is your money to keep, whether the stock goes above $20 or stays below $20.

If the stock stays below $20, you get to keep the $1,000 *and* you still own the stock. Maybe the stock has moved to $19, maybe it has moved down to $18, so nobody is going to pay $20 per share to buy the stock away from you. If the stock goes up to $23, then the stock will be taken away from you if you leave the sold call option position open up to the expiration date.

Without getting into all the details of buybacks and rollouts and other strategies that allow you to take back control of the stock, let it suffice to say that this $1,000 represents that particular month's cash on cash return. To figure the rate of return, you would take the amount of money you spent on the stock, which would be $18. You would have either spent $18,000 to own these 1,000 shares of stock, and generate the $1 on the sell of the option, which would be a 5.5% rate of return; OR, you could purchase the stock on margin. This means, you put up half the money and your broker loans you the other half and uses the stock as collateral for his loan. In short, you would have put up $9,000. Now if the stock is not bought away from you, that particular cash on cash return would be $1,000, or 11%.

However, there is another angle to this: The capital gains if you sell the stock at a profit. In this case, if the stock is purchased away from you at $20, you would make an additional $2, or for your 1,000 sold shares, a total of $2,000. This $2,000 combined with your $1,000 profit on writing the covered call, gives you a $3,000 cash return on your $9,000, or a 33% return. This $3,000 is calculated by the $1,000 option premium and the $2,000 capital gain for selling the stock at a $2 profit.

Please note: in none of these transactions did I figure in the transaction cost or commissions. Of the $3,000, that could easily be $100 to $300, as we actually have three transactions: 1) the purchase of the stock, 2) sale of the option , and 3) the sale of the stock which happens electronically on the weekend *after* the third Friday of the month.

Writing Covered Calls is a significant strategy for generating cash, especially for those people who have had stocks go down in value. It allows them to build cash back into their account.

Now let's move on from this set of informational material to the actual proof that we, "Continue to use honest advertising," in our advertising materials, including our seminars. We submit the following: I asked our Research and Training Department to select an index and then pick certain stocks out of the index with some random criteria. They were to look at the covered call options for the month of March, for which the expiration date is not a *month* away, but only two weeks and one day away.

To be fair, we also looked at the April covered calls, which would make it a six-week rate of return, as compared to a two-week rate of return. To put this information together today is almost like comparing apples and oranges, in that it will not be a full month. However, you will at least get the gist of the returns that are available. And, more than likely will be excited with the outcome.

We did not go through several indices selecting only stocks that would fit the criteria to make our point. We chose one index, the Nasdaq 100, from which we selected our stocks. These are also the same stocks that trade in a trust (a SPDR), known as the Q's, and traded under ticker symbol QQQ.

In our seminars, we teach that Writing Covered Calls should be done with stocks between $5 and $25. The reason is simply that you get a bigger bang for your buck by doing so. In short, an $18 stock with a $20 call may generate a dollar. A $98 stock with a $100 call may also generate a dollar. Notice that in each case you would have the potential of $2 capital gains. But, if you had to choose between putting up $18 or $98, you see that there will be a world of difference in the rate of return as the amount of cash required to invest in the $98 stock would be substantially more.

We chose stocks out of the Nasdaq 100 that were between $5 and $25. There were 35 such stocks. In the following tables you will see a listing of those stocks, including their ticker symbols, the March strike price and the premium on the option for both March and April. We also randomly chose some of those stocks to show what it would be like if the stock did *rise* in the meantime, and if you as the investor were called out at that higher strike price. You'll see what the adjusted rate of return would be when you add the profits or the capital gains into the mix.

## Covered Call Study

On February 28, 2002 we took a snapshot of the stocks in the Nasdaq 100 Index that were trading between $5 and $25. We then checked the covered call premiums for March and April. Here are the results and potential rate of return. All numbers use 50% margin for purchase of the stock. Our spreadsheet uses a purchase of 1,000 shares and selling 10 contracts of the nearest higher strike price options. No commissions are included. The March expiration is just over 2 weeks away on March 15 and the April expiration is about 6 weeks away on April 19.

## MARCH

| | Ticker Name | Stock Price $ | Opt. Strike | Opt. Price $ | % if not called out | % if called out |
|---|---|---|---|---|---|---|
| 1. | ABGX Abgenix | 18.45 | 20 | .65 | 7.05% | 23.85% |
| | ADLAC Adelphia | 22.34 | 22.5 | 1.15 | 10.30% | 11.73% |
| | ALTR Altera | 19.20 | 20 | .80 | 8.33% | 16.67% |
| | AAPL Apple | 21.47 | 22.5 | .50 | 4.66% | 14.25% |
| 2. | AMZN Amazon.com | 14.02 | 15 | .40 | 5.71% | 19.69% |
| | ATML Atmel | 7.43 | 7.5 | .30 | 8.08% | 9.96% |
| | BEAS Bea System | 12.72 | 12.5 | 1.00 | 15.72% | 12.26% |
| | CHTR Charter | 10.56 | 10 | .95 | 17.99% | 7.39% |
| | CIEN Ciena | 7.91 | 7.5 | .75 | 18.96% | 8.60% |
| | CSCO Cisco | 14.55 | 15 | .55 | 7.56% | 13.75% |
| | CTXS Citrix | 15.18 | 15 | 1.00 | 13.18% | 10.80% |
| | ABGX Abgenix | 18.45 | 20 | .65 | 7.05% | 23.85% |
| 3. | CPWR Compuware | 11.45 | 12.5 | .05 | 0.87% | 19.21% |
| | CNXT Conexant | 10.36 | 10 | .80 | 15.44% | 8.49% |
| | CYTC Cytyc | 23.46 | 25 | .25 | 2.13% | 15.26% |
| | FLEX Flextronics | 14.40 | 15 | .75 | 10.42% | 18.75% |
| 4. | GMST Gemstar | 18.39 | 20 | .65 | 7.07% | 24.58% |
| | HGSI Human Gen. | 20.65 | 20 | 1.85 | 17.92% | 11.62% |
| | IMCL Imclone | 21.82 | 22.5 | 1.35 | 12.37% | 18.61% |
| 5. | JNPR Juniper | 9.52 | 10 | .55 | 11.55% | 21.64% |
| | MLNM Millenium | 19.06 | 20 | .75 | 7.87% | 17.73% |

# 19-Writing Covered Calls: The 20% Monthly Cash Flow Challenge

| | Ticker Name | Stock Price $ | Opt. Strike | Opt. Price $ | % if not called out | % if called out |
|---|---|---|---|---|---|---|
| 6. | NTAP Network App. | 15.82 | 17.5 | .50 | 6.32% | 27.56% |
| | NXTL Nextel | 5.05 | 5 | .40 | 15.84% | 13.86% |
| | ORCL Oracle | 16.65 | 17.5 | .30 | 3.60% | 13.81% |
| | PMCS PMC-Sierra | 14.91 | 15 | 1.20 | 16.10% | 17.30% |
| 7. | RATL Rational | 18.20 | 20 | .50 | 5.49% | 25.27% |
| 8. | RFMD RF Micro | 16.18 | 17.5 | .60 | 7.42% | 23.73% |
| 9. | PDLI Protein Design | 16.25 | 17.5 | .80 | 9.85% | 25.23% |
| | SANM Sanmina | 9.92 | 10 | .70 | 14.11% | 15.73% |
| | SSCC Smurfitt | 16.40 | 17.5 | .15 | 1.83% | 15.24% |
| | SPLS Staples | 19.78 | 20 | .40 | 4.04% | 6.27% |
| | SBUX Starbux | 23.26 | 25 | .05 | 0.43% | 15.39% |
| | TLAB Tellabs | 10.59 | 10 | .90 | 17.00% | 5.85% |
| 10. | VRSN Verisign | 23.50 | 25 | .95 | 8.09% | 20.85% |
| 11. | VTSS Vitesse Semi | 7.11 | 7.5 | .35 | 9.85% | 20.82% |
| | YHOO Yahoo! | 14.73 | 15 | .70 | 9.50% | 13.17% |

March 2002 Covered Call Documentation: JUST TO RUB IT IN

1.  We buy 1,000 shares of Abgenix Inc. (ABGX) at $18.45. That costs $18,450 ($9,225 on margin). We sell 10 contracts of the March $20 call for 65 cents, or $650, generating a 7.05% two week return. If the stock rises to or above $20, we are called out, or sell, the stock and the rate of return becomes: 23.85%.

2.  We buy 1,000 shares of Amazon.com (AMZN) at $14.02. That costs $14,020 ($7,010 on margin). We sell 10 contracts of the March $15 calls for 40 cents, or $400, generating a 5.71% two week return. If the stock rises to or above $15, we are called out, or sell, the stock and the rate of return becomes: 19.69%.

3. We buy 1,000 shares of Compuware Corp. (CPWR) at $11.45. That costs $11,450 ($5,725 on margin). We sell 10 contracts of the March $12.50 calls for 5 cents, or $50, generating a 0.87% two week return. If the stock rises to or above $12.50, we are called out, or sell, the stock and the rate of return becomes: 19.21%.

4. We buy 1,000 shares of Gemstar-TV Guide (GMST) at $18.39. That costs $18,390 ($9,195 on margin). We sell 10 contracts of the March $20 calls for 65 cents, or $650, generating a 7.07% two week return. If the stock rises to or above $20, we are called out, or sell, the stock and the rate of return becomes: 24.58%.

5. We buy 1,000 shares of Juniper Networks (JNPR) at $9.52. That costs $9,520 ($4,760 on margin). We sell 10 contracts of the March $10 calls for 55 cents, or $550, generating a 11.55% two week return. If the stock rises to or above $10, we are called out, or sell, the stock and the rate of return becomes: 21.64%.

6. We buy 1,000 shares of Network Appliance (NTAP) at $15.82. That costs $15,820 ($7,910 on margin). We sell 10 contracts of the March $17.50 calls for 50 cents, or $500, generating a 6.32% two week return. If the stock rises to or above $17.50, we are called out, or sell, the stock and the rate of return becomes: 27.56%.

7. We buy 1,000 shares of Rational Software (RATL) at $18.20. That costs $18,200 ($9,100 on margin). We sell 10 contracts of the March $20 calls for 50 cents, or $500, generating a 5.49% two week return. If the stock rises to or above $20, we are called out, or sell, the stock and the rate of return becomes: 25.27%.

8. We buy 1,000 shares of RF Micro Devices (RFMD) at $16.18. That costs $16,180 ($8,090 on margin). We sell 10 contracts of the March $17.50 calls for 60 cents, or $600, generating a 7.42% two week return. If the stock rises to or above $17.50, we are called out, or sell, the stock and the rate of return becomes: 23.73%.

9. We buy 1,000 shares of Protein Design Labs (PDLI) at $16.25. That costs $16,250 ($8,125 on margin). We sell 10 contracts of the March $17.50 calls for 80 cents, or $800, generating a 9.85% two week return. If the stock rises to or above $17.50, we are called out, or sell, the stock and the rate of return becomes: 25.23%.

10. We buy 1,000 shares of Verisign (VRSN) at $23.50. That costs $23,500 ($11,750 on margin). We sell 10 contracts of the March $25 calls for 95 cents, or $950, generating an 8.09% two week return. If the stock rises to or above $25, we are called out, or sell, the stock and the rate of return becomes: 20.85%.

11. We buy 1,000 shares of Vitesse Semi (VTSS) at $7.11. That costs $7,110 ($3555 on margin). We sell 10 contracts of the March $7.50 calls for 85 cents, or $850, generating a 9.85% two week return. If the stock rises to or above $7.50, we are called out, or sell, the stock and the rate of return becomes: 20.82%.

Now, what about April? Here it is. Yes, it's six weeks instead of two, but think—the stock has one more month to rise, and for many companies this will be in their earnings reporting season. Potential problem: you have to hold the position open for six weeks instead of two.

APRIL

| Ticker Name | Stock Price $ | Opt. Strike | Opt. Price $ | % if not called out | % if called out |
|---|---|---|---|---|---|
| ABGX Abgenix | 18.45 | 20 | 1.50 | 16.26% | 33.06% |
| ADLAC Adelphia | 22.34 | 22.5 | 2.15 | 19.25% | 20.68% |
| ALTR Altera | 19.20 | 20 | 1.80 | 18.75% | 27.08% |
| AAPL Apple | 21.47 | 22.5 | 1.30 | 12.11% | 21.70% |
| AMZN Amazon.com | 14.02 | 15 | 1.15 | 16.41% | 30.39% |
| ATML Atmel | 7.43 | 7.5 | .60 | 16.15% | 18.03% |
| BEAS Bea System | 12.72 | 12.5 | 1.70 | 26.73% | 23.27% |
| CHTR Charter | 10.56 | 12.5 | .45 | 8.52% | 45.27% |
| CIEN Ciena | 7.91 | 10 | .30 | 7.59% | 60.43% |
| CSCO Cisco | 14.55 | 15 | 1.15 | 15.81% | 21.99% |
| CTXS Citrix | 15.18 | 15 | 1.60 | 21.08% | 18.71 |
| CPWR Compuware | 11.45 | 12.5 | .35 | 6.11% | 24.45% |
| CNXT Conexant | 10.36 | 10 | 1.40 | 27.03% | 20.08% |
| CYTC Cytyc | 23.46 | 25 | .95 | 8.10% | 21.23% |
| FLEX Flextronics | 14.40 | 15 | 1.40 | 19.44% | 27.78% |
| GMST Gemstar | 18.39 | 20 | 1.70 | 18.49% | 36.00% |
| HGSI Human Gen. | 20.65 | 20 | 2.90 | 28.09% | 21.79% |
| IMCL Imclone | 21.82 | 22.5 | 2.60 | 23.83% | 30.06% |

| Ticker Name | Stock Price $ | Opt. Strike | Opt. Price $ | % if not called out | % if called out |
|---|---|---|---|---|---|
| JNPR Juniper | 9.52 | 10 | 1.05 | 22.06% | 32.14% |
| MLNM Millenium | 19.06 | 20 | 1.60 | 16.79% | 26.65% |
| NTAP Network App. | 15.82 | 17.5 | 1.40 | 17.70% | 38.94% |
| NXTL Nextel | 5.05 | 5 | .80 | 31.68% | 29.70% |
| ORCL Oracle | 16.65 | 17.5 | .80 | 9.61% | 19.82% |
| PMCS PMC-Sierra | 14.91 | 15 | 2.10 | 28.17% | 29.38% |
| RATL Rational | 18.20 | 20 | 1.40 | 15.38% | 35.16% |
| RFMD RF Micro | 16.18 | 17.5 | 1.50 | 18.54% | 34.86% |
| PDLI Protein Design | 16.25 | 17.5 | 1.45 | 17.85% | 33.23% |
| SANM Sanmina | 9.92 | 10 | 1.10 | 22.18% | 23.79% |
| SSCC Smurfitt | 16.40 | 17.5 | .25 | 3.05% | 16.46% |
| SPLS Staples | 19.78 | 20 | .90 | 9.10% | 11.32% |
| SBUX Starbux | 23.26 | 25 | .50 | 4.30% | 19.26% |
| TLAB Tellabs | 10.59 | 10 | 1.35 | 25.50% | 14.35% |
| VRSN Verisign | 23.50 | 25 | 2.00 | 17.02% | 29.79% |
| VTSS Vitesse Semi | 7.11 | 7.5 | .85 | 23.91% | 34.88% |
| YHOO Yahoo! | 14.73 | 15 | 1.40 | 19.01% | 22.67% |

## Special Note:

1) We used the same 34 stocks. Maybe better deals could have been found, but we wanted to compare apples and apples.

2) You don't have to do just one month. You could do the Marches and then the Aprils after the March expiration.

3) We might have made much more by selling slightly in-the-money calls, especially in a weak market.

4) Many people get good at buying a stock and waiting for a rise in price and selling the call for more money at that time.

5) We did not do Buy/Writes, which is a double transaction, but with a) the commission of one transaction, and b) better overall pricing. A Buy/Write is done when the broker buys the stock and sells the call simultaneously. The trader can usually get one of these prices "in the spread," and save 20¢ (per deal) or $200. Hey, that's not much, but it may cover all or even half of the commissions. Question: By a show of hands, how many of you think these Government agents should pay for and come to our seminars? Buy/Writes are a Writing Covered Calls Power Strategy.

## Vindication!

I love getting challenged on the educational materials I present. I really have never been challenged on any of my strategies by anyone in-the-know. Oh how I would love to have a discussion on how covered calls work, or how selling puts works, or calls and puts on different quarterly news cycles, or rolling stocks, or *any* of the other strategies we teach, but it just never happens. It's a classic case of, "If you can't kill the message, kill the messenger."

In this case, a simple request to prove a statement made in a seminar has once again led our Research and Training Department and other people in management to really define who we are; to put forth that what we are teaching is worthy to be taught and valuable to people who want to use the stock market as a business. Or in other words, to have the cash flow produced on a monthly basis support their family.

*Please note:*

1. In the above example, we did not deal with the issue of commissions. This will, in fact, take away some of the profits.

2. We also did not deal with the fact that some of these stocks may go down in value. For a lot of people, this was a purchase of stock for the sole purpose of Writing Covered Calls. But, for many people reading this, they already own existing stock, and the fact that it may go up or down is not a new risk created by writing a covered call.

3. If the stock does go down, there are many things that can be put in place as protective measures. For example: the trader or investor could have purchased a $17.50 put, a $15 put or even a $12.50 put, which would go up in value if the stock went down, and would cover some or all of the losses in the devaluation of the stock. A trader could also have put in a stop-loss order on the stock for $15 to $18, and if the stock dipped down it would trigger a sell. In this case, they would have to buy back the call op-

tion—which means to purchase the same option, same strike price, same month—and end the open position.

4. One of the added risks a person has in writing a covered call is what we call a "lost opportunity risk," in that the stock may go up to $23 or $24. When you write a covered call, you are basically selling the upside potential of the stock. In our previous example, we're selling everything above $20.

So, if you have a stock which you think is going to go way up in value, it might not be prudent to write a covered call and give away that upside potential. You might make more money by hanging onto a stock either for a short-term bounce or for longer-term growth.

Writing a covered call is designed to be a cash flow strategy—to generate actual cash into your account—which you could take out to pay your bills, usually on a monthly basis.

5. <u>Variation on a theme</u>: Obviously, all of these numbers change every morning. This was a snapshot in time. You will have to develop an expertise to repeat this. Most people don't accomplish this every month. Yes, it's possible, but unlikely.

The following is excerpted (and edited) from my book *"FREE STOCKS: How to Get the Stock Market to Pay for Your Stocks."* We will discuss a variation on writing covered calls, known as *Large Option Covered Calls* (LOCC®).

## Flying In The Face Of Tradition

In this section I want to talk about the difference between traditional covered calls and the LOCC variation.

How are LOCCs different from traditional covered calls?

Traditional covered calls have you buy lower-priced optionable stocks with lower volatility and then write covered calls for the same month or the next month out. These stocks are purchased on margin, if possible.

The LOCC variation has you buy higher-priced optionable stocks with higher volatility and write covered calls that expire five to seven months out. These stocks are also purchased on margin, if possible. You are choosing stocks you feel will go up, as you definitely set up the trade to get called out.

LOCC allows you to use any-priced stocks with lower amounts of cash tied up. For example, if you purchase 100 shares of a $14 stock on margin, you are only putting up $7 per share. If the stock is relatively volatile, the call options should be more expensive. You may be able to sell a six to seven month call option on that stock and collect $4, which would give you an adjusted cost basis of $10 on the stock ($14 minus the $4 premium). The main disadvantage of selling this option is that you are giving up your upside potential on the stock.

Okay, the main thing to keep in mind when writing LOCCs is that our goal in this strategy is to get called out for maximum profit. I repeat, you want to get called out. That way you get the premium, plus you make or lose the profit part of the stock sale. In this example, we'll write the $12.50 call option. We'll take in $4,000 but we'll lose $1.50 or $1,500 on selling the stock at a loss. Our net will be $2,500, and even a little less after expenses.

Note: I usually sell these options slightly in the money. Why? 1) I set up the trade to get called out. 2) The sale of the options generates more in-the-money cash now, so I have less tied up.

As you can see, covered call writing is for the safety conscious investor. Remember that you can put in an order to sell the call just as you can a stock. If there is a small movement in the stock there may be a magnified movement in the option. By waiting for the stock to strengthen a bit, the call premiums might also strengthen.

> *"The LOCC training Wade presented allowed me to trade on [one] morning for a $2,000 profit. Thanks for the help.*
> *—John B., NV*

## Tips For Traditional Covered Calls

- Trade on margin if possible. When we speak of 20% returns, you will not get these returns without trading on margin. IRAs won't allow margin trading.

- You are looking for stocks that are within the $5 to $28 price range.

- The stock should be mildly (that's "mildly," not "wildly") volatile.

- Buy stock in 1,000-share increments if possible. Diversify with 100 to 1,000 shares in 10 different companies.

The Large Option Covered Call system is easy from a "you can do it from wherever you are here and now" point of view. That's what I'd like to address.

This LOCC process requires work, study, research. A certain element of risk—however mitigated by so many corrective methods—and a fair amount of dedication. However, the mechanics of LOCC deals are quite easy. They are definitely learnable and can be done from anywhere—even on vacation.

Okay, we spent a little over $14,000 ($7,000 on margin) to make $4,000 minus the $1.50 we lose by selling the stock for $12.50. These were real numbers. Think about it—$14,000 or $7,000, producing $2,500. It's probably really around $2,200 after commissions and margin interest, but it's still an impressive rate of return from five to six months of having that money tied up. Remember, most of these are close to or at the money. If all goes as expected, you may lose or make a little when you get called out—but you'll still be well ahead. Remember, you're only using a small part of your portfolio for these volatile deals. Practice the strategy thoroughly before using your actual cash. Even then, with these kinds of returns, a couple of trades could sour and you could still come out ahead.

But tell me—where can you find actual cash profits like this with minimal risk and several back door opportunities? Follow me on W.I.N.™ at www.wadecook.com as we play out trades like these.

## Conclusion:

Writing Covered Calls is a workhorse. It is not easy, but it is definitely a skill that can be learned. In my book, **Wall Street Money Machine**, I spend four chapters on Writing Covered Calls. I mention Writing Covered Calls in virtually every one of the other volumes, which are currently available in bookstores. Writing Covered Calls is also a major portion, in fact the most extensive portion, of our two-day *Wall Street Workshop*, sometimes taking between three and five hours in presenting the strategy and all of the fine-tuned power strategies that go with it. This strategy allows people a way to truly treat the stock market like a business in a relatively safe manner. I have said it once and I'll say it a thousand times: Twenty percent monthly returns are just not that uncommon. Skill, patience and connecting the dots are what are needed to safely make the stock market produce monthly cash flow income for you.

*IF YOU'LL DO FOR TWO YEARS WHAT MOST PEOPLE WON'T DO, YOU'LL BE ABLE TO DO FOR THE REST OF YOUR LIFE WHAT MOST PEOPLE CAN'T DO.*

*WADE B. COOK*

# 20

# Writing In-The-Money Covered Calls

Do you have stocks that are down in value? Do you feel like you are in a market place that doesn't seem to be going anywhere? Do you want to be a victim or do you want to learn strategies designed for creating cash flow and building up your asset base? Do you want to and are you ready to fight back?

We are here to give you the ammunition to fight back and the determination to achieve the American Dream, whatever that dream is to you. Do you want more time to spend with your family or would you like to retire early? Would you like to generate a little extra cash flow each month to help pay the bills? We want to rekindle the flame in you that no matter what the economy looks like now, it is still possible to get rich in America and see the light at the end of the tunnel.

Can the stock market be the answer to your income needs? We submit to you the answer is "no" if you look at investing the old fashioned way. Very few financial professionals know how to really "work" the market. The answer is "yes" if you learn to trade on good investments. Look at these two testimonials written about Wade Cook and his strategies.

*I have a background as a stockbroker and have been investing for about 15 years. I thought I knew how to make money in the market, but I wasn't even close!...*      *-Neil W., PA*

*I wish to take this opportunity to advise you how impressed I was with the learning experience. I have 25 years experience as a broker with 3 major firms, and I was convinced I had nothing to learn from Wade Cook. How wrong I was! It was the most professional, dynamic and thoroughly enjoyable series of meetings I have ever attended. I plan to write my clients and advise them to seriously consider attending. Once again, it was a profoundly educational seminar.*

*-Carl G., CO*

So, just who is this Wade Cook, and why should you get to know him and what he teaches?

Wade Cook is an educator, dare we say the most effective instructor in the country. He has taught tens of thousands of people and has sold millions of his books—many selling because of word of mouth. He started as a cab driver in Tacoma, Washington, and there learned and developed his now famous "meter-drop™" system. He first applied this strategy to real estate and even today his books *Real Estate Money Machine, Real Estate for Real People, 101 Ways to Buy Real Estate Without Cash* and *How to Pick up Foreclosures* continue to sell and help people do better at their real estate investing. Robert Bruss, of the Tribune Media Services said about Real Estate for Real People, "On my scale of one to 10, this excellent book rates 10."

In the 90's, Wade took his keen sense of cash flow development and applied it to the stock and options market. Soon, hundreds of thousands of people were flooding into his seminars, so they could find out how the stock market really works. Not long after that, four of his books, *Wall Street Money Machine, Stock Market Miracles , Bear Market Baloney* (now *Bulls and Bears*) and *Business Buy the Bible* hit virtually every best seller list that exists.

Currently, Wade continues to write and develop seminars and workshops, and manage.  He lives with his wife Laura and their children on a beautiful Arabian horse farm.

He now helps manage Liberty Network, Inc. This company promotes knowledge and education about ways to cash flow the market which many people know little about. If you want boring, old, stodgy information then call your stockbroker, you don't need us. If you want to buy mutual funds, then we can't help you. If you want someone else to manage your money and control your financial destiny, then what we teach and share will probably rub you the wrong way.

**We are pure educators.** We want to teach you strategies designed to generate cash flow. We get nothing out of what you do. Look at four testimonials that show the "big bucks" people have actually made in the stock market, using our strategies. Obviously, these results are particular to these people. We hope you make more and we'll show you how.

> *I had $36,000 and turned it into $460,000 in less than 3 months. In another account, I took $100,000 and turned it into $400,000 in 4 weeks, and in another, I made $30,000 in 1 week for a total (account balance) of $960,000.* -John T., OK

> *I turned $200,000 approximately into $1,200,000 in 6 months.* -Larry G., CA

> *I've made $1,338,081.43 net profit in 11 1/2 months. I originally started with $36,000.* -Myke L., WA

> *I started trading with $2,900. . . recently took an account from $16,000 to $330,000 in 2 weeks, and $35,000 to $2,484,000 in 6 weeks. I made $1.25 million in one day.* -Glenn M., IL

Now, when you read this, what are you thinking? We hope you're thinking, "WOW, I finally have someone on my team; who gets nothing out of what I do; who is not trying to hustle me on their next 'investment du jour'." Read the following testimonial from David S., who is a stockbroker who really sees the difference between us and "them."

> *"This seminar and Wade's books filled in the gaps in my stockbroker education. As a stockbroker, I learned how the markets work but not how to personally make money. The firms I have worked for focus on selling and on customer service. . .not on learning strategies beyond buy and hold. Thanks for showing me what I was missing."*
>
> *-David S., TX*

Read again the results: $960,000, $1,200,000, $1,338,081, $2,484,000, and ask yourself—"Where do I go to learn how to make this kind of money?" For example—go to your stockbroker and tell them you want to put in $36,000 and in 11 1/2 months have $1,338,081. Tell them: Wade Cook can show me the formulas that have been used to make this kind of money — why can't you? Point out that Wade Cook put all of his trades on an Internet site www.wadecook.org for the whole world to see, how about you?

**Here is one question in everyone's mind right now, "Is this the right time to get into the market?" The answer is YES!**

In 160 years of tracking the stock market, only eight times has the stock market been down two years in a row. Here is a list of reasons from one of Wade's seminars that share  why we feel the stock market is coming out of a bearish mood to become a BULL MARKET; albeit not a fast-climbing Bull Market:

1.  Because we want the market to go up, and we Americans usually get what we want.

2.  After three bad years, the market is poised to go up.

3.  Negative (Bears) are out of the woods.

4.  Bad investments have been written off—company's values are more stable.

5.  Companies have shed bad debt.

6.  Price / Earnings ratios are getting back in line—good again.

7.  Retail sales are solid—consumers are leading the way.

8.  Inventories are low and companies need to beef back up.

9.  Income Taxes will be lower, putting more money into the economy.

10.  Americans are eager to invest in good American Companies.

The next question is simple. "How do I take advantage of this?" One thing is for sure, you can't take advantage of it sitting on the sidelines. You have to be involved some way. By learning; by experiencing; and by doing.

# 20-Writing In-The-Money Covered Calls

So what does this mean to you? It means you are aligning with a company that walks the walk. It means you can learn their strategies, practice them and get good at them. Now is the time to look at the stock market as an opportunity and work toward fixing your portfolio and your investments to achieve the results you need to realize your American Dream.

Is that important to you? Think—more steady income. Why not pay off bills or your mortgage? Or even retire early? What would you do with an extra $4,000 to $9,000 per month? One of our greatest benefits as a company is seeing what others do with this extra (newly-earned) money:

*"You are not here merely to make a living. You are here to enable the world to live more amply, with greater vision, with a finer spirit of hope and achievement. You are here to enrich the world, but will lessen yourself if you forget the errand."*                    *-Woodrow Wilson*

*I committed myself to getting all of the education I could. I LOVE THIS STUFF! The best part of this, is the fact that I have been able to help my Mom and Dad retire in comfort (and lots of it) and I have been able to not worry about finances AT ALL! I plan on retiring in about 6 months, but probably sooner.*                    *-Jason A., UT*

*I have increased my faith promise to $1,000 per month for missions, and have been able to help some others whose needs were being challenged.*                    *-Doug C., FL*

*Bought a new home and now financing the upcoming birth of triplets.*        *-William S., GA*

*I am excited about my future. I am 72 years old and have a new burst of energy. I have made over $250,000 in just 3 months selling covered calls and have definite plans to realize all my life's unfulfilled goals. What a rush!!*                    *-Dwight H., CA*

*"Our purpose in life should be to build a life of purpose."*                    *-Wade Cook*

What wonderful things can you do with your life? What good things can you do? Then ask yourself: "Do I know any people investing in boring investments or mutual funds that are able to generate cash flow to do those things?" Again—is the stock market the answer to your cash flow needs? Yes, it potentially and unequivocally could be, if you use Wade Cook's safe, time-tested cash flow strategies. We realize you may get angry at your stockbroker or other financial professionals for not showing you these things, but remember, that's not their job. Their job is to sell you things. Our job is to educate you. That's why so many "in-the-know" financial professionals recommend our books and send their clients to our workshops.

This chapter will get you started and headed in the right direction—the direction of more cash flow in numerous "small chunks."

Do you need a lot of money to get started? Well, if you have thousands of dollars that would be nice, but look at the following testimonials. The first is from Jodi L. Her words are touching and we want you to see her letter in her own words. (See Book One)

*I just wanted to let you know, that I was able to play one (rolling) stock over a three week period, seven times, and was able to realize a $7,000 profit from a $500 investment. -Thom A., TX*

Hold it! Did you catch that? $500 to $7,000 in three weeks. Can your stock-broker help you do that?

*Just getting started in the last six months. Started with $600 in an on-line account, trading calls. At present, I have $6,000 in this account. Thank you for the continuing education!*
*-Clark R., FL*

Now, you would think that all financial professionals must assume everyone has $1,000,000 to $5,000,000. Seriously—they're into things like "asset allocation" and the completely ignorant concept of "dollar cost averaging." I guess we'd be the same if people attracted to Wade's books had those high net worths. What about the people with $200, $2,000, $20,000—the butchers, bakers, and candlestick makers? For those who need more income, we say, "Formula Allocation." Pick a formula; learn it, practice it, get good at it, and retire off of it.

You see, we get excited about our students who make millions, but we also love hearing from the ones who literally start with very small amounts. We want you to know that our theme is "monthly cash flow." Rolling Stocks, Writing Covered Calls, even options on stock splits are designed to generate monthly income.

Here's what our students say about monthly income:

*I am now a retired chiropractor at age 37… Averaging about $30,000 a month.*
*-Alan P., AZ*

*I currently make $8,000 to $15,000 per month. Thanks for changing my life.*
*-Kathie L., CA*

*I've made $7,000 to $10,000 per month since January 1, 1999.*          *-Stephan H., CA*

Can we help you? We've helped thousands and we have drawers (huge drawers) full of testimonials that speak of our teaching effectiveness. Can you afford to listen to these "so-called professionals?" Use them for placing orders, but you need to control your financial destiny—not some commission based, barely trained financial pro. Come, walk the walk with us.

*"If a man empties his purse into his head, no one can take it from him. An investment in knowledge always pays the best interest."*

*-Benjamin Franklin*

## Now On To Selling In-the-Money Calls

A variation on the theme of writing covered calls is to sell in-the-money calls. Remember, in writing covered calls, we are selling an option for the purpose of generating cash into our account. We take on an obligation in doing this: the obligation is to deliver the stock at a set price. Hopefully this price would be profitable to you.

In normal covered call writing, there is a tendency to write a slightly out-of-the-money call. If you have a $28 stock, you would write the $30 call. If the stock price moves up to and over the $30 price, you would be called out, or sell the stock. Most people write a slightly out-of-the-money call to not only generate the income from selling the call premium, but to capture the capital gain by the upward movement in the stock.

The overriding question which must be asked when writing a covered call is, "Do I want to get called out of the stock?" By answering this question, you can determine one of the following:

1)  Should I even write a covered call, or should I just go ahead and sell the stock right now? You might find that by selling the stock and using the cash for better purposes, you will generate more income.

2)  If the stock is on a serious downturn, and I sell a call against that position right now and get called out, I would lose money on the stock. I don't particularly want to lose money on the stock, therefore I will sell a slightly out-of-the-money call.

3)  I really don't care whether the stock is taken away from me or not, so I will sell a call close to the current stock price. If the stock goes above the strike price I will sell it. If the stock goes below the strike price, I will keep the stock and have it to write a covered call again on another day.

4)  If I want to sell the stock I will sell a slightly in-the-money call. In the example using the $28 stock, I would sell the $25 call.

5)  If I really want to get called out of the stock, then I would sell the $22.50 call. Even if there is then a downturn in the stock price, as long as it stays above $22.50, I will get called out.

6)  There are even variations on each of the five above. If you have a lot of time to monitor the position, you could try to do multiple trades on the same stock before the same

expiration date. This would involve selling a call when the stock has risen, and buying it back when the stock has gone down.

For example: if the stock is at $28, but is at a near-term high-point, we could sell the $25 call for around $4. Then, if the stock backs off to $26, we could buy back the $25 call for around $2. If we did ten contracts, we would have generated $4,000 into the account, and would now be spending $2,000 to buy back the option position, thereby netting the other $2,000.

Now, as the stock rises to $27 or $28, we could either sell the $25 call or the $30 call a week or two later. On the next dip, we could buy back that call and sell it again on the next rise. This could go on ad infinitum. The stocks take two to three weeks to roll up and down, so it probably could not be done numerous times within one month; but it is not uncommon to have the opportunity to do this two to three times in one month. This would be a nice cash flow generation machine.

Even on doing this strategy, you would still ask the same question—"Do I want to get called out of the stock?"—each time you sell a covered call. Your opinion could change, even in a one- or two-week period of time.

## A Study

Recently, we performed a study on trying to generate a 20% monthly return. The results of this study are found in the last chapter. In that study, we sold slightly out-of-the-money calls. We also took the assumption that these stocks rose in value to the strike price and we were called out to generate the 20% monthly premium. If we did not get called out of these stocks, we simply still owned the stock and could write covered calls again and again.

Now, however, as a follow-up to that study, we changed the strategy slightly, but you'll soon see that there were dramatically different results. This time, we wrote slightly in-the-money calls, but took the assumption that we were called out. There is an unusual phenomena in doing this, which we should explore before we show you the results of this study. This phenomena will generate a new word or two for you—jargon in the stock market.

The term is, "give back." Let's explore what this means. If we own the $28 stock and sell the $25 call for $4, you can see we are writing an in-the-money call. Of the $4 option premium, $3 is in-the-money. Another way of looking at this, is that $3 of the option premium is actually part of the stock price. If the stock is at $28 and we write the $25 call, the stock is $3 above the strike price. If we sell the call for $4 and if we are to get called out at $25, then out of that $4, we have to "give back" $3.

Another way of looking at this, is to say we are losing on the stock price. Remember, we bought the stock at $28 and we sold it at $25. In anyone's book this would be calculated as a $3 loss. Question: "Do you have the right to lose on a stock price?" The answer is, "Yes." But, it's not as bad as it looks. You see, in fact, we are *pre-capturing* part of the profits in the stock, or the last run-up in the stock.

When I say we own the stock at $28, I do not mean we *bought* the stock at $28. We could have purchased this stock at $24 or $26. We would have to then consider the price at which we purchased the stock and the price at which we sold the stock in order to determine our profits. Let's say for example that we bought the stock at $24 and we have seen it run up to $28. If we were to simply sell the stock in this case, we would have a $4,000 profit. Let's see if it's better with writing the covered call.

We'll take the same stock, different example, in that we're going to buy the stock this time at $24. When the stock hits $28, we sell the $25 call for $4. This would generate $4 of profit. If the stock stays above $25 before the expiration date, or even on the expiration date, and we get called out, we would then generate another $1 in capital gains. Our total profits would be $5,000. This is a mild example. There are many examples where the option premiums are substantially more than $4, when the stock is $3 in-the-money. Even using this lower-profit example, you can see that writing covered calls is a method of enhancing the assets in your account. We simply generate more cash into the account.

Now let's see what happens if the stock drops back below $25. If it happens on or around the expiration date we would not get called out of the stock. We would still own the stock and could then write more covered calls. We could do so right now by:

a) Writing a further-out covered call. Instead of writing again for the one week left until this month's expiration, we could write the call out for two or three months, thereby generating a larger option premium, which puts cash into our account.

b) If the stock acts like it's going to rise again, we could put in our order to sell the $25 call, or just wait it out and sell the $25 call on the next rise in the stock.

c) If the stock is showing signs of weakness, we could sell the $25 call. Or, maybe it would be better to sell the $22.50 call. Once again, picking up a larger premium now and getting called out at the $22.50 price if the stock continues to slide. Depending on where the stock was on the expiration date, we would either keep or sell the stock.

## Why Do This?

By selling an in-the-money call, we are simply generating more cash into the account. If that is important to you, then this just might be the way to go. In some regards, it is better to do so; for instance, when the cash in your account could be better used to serve other purposes. Let's stick with a pure comparison of the $28 stock.

Now let's take another look at both of the transactions in Column A and Column B above, from a rate of return point of view. Many of you will not use margin. Margin means you would borrow half of the stock price from the stockbroker. However, many people use margin purchasing so that they only have half of the amount of money tied up.

We will buy the $28 stock for $28 and use margin for this purchase. In this case, with purchasing $1,000 shares, we will put up $14,000 and our broker will loan us the other $14,000. Now let's go back through Column A and Column B:

## Summary:

### A

The stock is at $28 and we write the $30 call. We sell it for $2 and with 1,000 shares of the stock, we sell ten contracts and generate $2,000. We have agreed to give up everything above $30. If the stock does not rise above $30, we keep the stock and we keep the $2,000. We would still have the stock and could write more covered calls in the future.

### B

We write the $25 call for $4. We generate more cash into the account (the $4,000). We are giving back everything in the stock above the $25 strike price. The extra cash can be used for other stock purchases or even other option purchases. We would execute this strategy when we want to get called out of the stock.

There is more profit in the Column A trade, but remember that the stock has to rise to $30 or above in order to get called out and generate the complete $4,000 profit. If the stock remains right at $28, all we're going to make is the $2,000 option premium. In this case, we would calculate our profits by taking the $2,000 and dividing it by $14,000, leaving us with a rate of return of 14%. While there might be less profit in the Column B trade, there is definitely more certainty of getting called out.

## Capturing The Last Run-up

Many of the stocks we own are very volatile. Let's continue to use the same $24 to $28 stock example we used before. I'm going to use the same one, but this time, hopefully help you come to a slightly different conclusion about how to look at your stock purchase. Specifically the last run-up in the stock.

Whenever you have a run-up in a stock, you must ask yourself the question, "Is this going to continue? Can this new price be sustained?" As you come to a determination of what you think the stock will do now that it has hit a high, or has had a nice run-up in price, you will also be able to determine at which strike price to write your covered call.

## A

If we purchase a stock at $28 and sell it for $30, we would have a $2 capital gain and we would keep the $2,000 from selling the $30 call. We would have $4,000 profit. On our $14,000 investment, that would represent a rate of return of 20%. This was a three- or four-week trade. If you use the $2,000 generated from selling the call to offset the amount of your own personal cash you have tied up, you'll see a slight change in the rate of return. You would take the $4,000 profit and divide it by $12,000. The reason we would only use $12,000, is because the $4,000 we generated by writing the covered call is just cash in the account. The computer at your brokerage firm will do what is best with that money on your behalf. Basically, it would lower the amount of margin your broker is putting in to the trade.

## B

If we sell the $25 call and get called out at $25, the rate of return would be 7%. When we write a covered call in this example, our only profits are going to be the option premium. In fact, we're going to lose money on the stock purchase, and we'll subtract that loss from the option premium of $4. The loss would be $3 from the $4, which leaves us with $1, or a $1,000 profit. We would then take the $1,000 in profits and divide it by the $14,000, for a rate of return of 7%; or we would use the $4,000 to offset our $14,000 for the stock purchase, and divide the $1,000 by $10,000, for a 10% rate of return. It doesn't sound like much, but remember, this is a three- to four-week trade. And, I must add, there is more certainty in this trade. Nothing is ever one-hundred percent certain, but there is a higher likelihood of getting called out at $25 than there is of getting called out at $30.

Our example is that we bought this stock at $24, and in a matter of weeks it has run up to $28. You really think it is going to back off. Should you sell the stock right now and capture all the profits? Should you buy a put on the stock to protect the downside? Could you put in a stop-loss order at around $26, and then if the stock does back off, you could sell it at $26, thereby capturing a $2,000 profit?

One other way to look at this, and I hope this will drastically change your mental picture of the stock, is to sell a call option which represents much of the last run-up in the stock price. The stock has gone from $24 to $28. Then, by selling the $25 call option, you have pre-captured everything above $25 into your account. Yes, you have given up the balance of the upward movement in the stock. If you still think the stock is going to continue to go up drastically, you should not write the covered call.

When we write the covered call, we take on a new form of risk, that which we call "opportunity lost risk." You are selling the future upward movement of the stock. However, you could pre-capture the *last* upward movement of the stock by selling the call at this time. You would only do so if you think the stock has peaked out and is going to back off.

Again, if you really feel this way, your choices would be one of four things:

(1) Sell the stock

(2) Put in a stop loss order and capture a portion of the last upward movement

(3) Buy a put, which would increase in value as the stock takes a downturn, or

(4) Sell a covered call.

I like selling the covered call, because one of the advantages of selling an option is that we have a two in three chance of making money. Remember, in the stock market in general, as well as in each stock in particular, one of three things will happen: the stock will go up, down or sideways.

Let's explore each of these possibilities with our $28 stock, wherein we write the $25 call option. If the stock goes up, we will definitely get called out at $25 *and* we have made our profit. We have captured our $4,000 premium, of which we have to give back $3,000 (remember, we sold the call for $4, $3 of which was in-the-money), thereby leaving a $1,000 profit. We also have a 1,000 capital gain.

If the stock stays the same, say around the $28 price, we *will* get called out and our profit will be the same $1,000, plus the $1,000 capital gain.

If the stock goes down *below* $25, we still get to keep the whole $4,000 option premium, and we would determine whether we are in a profit or a loss situation, dependant on what price we paid for the stock.

If we buy a stock, the only way we make money is if it goes up in price. If we buy a put option to protect the downside movement in the stock, the stock must move down for the put option to go up in value. Again, a one in three chance of making money. By *selling* the call we have a two in three chance of making money: *actually,* we have a two-and-a-*half* in three chance of making money because the stock could go down a little bit and we still make money.

If you need more information on this two in three chance of making money, see *Writing Covered Calls* in virtually all of my books, but especially Wall Street Money Machine and *"FREE STOCKS: How to Get the Stock Market to Pay for Your Stocks."*

It is so easy for stocks to spike up and then immediately retrace (pull back from) the last run-up. Writing covered calls gives you a way of selling part of the stock—that part which is above the strike price. If that part represents the last run-up in the stock and the part of the profits that is most likely to be lost as the stock retraces itself to a lower level, we will benefit greatly by selling the call option at the current time, and then if and when the stock backs off, buy back the call option to either sell it again or to sell the stock.

One of the reasons I like writing covered calls is because it allows you the opportunity to get involved, get uninvolved by buying the option back and then get involved again. In my seminars I have taught that it is more important to make correctable decisions than it is to make correct decisions.

This strategy of writing covered calls lets us stay in the game and allows us to keep making correctable decisions.

## Back To The Study

The following is a chart of the same stock we used in our 20% Monthly Covered Call Challenge. (See chapter 8). This time we wrote in-the-money calls. You can see that the numbers speak for themselves. The rates of return are quite substantial, but could even be higher had we written further-out-of-the-money calls and had all of the stocks risen.

In that last sentence is a hidden secret. I used the expression, "all of the stocks." Very seldom will *all* of your stocks rise. A decision you need to make is, how big of a rate of return do you want to go for? "Do I want a bigger rate of return, or do I want more certainty?" Oddly enough, the answer to those questions is also found in the same overriding question I keep reminding you to ask yourself, which is: "Do I want to sell this stock?"

### APRIL

| Ticker Name | Stock Price $ | Opt. Strike | Opt. Price $ | % if not called out | % if called out |
|---|---|---|---|---|---|
| ABGX Abgenix | 20.83 | 20.00 | 2.30 | 22.08% | 14.10% |
| ADLAC Adelphia | 24.30 | 22.50 | 3.00 | 24.68% | 15.14% |
| ALTR Altera | 23.75 | 22.50 | 2.75 | 23.15% | 12.60% |
| AAPL Apple | 24.68 | 22.50 | 3.00 | 24.31% | 6.64% |
| AMZN Amazon.com | 16.43 | 15.00 | 2.35 | 28.60% | 12.26% |
| ATML Atme l | 9.01 | 7.50 | 1.65 | 36.62% | 3.10% |
| BEAS Bea System | 16.26 | 15.00 | 2.30 | 28.29% | 12.79% |
| CHTR Charter | 13.29 | 12.50 | 1.60 | 24.07% | 11.88% |
| CIEN Ciena | 10.79 | 10.00 | 1.60 | 29.65% | 15.00% |
| CSCO Cisco | 17.25 | 15.00 | 2.65 | 30.72% | 4.63% |
| CTXS Citrix | 17.54 | 15.00 | 3.00 | 34.20% | 5.24% |
| CPWR Compuware | 12.42 | 10.00 | 2.45 | 39.45% | .50% |
| CNXT Conexant | 13.17 | 12.50 | 1.50 | 22.77% | 12.60% |

| Ticker Name | Stock Price $ | Opt. Strike | Opt. Price $ | % if not called out | % if called out |
|---|---|---|---|---|---|
| CYTC Cytyc | 25.51 | 25.00 | 2.10 | 16.46% | 12.15% |
| FLEX Flextronics | 19.68 | 17.50 | 2.95 | 29.97% | 7.80% |
| GMST Gemstar | 21.43 | 20.00 | 3.40 | 31.73% | 18.38% |
| HGSI Human Gen. | 23.16 | 22.50 | 3.00 | 25.90% | 5.69% |
| IMCL Imclone | 26.29 | 25.00 | 3.50 | 26.62% | 16.81% |
| JNPR Juniper | 14.08 | 12.50 | 2.65 | 37.64% | 22.44% |
| MLNM Millenium | 24.64 | 22.50 | 3.10 | 25.16% | 7.79% |
| NTAP Network App. | 21.28 | 20.00 | 2.90 | 27.25% | 15.22% |
| NXTL Nextel | 6.45 | 5.00 | 1.65 | 51.16% | 6.20% |
| ORCL Oracle | 14.32 | 12.50 | 2.15 | 30.02% | 4.60% |
| PMCS PMC-Sierra | 19.21 | 17.50 | 3.20 | 33.31% | 15.51% |
| RATL Rational | 20.41 | 20.00 | 2.30 | 22.53% | 15.68% |
| RFMD RF Micro | 20.95 | 20.00 | 2.55 | 24.34% | 15.27% |
| PDLI Protein Design | 16.68 | 15.00 | 3.00 | 35.97% | 15.82% |
| SANM Sanmina | 14.42 | 12.50 | 2.50 | 34.67% | 8.04% |
| SSCC Smurfitt | 16.82 | 15.00 | 1.95 | 23.18% | 1.50% |
| SPLS Staples | 20.00 | 20.00 | .90 | 9.00% | 9.00% |
| SBUX Starbux | 23.03 | 22.50 | 1.30 | 11.28% | 6.68% |
| TLAB Tellabs | 12.80 | 12.50 | 1.15 | 17.96% | 13.28% |
| VRSN Verisign | 31.97 | 30.00 | 3.90 | 24.39% | 12.07% |
| VTSS Vitesse Semi | 9.57 | 7.50 | 2.40 | 50.15% | 6.89% |
| YHOO Yahoo! | 19.71 | 17.50 | 2.90 | 29.42% | 7.00% |

The first is an article by Dr. George Park. The second is an update on his article about In-the-Money Covered Calls. These articles were written several years ago, but the knowledge is still pertinent.

*THE MOST IMPORTANT KEY TO ACHIEVING GREAT SUCCESS IS TO DECIDE UPON YOUR GOAL AND LAUNCH, GET STARTED, TAKE ACTION, MOVE.*

*JOHN WOODEN*

# 21

# 22 Ways to Build Wealth: Learning from the Mistakes of Wade

I try to put all of the good trades and all of the bad trades I do on M.U.S.T., but in looking over my portfolio for the last year, I realized I've made a whole bunch of mistakes. Many I know could have been corrected, so I decided to do a presentation called *Learning From the Mistakes of Wade*. I've isolated 22 different things I have done *wrong* in the last year. Remember, every one of these mistakes is correctable. I hope everything I share with you and teach you here, will help *you* make better trades.

I'm amazed at how many people think they can get extraordinary results with mediocre or ordinary efforts. Teenagers look at that big nice car when they get out of high school—16 to 18 year olds—looking at every Viper, Prowler and Corvette out there. They want the big car. They want the big house. They want everything. And then all of a sudden reality sets in. If you're going to get that Corvette, *you're going to have to work for it.*

I'm trying to teach the teenagers in my Sunday School class that *everything starts with a thought*. Our thoughts control everything we do. How dare we think that we're going to get some action or result different than what we're thinking about? You will get what you think about. If you want to make millions of dollars, think about it all the time; hopefully also keeping your relationship with God intact. Think about the process. Don't focus on the prize, focus on the *price*. What is the price that has to be paid? Are you willing to pay the price, do you even know the price? I contend that most people are not successful because they don't know the price that has to be paid; but when they understand the price that has to be paid and they pay the price, then and only then will the prize come.

> *"We choose our joys and sorrows, long before we experience them."*　　　　　*~Kahlil Gibran*

> *If you think about disaster, you will get it. Brood about death and you hasten your demise. Think positively and masterfully, with confidence and faith, and life becomes more secure, more fraught with action, richer in achievement and experience.*　　　　　*~Swami Silvanada*

You see, it all starts with our thought process. In light of all this, I stand before you as one student of the stock market, and I am ever learning. How dare I think that all of a sudden one day, I'm going to reach the pinnacle of success, and to know everything there is to know about the stock market? The stock market is a moving target—stocks are a moving target, and strategies change. Different strategies are needed at different times. We need to adjust, we need to continually adapt.

MISTAKE #1 is ignoring the natural movements that exist, with or without me. I don't want to get my money in the way of a possible movement of a stock, if that position is going to go against any natural movements. For example, you've heard me talk a lot over the years about this *Red Light, Green Light* phenomenon. Let me share that with you very quickly.

I have noticed, because I was the President and CEO of a publicly traded company, that there are specific times when stocks rise and stocks fall. There can be really bad economic times, a year or two of really downtrending stocks, which pretty much supercede everything I'm going to say. I suggest to you, though, that in most traditional years, regardless of whether we're in an uptrending or a downtrending market, there are still better times to buy and better times to sell.

What I have noticed is, as the stocks move through each calendar quarter, there's the anticipation of news, the actual quiet period, and a time when all of the news starts to hit the streets: company reports, earnings reports, other kinds of news, dividends increases or decreases, share buybacks, etc. There are market moving kinds of news you need to look for. One is the earnings—the earnings and the anticipation of earnings.

Virtually every stock price today is a reflection of the anticipation of future earnings. Take that sentence to the bank. It is true. If the company's earnings are growing, and they're expanding overseas, the anticipation is that earnings will increase. The stock moves up. For example: Krispy Kreme donuts is all over the country. They're expanding right now, so the stock is going to reflect the anticipation of the earnings resulting from this expansion. For those of you in the Northwest, we're going to have one right out in Issaquah, down the hill from my house. Next time you see me I will be 400 pounds.

When the Federal Reserve raises interest rates, raises the discount rate at which the banks have to hold money, what happens to the future earnings of companies? If they raise interest rates today, what is the perception about earnings in a year to a year and a half? Profits will go down, earnings will go down, therefore stock prices will follow. Do the stock prices wait a year to go down? Or do the stock prices go down *today*, based on the anticipation nine months or a year and a half from now? Stock prices today are the *anticipation* of future earnings. By the way, has Alan Greenspan taken on almost god-like status? My goodness, God would be *happy* if he could have that much attention, I think. Every move he makes, the way he breathes, the way he talks, everything he does is watched. (2003 Update: The rates were lowered to 1.00%. If these continue, companies who rely on a lot of debt will probably eventually start making more money.)

The pendulum is always swinging. That's my point in mistake number one. I got behind the eight ball because I didn't follow the natural movements. All right. Starting today, I, Wade Cook, am going to pay a lot more attention to what Alan Greenspan has to say. When he talks, when the Federal Reserve moves, the marketplace follows to a certain extent. Not every stock follows, and some stocks will countertrend, but the marketplace in general follows his statements.

MISTAKE #2 also involves this *Red Light, Green Light* period. Is it possible to have a whole one or two *year* Red Light period, and a whole one or two *year* Green Light period? Back in the year 1998 and the first part of 1999, almost any trade we did worked. We could buy stock anytime.

One of my big mistakes is, even though I discovered the *Red Light, Green Light* phenomenon and have created a whole Home Study course around it, I'm a classic case of "Physician, heal thyself." I read my book again and I ask, "Why did I do this? I do trades that are against everything I know." Is that a pretty common thing? You just know something, you have it locked down and know it inside out, and then you continue to do stupid things. I think we're all like that, I'm no different.

Back to the point: I decided to pay even more attention to these Red Light periods. Through the month of February stocks go down. About the middle of March, when the anticipation of the news and the news reports start coming out with forecasts, they start to go up again if the news is good. Understand that about 50% of the news is bad and about 50% of the news is good; it's not always based on the fact that news is out, it's based on *who's* giving the news, and the *quality* of the news. How many of you have seen this simple little statement by Dell computer a few years ago? "We're meeting our numbers and we're growing for the future. The worst is behind us." That day, the whole stock market was up a couple of hundred points (398). It just took off. *One* statement, *one* sentence by *one* person on *one* news release changed the *whole market* for the day. The news was good, and it was perceived that it was going to ripple through the system. Then someone else will come out and say, "Well, we just barely made our numbers, and we're doing OK, but we're expecting lower revenues for the next six to nine months." What happens to the stock today? The $58 stock goes to $50 because of *the anticipation of future earnings*. Pay attention to these comments.

When I say Green Light, I just mean "news" period. It's not a time to get involved necessarily. It can be a Green Light period with a lot of bad news and the stock prices will go down. The only thing Green Light signals is that *the news starts*. It's not the *quantity* of the news, it's the *quality* of the news, and that's what you have to monitor. Don't go, "Well Wade says this is a Green Light period, therefore I need to get involved in stocks," *No*! This is a Green Light Period—*be careful*. Maybe I should change it to Red Light, Yellow Light: Caution, be careful.

MISTAKE #3 When I was buying stocks over the last couple of years, my biggest mistake was that I was not following earnings. I was buying stocks on the momentum. I was buying stocks because everybody else was buying stocks. I got caught up in that too. Everybody is talking about it, everybody is thinking about it, therefore go buy it. I bought Qualcom as it was just climbing up, $100, $200, $300, it got up to $800 and did that 4:1 split. That $200 stock has backed down around $50. It's amazing! But, if you look at it, that's where it *should* be. Even at $50 it's a little bit high.

There are two ways you're going to make money if you watch Price/Earnings ratios. The P/E ratio refers to the money you have to spend to get at $1 of earnings. If you hear about a P/E of 18, or a P/E of 43, or a P/E of 608, it means you're going to pay $18 to get at $1 of earnings for that stock. If the P/E is 43, you're going to pay $43 to get at $1 of earnings. If the P/E is 608, you're going to pay $608 to get at $1 of earnings.

Here's the point: do you know what 608 times earnings means? This is what AOL stock was selling for several years ago. Don't get me wrong, AOL is a good company. AOL was making money. AOL was trading at 608 times earnings. Do you have any idea what that means? That means, at 608 times earnings, Americans are willing to spend *sixty million, eight hundred thousand dollars* to get at $100,000 of earnings. Are we that stupid? Obviously, we were. Because we were buying these kinds of companies. We have companies trading at 900 times earnings, *2,400* times earnings. We thought that was the new game, the new paradigm in the stock market. "One thousand times earnings, ah, that's a piece of cake." Prices had to come down. Everything returns to the norm.

If you want to buy a stock today, check out its *earnings growth* for the last three years. Would that be a telltale sign of where it's heading? I think so. Not just what it's earning this year, or what it's projected to earn next year, but what *has* it been earning? Has it been growing, has it been expanding, how has it been doing *over a longer period of time*? I didn't check that out. I took too many risks buying stocks I shouldn't have been buying.

Let me deal with this whole risk factor for just a second. You have the potential to go broke in one of two ways: (1) is to take too much risk and (2) is to not take enough risk. Ah! There's the dilemma in life. What is the happy medium for you? Too much risk will wipe you out. Too little risk will cause you to go nowhere. You'll end up broke either way. A lot of you have said, "Yep, I took too much risk on that stock, I should not have bought it." Every one of you now can point to a stock you bought that, if you could go back now and check out all the data that existed at the time you purchased the stock, you'd probably say, "I shouldn't have bought that stock." Earnings were flat, earnings were going down, it wasn't making any money, but boy was it the hot stock of the day. It is a harsh reality. A lot of us messed up. We got involved in stock purchases, and sometimes options and LEAPS® for the *wrong reasons*. We got involved thinking that that current marketplace would never end; and it ended harshly.

Now let's shake it off and step up. Let me tell you about Dudley the Mule. Dudley kept kicking things and knocking things over. They called him Dudley-Do-Wrong. Dudley-Do-Wrong one day happened to trip and fall into the well. After expansive study on how they could get him out of the well, they determined it would cost almost $10,000 to excavate and get him out. They determined that the well was going to have to be his grave. The farmer invited some friends over. They brought their shovels and started shoveling dirt down to bury Dudley. He didn't like the dirt on his back, so he shook it off. They shoveled more dirt and he shook it off and stepped up. They threw more dirt down the well, he shook it off and stepped up. Every time he got dirt on his back, Dudley would shake it off and step up. After several hours of doing this, Dudley was finally able to step up, and step *out*, of the well. That which was meant to kill him, actually saved his life. That which could hurt us, could actually save us if we have the right attitude.

I'll submit to you one powerful statement made by one of the people in our Research and Training Department. He was hurting too. Here's a guy that came in with $5,000 and took it to over $2,000,000 in a couple of years. He was down several hundred thousand dollars on several options, and he said, "With the Wade Cook strategies, used the right way, the way they were intended to be used, anyone out there has an *infinite ability* to make it back." So don't quit trying. *Learn* from your mistakes, figure out what you did wrong, and get on with it.

MISTAKE #4: I think a lot of us often do not clearly define the strategy we're working. You might have $100,000 in a brokerage account, and you have $25,000 allocated for rolling stock, $20,000 for some Blue Chips investing and $25,000 allocated for writing covered calls. You should allocate your money and clearly define your strategy. More importantly than that, you should clearly define the strategy with, for instance, your stockbroker. You determine your exit points and your team—make sure they really, truly understand your intentions. I do this a lot. Here is my mistake: I say, "Yeah, if it hits $4, go ahead and sell it, but I'll talk to you later about it." I made that statement once, because I was getting out of the car. That statement by me caused my broker to not sell the stock when it hit $4. "Didn't you sell it at $4?" I asked him. "Well you said you were going to call me later," he replied.

When the people around you, your team, do not *clearly know* what you're after, mistakes will be made.

MISTAKE #5: I forget who I am, and how busy I am. I was the President and CEO of a publicly traded company. I don't like being as busy as I was. I would have rather spend more time with my kids. But right then, I had companies we were running. We also had some companies getting ready to go public. It was really a lot of fun, but it was very time-intensive. Therefore, I didn't have a lot of time to watch my computer screen all day. Some of you have a lot of time and can call your stockbroker ten to fifteen times a day; get out of positions, monitor things, check on things. I didn't have that luxury. I personally needed a strategy I could put in place and let go.

MISTAKE #6 is not getting out of bad positions. I've got to quit letting bad positions ride. A few months ago, I was a most brilliant trader for a day or two. My family was at a horse show and I had a lot of time to call my stockbroker. I did thirteen trades in a row on about three or four different stocks. *Thirteen trades!* Eight hundred here, twelve hundred there, I made $23,000 on those thirteen trades. It was awesome, it was incredible, you would think I was a genius. However, in the same account I had 1,000 shares of a $50 stock that went down to $20. So my $50,000 was now sitting at $20,000. Oh yes, I made $23,000 in the active part of the account, but I lost $30,000 by not keeping track of the other stuff! It's kind of like you're hoeing the ground over here in one part of your vineyard while there's a fire in the other part. If you don't take care of the fire it just might burn down the whole farm.

I should have had a $45 stop-loss in place; an order to sell it on a 10 or 20% dip. And that would have been horrible enough! $50,000 down to $40,000. As it turned out, I got out at $20,000 and then the stock went to $1. I was really glad about that, because I didn't lose another $19,000!

MISTAKE #7: I've also hinted at this one: choose and get to be an expert at one or two strategies. You may know peripheral strategies, rolling stocks, rolling options and things like that. If you sell a put against a stock, and end up taking the stock, then all of a sudden you're a covered call writer. Writing covered calls requires a whole different and new level of expertise than selling puts. You have a whole different bid and ask, different events which move the stocks, etc. You start out selling puts and getting really good at that, but from time to time you take the stock, and that is what happened in my account. The account was doing really well selling puts, but from time to time I would go ahead and take the stocks. And guess what I ended up with in the account? About $300,000 worth of stock that eventually dipped down to about $150,000. I had this account making me a good 15 to 20% a month, and I ended up with a whole bunch of doggie stocks. Don't change strategies in the middle of the stream. Get good at one strategy and figure it out. You also need to get good at one small grouping of stocks.

Another mistake: you end up with too many positions to monitor. You get too many different things going on. You should take your top ten or twenty stocks or options and literally memorize everything about them.

MISTAKE #8: This is a real mistake I have made over the last two years. I keep thinking that the stock market is going to come roaring back. It's like I'm expecting those Go-Go Days of '97 through '99 to happen all over again; when stocks were up ten to twenty dollars a day, would back off five dollars the next day, then they'd be up thirty dollars, and back down fifteen. Those days are over. Our mental process has to come back to this current market.

I started teaching stock market seminars when we had a marketplace like we have today. In 1994 it was a sideways moving stock market. Ups and downs, but not so dramatic as in '98 and '99. Can you get good at playing a lot of ups and downs, even if the stock market doesn't go skyrocketing higher? There are always cash flow strategies—which is the one you need to get good at? I keep waiting for those ten to twenty dollar moves on the Qualcoms, and now we're getting two and three and four-dollar moves in a day. We have to get our brain set back a little bit and say, "This is the new reality. This is how I'm going to make money in *this* marketplace."

MISTAKE #9: We can use rolling options. We will always have stocks going up and down. Qualcom, Microsoft, QLogic, Cisco. How do you play these? If you buy the stock—which is even safer if you want to spend that much cash—you buy MSFT at $28 and you sell it at $30. If you have 1,000 shares you make $2,000. But when the stock gets up to $28 or so, and the earnings news is played out, if it's in a Red Light period, the stock is more than likely going to come back down. Take a rolling stock like a Microsoft that has a $2 or $3 swing. Make money on the $25 calls or sell the $25 or $22.50 puts.

Once again, I'm playing what is called a directional move. I just cautioned you against buying too many options. If you *buy* a call on a stock, you have all of the unlimited upside potential and limited downside risk, but the stock *must move* for you to make money.

You trade at the level at which you are not afraid of losing. Even if you have $100,000, two to six thousand dollars for options is enough. Qualcom is doing a two or three-day pattern, or about $3 to $6. Pick two or three stocks, get good at understanding them and set good exit points for either outcome—both if the trade works or if it does not.

MISTAKE #10: Mistake number ten is having too many positions in my account. I was keeping stocks I hoped would come back. I needed to clean them out, it was too much clutter. I put some stocks into a separate account and sold off others. Even if it was a $30 stock and it's at $3, it's out of there. That's what I mean when I say, pick your top ten or twenty stocks.

I mostly do three kinds of option trades. (1) Calls and puts on stock splits. (2) Bounces off of support levels, and (3) *selling* calls and puts.

For me, I'm limiting my rolling options trades to three principal companies. See these at www.wadecook.org (Note: this chapter is a few years old, but the point still is to get good at a few stocks.) It is better to get good at three different stocks and make money consistently, than to have a peripheral knowledge of 50 stocks. If you just have two or three stocks, with all the different strike prices and all the different roll patterns, it's enough to think about! Get to be an expert at two or three stocks, know when their earnings are coming out, know when all the news is coming out, know when their contracts are coming up, know the company inside out. Study them. Monitor them. Watch their patterns, and then place position trades in front of the next movement. Puts going down, calls going up.

MISTAKE #11: We need to get better at monitoring our whole account. We need to look at each strategy, even if it's buy and hold, a blue chip investing account. You might have the best stock out there at $60, and if you don't have a stop-loss on it, if you're not monitoring it, it can go down to $30 behind your back! Now, you might have $100,000 again in your account, and you're really doing well with this $5,000 or $6,000 on these rolling options; you also have $20,000 allocated for trying to get 20% a month on selling puts. But then in a different part of your account are your other blue chip stocks. Keep track of those too. The point is, you're managing a *whole account*. I got caught not managing the whole account and that hurt my portfolio.

MISTAKE #12: Understand that when you buy options, *time becomes the enemy*. When you buy stock, in theory, time becomes your friend. Stocks can be very forgiving over a long period of time. Options don't give you the time to be forgiven. If you buy a two-month-out option, that stock has to move within a very specific time frame, or you are going to get burned. A reminder of the Rule of Three. We don't always accomplish this, but I'll give you the rules once again.

*RULE #1: Shoot for a 300% return.* Let's assume you're going to take $10,000 of your two to three hundred thousand dollars, and put it into option trades. Now you need to remember, always only around 4-6% of your account should be in these riskier options. A lot of us, including me, got burned the last couple of years, because we thought we were invincible with options. When those $80 stocks took a tank down to $18, what happened to our $75 call option? We thought it was going to go up, but, it's down there at $12 right now, and it won't recover fast enough.

I consistently try to teach my students how to get 20% a month. We don't always make it, but our target is to pound out profits with part of our account in the 10-20% range. Which means that if you have $10,000, it would be nice to make $2,000 a month. From time to time, you'll have $10,000, you'll get lucky, and it will turn into $20,000. Great. But those events are usually the exception to the rule.

If you want to make a consistent 20% a month, you need more discipline. This is where most people fail in option trading, because they're not willing to discipline themselves. When you go into an option trade, you need to plan for a 300% return. You won't always make it, but you *shoot for* a 300% return. For example, if you invest $4,000 in some call options, that stock, in theory, needs to move enough so that you can make $12,000 and have $8,000 profit. How much does this stock have to move for me to get that option from $4 up to $12? Try this method. By the way, this will help you quit doing most riskier option trades.

*RULE #2: Cut your losses early.* You're going to stop out at a 50% loss. If you have $4,000 and you hope it's going to go up, but it goes down to $2,000, you're out of the trade. You have to weed the garden better. It's not working, get out of there. We talk about being right one out of three times, or two out of three times, we're hoping we can be right six to nine times out of ten.

*RULE #3: Do even trades.* If you have $10,000, you should do five $2,000 trades, or you should do ten $1,000 trades. Think it through. You could, for example, if you have $10,000, put $4,000 into one trade,

$4,000 into another trade and $2,000 into another trade. Let's say that your $2,000 turns into $3,000 and you have $1,000 profit. You also get out of your $4,000 at a $1,000 profit and your other $4,000 goes down to $1 and you get out with a $3,000 loss. Tell me where your account is. How do you like that, being right two out of three times and losing money?

If you are right more times than not, *and* have equal amounts of money in the trades, *then*, if you're right three out of five times, or seven out of ten times, or even five out of ten times, you're going to make money. That is a discipline most people are not willing to stick with. People get really excited about a stock, and out of $10,000, they put $8,000 into one trade. Then, guess what? On their $2,000 trade, they get a triple. They turn it into $6,000, a $4,000 profit. But the $8,000 trade went down to $2,000. How does their account look? Where are they? Losing money again. *Do even trades.* You literally have to say, "I am a $1,500 per trade trader. That's what I trade." You can determine a percentage or a dollar amount, although I suggest a dollar amount is a better route. That may force you to buy seven contracts on one stock and thirteen contracts of another. And you don't do $3,000 or $4,000 trades until you conscientiously, in all of your positions, say, "Now, I am a $4,000 trader."

In the options marketplace, if you will shoot for a 300% return, if you will cut your losses early, and if you will do even trades, you can be right three out of ten times, and you'll still get close to a 20% returns. That is across the board in the industry; option traders have proven this day in and day out. Guess where most of those profits come from? Getting out. We hope against hope that an option will turn around. That option has gone from $5 down to $2, and we say, well, we have two weeks left, it will bounce back. Then it's at $1, well, we're still going to wait for it to bounce back. Then it's at 50¢ and we say, what the heck, just let it go, and there goes our whole $5,000. We could have had $2,000 back on our $5,000, but we're not very good at weeding the garden. It's painful to do and we don't like doing it.

MISTAKE #13: This is a simple one. I found myself not reading as much as I used to read. I was studying many newspapers and magazines. I was reading five to ten magazines a week. I read all kinds of stories about companies. This last year, I have been very, very involved writing some new reports based on the Bible and other spiritual topics. It was very important to me, by the way, and I wouldn't trade it for anything.

I believe readers are leaders. If you're going to be active in the stock market you have to read and study more. I got away from my studies of the stock market. Now again, I wouldn't trade it for all my studies of Hebrew and the Bible and all that I've done, but there is a price to pay. You need to determine how much reading you have to do. I suggest to you that you need to keep up on the news.

MISTAKE #14: I had too much money in options. LEAPS can get hurt really fast too. The time value of LEAPS can expire very quickly. Don't have more than 4-10% of your money tied up in options, long calls or long puts. For those of you who are a little bit faint of heart in this area, 2 to 4%. Those who are a little bit riskier, 5 to 9%. For those who are *really, really* risky, and don't need the money anyway, 10%. Quit putting so much money into options over which you have no control. I now do NORM trades: No required movement. I want to do a lot of trades that require no movement in the underlying stock for me to still make money on the option. It comes down to selling–as in selling puts or writing covered calls. I've tried to show you how to do directional trades through rolling options on support and resistance levels, but *this new* theme is no directional trades. If the stock doesn't move, we will be able to keep the option premium? Yes, we don't need any directional movement to make money. I think that's an interesting philosophy. Put yourself in a position where nothing has to happen, and you make money. Then if things *do* happen, you still make money.

MISTAKE #15: Change is imminent. Trust change. Change is always going to happen. As soon as the options market makers figure us out, they make changes and take advantage of us.

Here's another thing. Do we all wake up in the morning, thinking that there must be some options market makers in Chicago and New York who get up, drive across town, and go to work saying, "I have to figure out some ways today to help all those investors out there make more money"? Do some of us think this? Are we that naïve? "Oh, especially those Wade Cook Seminar people, those are a *good* bunch of people. You know, I need to help all of those people make more money." What do you think? No way! They have to get you to lose before they can make their house payment. To put their kid through college, they have to get your money and they are *professionals* at it. They sit there all day long trying to figure it out. As soon as Wade Cook comes out with a bestselling book about Stock Splits, they think of what to do to counter us. How can they counter? They say, "We're hiking up those option premiums!" Guess what we do? We chase them, and end up with an option premium that's way overpriced and a couple days later we can't sell it at a profit. How did that happen? Because there are people behind the scenes that are specifically there to <u>get us to lose money</u>. And as soon as they figure us out, they will counter any movement we make and figure out a way to make money off of us. So, if we're going to be ahead of this game, except for that devious part of their nature, I'm going to suggest that you act more like them. They make money by selling, I think you should make more money by selling (going short, or in writing [selling] calls and puts).

MISTAKE #16: Straddles. We'll cover straddles and strangles very quickly. When companies do earnings, you can check the quarterly date and go back nine or ten quarters and punch up the day of or day before the earnings reports. You might see a two- to ten-dollar movement, almost every time, into the earnings. Even if it's good earnings, the stock might tank the next day. Because, they could have great earnings, but then right at the very end they announce some forward looking news. Boeing, for example, during earnings will do a charge-off of $280,000,000. The great earnings are now bad earnings, because they took a one-time expense and the stock goes down. How do you play that?

Here is a strangle. The stock is at $66. It has been up from $64 to $66, and earnings come out tomorrow. If you don't know for sure if it's going to go up or down, you could play it both ways simultaneously. You *do* know that the stock is going to move one way or the other. You could buy the $70 call, and the $65 put. These are cheaper to play. By buying the call and a put, you have now purchased two options. To make money, that stock has to move a lot. If you have a non-moving stock, you shouldn't be doing a strangle.

A pure straddle is where you buy the call and buy the put at the same strike price. The stock is at $64 or $66. You would buy the call and the put at the $65 strike price. A strangle is the next price lower for the put, and the next strike price higher for the call.

MISTAKE #17: I think we need to use a small amount of emotion. Everybody says to use no emotion. Most of you have heard me talk about computers. I don't do computers. I still don't know how to turn them on, but I call my secretary and tell her I'm almost there, and she pulls up my screens. I've learned how to click in a ticker symbol now—and all of a sudden I find myself very busily staring at a computer screen 15 or 20 minutes a day. It's almost destroying my personality.

My point is, I have watched a lot of people do this. They see a stock and it's at $62, and then it's at $63, and they have the call, and it's at $64, and they're still staring at it. "We should sell it," they say, and they let these streaming numbers on a computer screen dictate their emotion. That emotion then controls everything, and they usually end up selling badly.

I think we need to step back and say, "Why am I doing this? What is my exit strategy? I'm rallying into the split. There are earnings today. This is a rolling stock." If you have your sell points in, you *don't* have to sit and stare at the computer screen. The more I do that, the less money I make. You decide what you're going to do, that's just the Wade Cook method. I didn't tell you these were learning from the mistakes of you, these are learning from the mistakes of Wade.

MISTAKE #18: General to the Specific, Specific to the General. We think that just because any kind of broadband company moves, all of them are going to move. While this happens sometimes, it doesn't happen all of the time. We take a general thing happening in the market place, and make it specifically apply to every stock. It doesn't work very well. We take a specific thing that happened on one stock, and we think it's going to happen on every stock. That's a big problem. I've been caught several times. I'm going to avoid doing that, be very cautious and say, "What is the story of *this* stock, what is the story of *this* company?"

Don't get me wrong, a lot of things do move in sectors, but just because one bank stock does a stock split announcement, and others may follow, some may go *down* in the meantime. Look at *each* stock, *each* trade, isolate it, and make sure it is a good trade in and of itself.

Mistake #19: Keep a lot of cash in reserve. Need I say more? You need a lot of cash in reserve for margin calls and for opportunities. *Cash will always have an opportunity.* Stock and equities will not always have an opportunity. As always, know your exit point.

MISTAKE #20: Get better at your exit strategies. Do you really know your exit on every strategy? Are you happy with your exit? I submit to you that most people don't, and aren't. Someone will come to me and say they either made a lot of money or lost a lot of money, and I'll say, "What was your exit point? What was your strategy, what were you trying to accomplish?"

"Uh...uh... make money?"

That was their exit strategy, "make money", "Buy low, sell high." No! What specific dollar amount or price point did you have?

Or do they say, "The stock was around $74 and was on a major dip. I sold the $70 puts for $3. I was going to wait for the stock to go up and buy back the puts for $1 and the plan was to make a $2,000 profit." Man, I would give *anything* if I could get an answer like that! But I don't. I get answers like, "uh...uhhh." I'm suggesting to you that you will get better at profitable trades in proportion to how good you get at weeding your garden and at establishing your exit points.

Mistake #21: Don't forget your purpose. When you first come to know Wade Cook, what was your intent? When you heard me on a radio show, or you bought one of my books, why were you attracted to Wade Cook, our company, Liberty Network, Inc.? What did we say to you that got you excited? Cash flow? Monthly income? Training? Hopefully to make enough money so you could replace your income and quit your job, all of it or part of it. I'm about building monthly income, correct? Do you know what happened the last couple of years? Far too many people listening to this presentation made such good money off of the strategies that they were almost out of control. They bought some stocks and some options that just took off and flew. Now they're not flying anymore, and I'm saying to you, "What's the point? What are you doing?"

The mistake is not having a reason for the movement established ahead of time. Figure out what you want to accomplish so you can then figure out how much money you'll need. You set these targets and then put into place a process to accomplish it.

One lady started with $4,000. She took her $4,000 up to $30,000. She was writing covered calls on the $30,000. She was making around $4,500 a month on the $30,000 and her stocks tanked. Her $30,000 was now at $20,000. Would anybody else have bragging rights, taking $4,000 to $20,000? Yes! But it numbed her. It paralyzed her. She couldn't move. She couldn't shake it off. Her $30,000 was at $20,000. She didn't do trades for over *six months*. And her positions just sat there around $20,000, $18,000, $22,000. I talked to her and asked, "Look, how much could you make writing calls?" The second day, on her $20,000, she sold almost $3,000 in covered call premiums. So, it's not $4,500, it's only $3,000. Could some people still really use an extra $3,000 a month? But her paralysis caused her to lose out on $2,000 to $4,000 a month for six months. So what? Your $300,000 is down to $200,000. Your $30,000 is down to $20,000. _There's still money to be picked up_. So, what was your intent in coming into my life? I'm going to submit to you that your intent was to help you build up your monthly income to do whatever you wanted. To have your spouse quit their job, to buy a better home, whatever. Have you forgotten that? Have you become so wrapped up in making millions on options that you forgot what you really wanted was $6,000 a month?

Ask yourself, "What are my cash flow needs?" Let's work with that $6,000 a month plan. If you really want to make $6,000 a month, if that is your target, if that's what you need, then here's what you need to do. Back it down from there. Start with your exit strategy. Start where you want to be, and now let's goal-set backwards instead of forward. If you want to make $6,000 a month, what do you need to do? What strategy will work best for you? Is it writing covered calls, selling puts, or doing some options?

What purpose is the money going to serve? What do _you_ need to wind down _your_ business, what do _you_ need to do to spend more time with _your_ family? What do _you_ need to do to get out of _your_ job, if that's what you want? Then figure out how much money you need to generate that monthly income. Then put a plan in motion.

I've told this story before about a guy who came to our seminars. He made $180,000 in two months. He went to his wife and said, "I want to quit my job now." What's the typical wife going to say the first time a husband comes and says he wants to quit his job? "Do it again." She didn't want him to quit his job. He continued working options. He never made that kind of money again, but he got to the point where he was averaging $8,000 a month. Seven or eight months later he went to his wife and said, "I've been averaging $8,000 a month. Here are my accounts, here's the money, I've been averaging $8,000 a month, now I want to quit my job." What has he proven? That he can earn consistent money. What we need is consistent cash flow. Do you understand, eight months times $8,000 is only $64,000? He made $180,000 on a couple of hot deals before. $180,000! This time he only made $64,000. What's the point? It's consistent, it's doable, it's achievable! _That_ is the point!

Mistake #22: Remember to build quality into your life. When you came into my life, you probably didn't know what drove me. I started buying and selling houses at the age of 27 and was able to retire at the age of 29. I did real estate so I could go back to college, get a degree and teach college. That was my whole desire in life. I actually wanted to become a law school professor. I had no desire to be a lawyer, but I loved law, and I wanted to teach law school. That was my plan.

# 21-22 Ways to Build Wealth: Learning from the Mistakes of Wade

While in college, I bought a new house and the guy said, "Man, you ought to write a book!" I wrote a book, and he introduced me to Bob Allen who wrote the book *Nothing Down*. We became friends. I began speaking for him and suddenly I was in a whole new business. I didn't even know there *was* a lecture circuit. Now on a good weekend, I make as much as most college professors make in a year.

All I wanted was to help people better the quality of their lives. Buying a house, becoming a landlord and maintaining rental property ties up your life. I would go out and buy a house, fix it up, sell it and carry back the paper. I was able to retire at the age of 29, *not* from doing real estate, but from all the mortgages I created. People were paying me $60 and $90 a month and I had $5,400 a month coming in. That's more than I needed to live on, and I retired at the age of 29.

I didn't want to teach people how to buy houses; I wanted to teach them how to spend more time with their kids. I wanted to teach them how to have a better quality life. When the real estate business took a hit, I started doing stock market trades to support my own family and I realized, "Man! I'm able to support my family with rolling stock. Why don't I start sharing this with people?"

I used real estate as a means to an end. Today, I use the stock market as a means to an end. If I could call up a candy bar broker and say, "How about a couple cases of Snickers® candy bars at $23.50, and when they go to $26.50 I want to sell them." If I could do Snickers candy bars over the phone, if I could do real estate over the phone, I would do it. That's why I do the stock market. It's a perfect part time business. But it's a perfect business *not* to get you busier.

My point in number 22 is that you need to determine what you are doing to build up the quality of your life. What are you doing to *have* a wonderful life? Change that word "wonderful" to "full of wonder". How are you filling up your life with various "full of wonder" things? Do you really have time to smell the daisies?

We have a 30-acre pasture, and I went out walking through the pasture two nights ago, out among the horses. It was so quiet and so peaceful. That was my "smelling the daisies." I want to take time like that *every day* to be quiet. People think, "Gosh, you're so busy." You know what, I'm not. I go to a movie almost every day. I *love* going to movies. I love parts of my life. I don't want to be busy just for the sake of being busier. I am really, really busy about three hours a day at the company, training and building people up in all aspects of the company.

I'm not trying to encourage *you* to replace a 60 or 70 hour a week job working for someone else for a 60 or 70 hour a week job working in the stock market! If that's how it turns out, I haven't accomplished my job as an educator. Did you want to spend more time at home? Now you've locked yourself away in the back bedroom with all of your computers and you don't see your kids more anyway because you're telling them "Sh, sh, sh, Qualcom's moving, I can't talk to you." You're just so intense into your computer that it controls your life. That is not what I wanted to accomplish for you.

*Build the quality of your life*. Every day, I think you should make more inroads into increasing the quality of your life, more than you're spending trying to increase the quality of your option trade on Qualcom.

I'll end with this. This is a quote by President Woodrow Wilson. He said:

> *"You are not here merely to make a living. You are here to enable the world to live more amply, with greater vision, with a finer spirit of hope and achievement. You are here to enrich the world, but will lessen yourself if you forget the errand."*

*THE MONEY IS IN THE METER DROP. YOU GET IT IN, YOU GET IT OUT. YOU MAKE MONEY.*

*WADE B. COOK*

# Appendix 1

## Available Resources

The following books and CDs have been reviewed by Liberty Network Inc., and are suggested as reading and resource material for continuing education to help with your financial planning and stock market trading. Because new ideas and techniques come along and laws change, we're always updating our list.

To order a copy of our current list of educational products, please write or call us at:
Liberty Network, Inc.
1420 NW Gilman Blvd #2131
Issaquah, Washington 98027
1-866-579-5900
1-425-222-3760

Or, visit our website at:
www.wadecook.org

*CALL NOW for a FREE seminar on CD:*

How to Treat the Stock Market Like a Business. FREE CD.

This up-to-date skills training event is a wonderful introduction to Wade Cook and his time-honored, street-tested methods. This CD's sole purpose is to get your retired "Cash Flow Wealthy". $FREE ($19.95 Value)

# Appendix 1

### Power of Nevada Corporations—CD  Presented by Wade B. Cook

Nevada Corporations have secrecy, privacy, minimal taxes, now reciprocity with the IRS, and protection for shareholders, offices, and directors. This is a powerful seminar. $10 (plus $2 S&H)

## ON YOUR MARKET

COMBINATION OF FIVE REMARKABLE GROUPS OF SEMINARS: Five packages included together: (1) Investing and Trading; (2) Job Free Income; (3) Baseball the Stock Market and You; (4)Cash Flowing the Stock Market; (5) and Stock Splits.

That's 11 CDs, 9 Special Reports and 1 DVD. This is an INCREDIBLE offer.

It's also a limited offer. This one would make a GREAT present for the financial guru in your life. JUST $99 for this comprehensive package of financial power!! Total Value is above $400.

### *ORDER NOW!*

### Package 1: INVESTING VS. TRADING

This remarkable collection of trading knowledge will ready you to turn assets into a cash flow machine. "Income Producing Assets" is the best way to free up your time and energy. But, did you know you can trade (make extra cash) on your good investments? This collection shows you how to get your money to work as hard as you work. Why? So you can live a better life!

Includes:

1. SPECIAL REPORT: *What Makes Stocks Go Up* ($29.00) Finding Values. Sailing into Profits. P/E Ratios. Stock Prices: Follow Earnings. Cash Flow (sometimes two to three times a month!)

2. CD: *Powerful Income Formulas* ($14.95) This fast paced presentation will get you up-to-speed. Assets vs. Income, Formulas and Examples from the Real World, Consistency and Profitability, Pitfalls to Avoid.

3. DVD: *Dynamic Dollars* ($32.95) See Wade in action in this professionally produced demonstration of his Monthly Income Formulas. Rolling Stock, Stock Splits, Covered Calls, and Option Basics. The "How-Tos" shown so you can see them right away. Powerful information.

4. CD: *How to Treat the Stock Market Like a Business.* This up-to-date skills training event is a wonderful introduction to Wade Cook and his time-honored, street-tested methods. This CD's sole purpose is to get you retired "Cash Flow Wealthy". $FREE with this order. ($19.95 Value)

**Again, A Total Value of $96.85. . . YOURS FOR $55.00 (plus $5 S&H)**

## Package 2: JOB FREE INCOME

Wade Cook is in the retirement business. He uses the Stock Market as a business—which is a whole new concept for many. He gives details on how to get a second paycheck without getting a second job. Consistent Income comes from values, methods, and skills. This quote by *Henry Ford* says it best: *"If you think money is your hope for independence, you will never have it. The only real hope that a man (or woman) will have in this world is an abundance of knowledge, experience and ability."* In other words. . . useful skills.

Includes:

1. CD: *Job Free Income* ($16.95) Consistent Cash Flow, Little Known Ways to Capture Profits, Educating the Pros Around You, Finding Ways to Succeed.

2. CD: *Bargain Hunting* ($19.95) From Penny Stocks to IPO's, Wade shares his knowledge, from his years of experience and thousands of trades to show you how to find bargains and turn them into cash flow machines.

3. SPECIAL REPORT: *Make the Right Trade* ($29.00) From trade suitability to the in-and-outs of determining your own "how-tos" and "why-tos". A different look at procedures for eliminating risk and capturing profits.

4. CD: *More Income than You Can Spend* ($16.95) Double Dipping, or generating twice the cash flow each month, shared by Wade Cook, like only he can. Why? Because this knowledge is gained in the real world by trial and error, trying and trying again, to find ways to pound out excess profits.

**Again, a total value of $82.85... YOURS FOR $44.00 (plus $5 S&H)**

# Appendix 1

## Package 3: BASEBALL, THE STOCK MARKET AND YOU

America has two pastimes. One is baseball, a game with rules, set plays, teamwork and specific and reliable methods for success. The other is the stock market, a money game with rules, set strategies, teamwork and specific and reliable methods for success. Here is the good part: When you learn to play "small ball" and how to "manufacture" runs, you'll be in the stock market to "manufacture" repeatable small profits. This collection is designed to get you retired to a life of "one hour or less a day" $5,000 to $9,000/month. Obviously your results will vary—we hope you make more.

Includes:

1. CD: *Hitting Singles and Doubles in the Market* ($19.95) It's about repeatable small profits: made on autopilot. It's about diversity, but diversity in formulas. This is a great seminar to "realistically" put you in a position to make real cash profits.

2. SPECIAL REPORT: *Baseball, the Stock Market and You* ($29.00) This report is an extensive study of P/E ratios (finding values) and how earnings move stock. Small repeatable profits, manufactured like bunting a runner over to third for a run set up, then moving the runner in by base hits (rolling stock), upping your "batting average" with "covered calls" and an occasional home run. . . like IPO's, spin-offs and stock splits.

3. CD: *What it Takes* ($16.95) This mind-stretching seminar sets new standards in personal development. Success, both in life and finances comes from controlling your thought process. Every family member will love this knowledge.

**A total value of $65.90, YOURS FOR $22.00** (plus $5 S&H).

## Package 4: CASH FLOWING THE STOCK MARKET

This library of written and spoken words shatters the old, stale ways of investing—in other words, letting someone else control your financial destiny. **WRITING** (Selling) **COVERED** (you own the stock) **CALLS** (call options) generates cash into your account. You trade for income. This system will help you get retired. These reports and seminars will put you in the drivers seat. You can invest and trade this way in your IRA (and make profits tax deferred).

Includes:

1. SPECIAL REPORT: *The 20% Monthly Cash Flow Challenge* ($29.00) This explosive report shows the methods used with large popular stocks (8 out of 100) that show a 20% cash on cash profit for the month. You'll be amazed.

2. SPECIAL REPORT: *Selling In-the-Money Calls* ($29.00) This report continues with a little known, seldom used technique, which makes profits more certain. Useful for every Investor and Trader.

3. CD: *Classic Covered Call Writing* ($19.95) Wade is on fire in this motivating presentation of Writing Covered Calls. He shows the 2 1/2 out of 3 chances of making money. You learn how to capture profits now—to buy groceries or pay the rent. You'll learn to buy the stock on dips and sell the calls on strength.

4. CD: *Get Rich Steady* ($17.95) Wealth comes from a mind-set. This seminar literally "breaks through worn out and boring investment methods. This CD is formidable knowledge against the methods so often used.

5. SPECIAL REPORT: *Events Which Move Stocks* ($29.00) There are 31 events which move stocks up and down. This calendar, in conjunction with Red-Light, Green-Light information will help you invest and trade smart. You'll be angry with your stockbroker for not sharing this information with you.

**Again, that's a $124.95 Value... YOURS FOR $55.00 (plus $5 S&H)**

## Package 5: STOCK SPLITS

Wade Cook, author of *Wall Street Money Machine*, put his trading power of knowledge into this fine-tuned array of trading points. You can capitalize now! There are five times to trade on stock splits with options (low-cost, limited risk) or stock. 1) Pre-announcement: one of the best; 2) On the announcement: wait, don't trade here, the small guy gets hurt; 3) Between the announcement and the split: Great time as rolling patterns are formed; 4) Rally into the split--great 2 to 3 day trades—good for the busy executive or homemaker; 5) After the split: After a brief downturn (which can be played with puts), this trade is often a nice upward move (though slower).

Includes:

1. CD: *Outrageous Returns* ($19.95) Put market forces to work for you, not against you. Learn solutions to problems. Examples of entrance and exit points.

2. SPECIAL REPORT: *Stock Splits and Cash Flow* ($29.00) More in-depth details of finding and processing splits. Learn how to use market movement to make better trades.

3. SPECIAL REPORT: *Stock Splits with Leverage* ($29.00) Proxy Investing. Unlimited Upside Potential with Limited Downside Risk. When the stock splits... the Options split--a double whammy!

4. CD: *The Stock Improvement Seminar* ($14.95) Anyone who has a stock down in value will appreciate this timely and pertinent information from this seminar. Numerous topics and strategies given to fix your portfolio.

**Again, a total value of $92.90... YOURS FOR $33.00 (plus $5 S&H)**

**GET ALL FIVE PACKAGES FOR JUST $99** (plus $10 S&H)
***This is a LIMITED TIME OFFER.***
**CALL FOR CURRENT PRICES AND AVAILABILITY.**
**1-866-579-5900**
**1-425-222-3760**
**www.wadecook.org**

---

# Attention Speakers and Instructors:
Liberty Network, Inc. is looking for a few great teachers of stock market strategies, Real Estate techniques and asset protection methods.

Visit www.wadecook.org
and
www.johnchilders.com

---

# Appendix 2
## Tutorial Service

## M.U.S.T.

Liberty Network is the company of MORE. More cash flow, more freedom, more knowledge, and more time with your family. Once in a while there comes along a service that is so unique, so creative that renders it almost hard to explain. Our M.U.S.T. program is such a service. There is literally nothing like it in the world. If you want news, if you want stock prices and quotes, if you want pure motivation, then you need to look elsewhere. **M**onthly **U**pdate **S**kills **T**raining is a specific tutorial service to help individuals—small investors—to connect-the-dots better in the stock market.

## Investing Vs. Trading

There is a world of difference between investing and trading. Investing is where you use your money with a longer-term horizon—say 2 months to 2 years. It is what we call "semester investor".

Trading however is an action done with a shorter term horizon—say 2 to 4 days or 2 to 4 weeks. The beautiful thing about the way Wade Cook trades in the market is that you can trade on your good investments. A lot of people think that you either have to be an investor or a trader. Wade believes that no such choice has to be made. You can become a very good investor—studying fundamentals, book values, and other ways of measuring the health of a company—but you can also learn how to trade. Trading deals with peaks and slams, moving averages, making better entrance and exit points. And doing all of this with a cash flow purpose.

If you are a good investor it will help you make better trades. Conversely, if you are a good trader, it will help you make better investments.

Blending these two activities together is what M.U.S.T. is all about.

Wade Cook, author of the 4 New York Times Business Best-Selling books now puts his knowledge, experience, and wisdom together in our powerful internet site. Visit us at www.wadecook.org

# Appendix 2 Tutorial Service

## Experience Is The Best Teacher

What do you need to get ahead? What do you need to learn to help you connect-the-dots better? Everyone learns differently. Some people learn best by reading. Others learn by seeing. Many learn best by the spoken word or hearing. ***But almost everyone learns best by experience.***

You can study everything there is to know about snow skiing. You can read books; you could watch videos; you could even go to the slopes and watch various skiers. Though, at some point in time, if you are going to snow ski and be really proficient at it you have to hit the slopes. Nothing takes the place of experience.

The problem with experience is embodied in the following statement: "Experience is the best teacher, but it's so darn expensive." Also in this statement by Vernon Law, a famous baseball pitcher: "Experience is the best teacher, but she gives the test first and the lesson later."

It truly is a wise person who can learn through the experiences of others. Wade Cook has been in the trenches literally doing tens of thousands of trades, and not all of them have been successful. He has learned a lot from his unsuccessful trades. He has been trading in up-markets and down-markets. He has had investments go from $20 to $800 and he has had other investments go from $200 down to $2. He's learned how to avoid costly mistakes. He has learned how to protect both the upside and the downside: "Know your exit before you go in the entrance." Many of you have heard the expression before, but now with years of experience, Wade has two exit points. He has an upside exit point and a downside exit point.

What has this to do with a tutorial internet site? You can literally leap frog your way to wealth, by watching over the shoulder of a position trader who is willing to share what he knows and what he is learning on a daily basis. The stock market is a constantly moving target. Everyone needs a mentor. Even Wade has mentors—he brings in a team of experts to help him learn and make better trades.

## The Stock Market As A Business

We believe the stock market can make a perfect part-time business. Obviously it needs to be treated like a business. This means to buy wholesale and sell retail. The stock market gives you many opportunities to sell first and buy back later. You can't do this with a typical business. The stock market also makes a perfect part-time business without all the necessary expenses. Look at this list of what Wade has developed of what he wants out of a business and what he doesn't.

## What I Want

A) I want the freedom of owning my own business and not having to punch a time clock for someone else.

B) I want a lot of income with small expenses, not the other way around.

C) I want unlimited potential—with my only limitation being my creativity, my industry, and myself.

D) I want tax deductions and write-offs, growth of assets, and excessive income from the assets.

E) I want to set aside huge amounts of tax-deductible money for my future. I also want to make money in a tax-deferred account.

F) I want more quality time to be with my family and friends.

G) I want a small business with big profits. "Stay small and keep it all."

H) I want easy access, low start up costs and a way to grow the business without huge advertising costs.

I) I want to share with family and friends, and mentally, not financially support each other.

J) I want the ability to wind down, sell, or quit, or just walk away at my choosing.

K) I want to be happy with the process—and to use my knowledge of things to connect the dots.

L) I want to associate with "like-minded people", who, synergistically with me, want the best for others.

## What I Don't Want

A) I don't want the ball and chain of a retail establishment and its time demands.

B) I don't want high expenses, increasing costs and surprise cash outlays.

C) I don't want ambitions, drive, originality, or abilities to get eaten up by un-ambitious people—the parasites of enterprise.

D) I don't want to net 10%, with 90% going to operation costs—In fact, I want to net the 90%.

E) I don't want all the normal expenses of a business—rent, insurance, licenses, registrations, Research and Development, employees, etc.

F) I don't want to have to buy or lease and then take care of expensive office equipment.

G) I don't want a big business with big-time headaches.

H) I don't want large start up costs for me, or others, and huge expenditures to grow the business.

I) I don't want costly entanglements with agreements, contracts and messy relationships.

J) I don't want ongoing commitments with no exit strategy planned.

K) I don't want to live for the business, but have the business live for me—providing a nice life style.

L) I don't want to be around people who are there for the next paycheck and could care less about the enterprise.

# Appendix 2 Tutorial Service

## Value

In previous years Wade has sold a similar service to M.U.S.T. for $3,600 a year, or $300 a month. As a charter member you do not need to pay anything near that price. In fact you can subscribe today for $22 a month. The only contract to sign is to acknowledge that the stock market is risky, that you should seek your own professional help in making financial decisions, and that you will be responsible for your own trading activities. You can subscribe for $22 a month and pay with a credit card and quit anytime that you like. So if you do not find the service beneficial there is no ongoing commitment. This is a limited "charter membership" and may not be available very long, but even at $200 to $300 a month, M.U.S.T. is a bargain.

## J. O. T.

As we mentioned in previous years a service like this has cost thousands of dollars. Even at that high price one of Wade's commitments is to show one or two trades a month that any of his students can do, either that particular trade or, more likely a similar trade, and with the profits of "Just One Trade", be able to pay for the whole service—again $3,600. It is a process called J.O.T. or Just One Trade. *Now, with our service priced at only $22, Just One Trade could pay for 2 or 3 years with this particular service._*

## Four Steps

At M.U.S.T. we employ a very unique four step process. This process is designed to help you not just do these particular trades but to find ways of doing your own trades. You should come up with your own four steps; the scenario or what is going on with the stock, the particular trade you're trying to employ, the actual cost of the trade and then your expected and actual results.

> **Step 1**: *The scenario. What's going on with the stock, sector, or in the whole marketplace. Why are you doing this trade? What is the impending event?*

> **Step 2**: *What strategy is being employed. When possible, information from books, seminars and special reports expound on the formula.*

> **Step 3**: *The trade. What exactly did we do?*

> **Step 4**: *The expected results or actual results (when appropriate) of the trade.*

## Paper Trading

Our purpose is to get you ready to make great trades through education. We firmly believe in simulation trading or paper trading. Let us share with you what this means. Imagine getting on an airplane and the pilot gets on the intercom and says "Welcome on board ladies and gentlemen, I am a brand new pilot and this will be my first time taking off and landing". Most of us would head for the door. We want somebody with years of experience. Most airplane pilots spend years training in the right seat before they ever move over to the left seat to become captain or pilot. And even after they become captain they spend days and even weeks every year in simulators on how to take off and land and all other aspects of navigating a plane.

Another interesting point of pilot simulation training is they always learn how to take off and land in the worst of conditions. Isn't this applicable to all of us in our own businesses – especially the stock market? We need to learn how to trade in the worst of circumstances, and also how to fix any problems that come up.

We believe that everyone should learn the particular trading strategies through practice. The stock market unlike real estate or other distant activities allows us to make particular trades and study the results. Often times the results are almost immediate—at least within days or weeks—and we can fix any problem as we go along. We can develop our skills. You've heard the expression, "Practice Makes Perfect". Wrong. You can practice something the wrong way for ten years and it's still wrong. *"Perfect practice makes perfect!"*

May we put all these three words: knowledge, experience and ability, into one word: SKILLS. That is why the "**S**" in **M.U.S.T.** is *SKILLS* – Monthly Update Skills Training. Developing these skills is suggested so that you do not put your money in harms way. You use paper money or monopoly type money in studying, improving, connecting-the-dots and gaining experience.

We also believe you should trade each strategy at least 15 times of which <u>10 in a row</u> are <u>profitable</u>, before you ever use real money. If you are looking for 10 in a row to be profitable and you lose money on one trade, again you lose it on paper, so it does not hurt your pocket book. Start again. Remember, you need 10 successful trades in a row. We realize this takes a certain amount of patience and discipline. Read this quote by John Wooden the infamous past coach of the UCLA basketball team and 16 times National Basketball champion: "Discipline yourself and others won't have to." We suggest you discipline yourself in the stock market or any business activity.

## There are three specific times to paper trade.

(1) Wade Cook has 9 different cash flow strategies. We suggest you get to be an expert at one of them. Each one has a time and place—basically its own how to's and why to's. It is up to you to figure out the why to's. We suggest that a "why to" type person is the leader.

*"The person who knows how will always have a job. The person who knows why will always be his own boss."*
*—Dianne Ravitch*

Why you would use a particular trading strategy is very important. When you figure out what strategy you want to use we suggest you paper trade with that strategy many times before you use real money. When you get to be an expert at one strategy, and want to move on to a new strategy, don't think that the same rules apply. Each strategy has its own set of rules. So as you start to use a new strategy, you need to paper trade that strategy while doing real trades with the other strategy.

(2) You continue to paper trade when you run out of money. No one has an unlimited amount of money. Let's say you have $10,000 to invest and you have traded with one strategy and you are fully invested. You want to continue to trade that strategy but all your money is tied up for a temporary time – lets say until next expiration date. Do not quit trading. Move from trading with real money into paper trading so that when your money is available you are **in the know, on the go and ready to make additional trades.**

The opposite of this means you have to get good at that point and time if you have stopped trading just because you were out of money. So never quite trading, continue with paper trading. It would be good to do at least three paper trades a day so that you keep your cutting edge sharp.

(3) You paper trade or go back to trading anytime there is a significant change in the market place or with any particular stock that you are trading.

Let's say that a stock shoots from $40 to $80. You do not know if that price can be sustained. You don't know if it is going to roll again and have the same ups and downs it had in the $40 range. If you still like the stock go back to paper. Or try a new stock and remember to paper trade the stock before you ever use real money.

There are also a lot of minor rules with simulation trading. For example, being very truthful with the prices, either use the bid or ask when you buy and sell or use the last trade. You can figure out your cash profits or your rate of return if you use real numbers. You should keep very good records so that as you connect-the-dots and figure things out, you have accurate records by date, time and place.

## Getting Ready

There are many things to consider with the market place at hand. **The American economy seems to be turning around which will provide ample opportunities.** Option prices should pick up and be more expensive which will give us a better opportunity when we sell. There are a lot of things that we see on the horizon that make the upcoming economy a great place to trade in the market.

## Market Reloaded

**REINVIGORATED:** All indicators point to an uptrend. Don't get left behind.

**RENEW:** Learn to DIVERSIFY into different formulas. Stocks are just inventory.

**REBOUND:** Like a trampoline. Big money is ready. There is huge pent-up demand.

**RESET:** Poised and ready for growth. Opportunities are abundant if your knowledge and mindset are right.

**REBUILD:** Use corrective measure to fix your portfolio. Don't be a victim. Fight back!

**RETHOGHT:** An added dimension of safety with new corporate governance issues in place.

**RESURRECTED:** Many stocks are back from the dead: slimmed down, trim and fit.

**REGAIN:** Yes, we've had a major correction, but new corporate profits and earnings forecasts look brighter.

**RESTATE:** A reality check has brought earnings growth to realistic expectations.

**REGROUP:** Get ready before the next wave. Position trade—get your money in the way of movement.

Imagine if you will that you want to learn how to surf. If you have ever surfed yourself or watched it on TV you will note that as the surfers see a good wave coming in the distance they do not wait for the wave to get upon them and rush over the top of them. The first thing you do is turn your surfboard toward shore. As the wave starts approaching you start paddling and get up your speed so as the wave comes close to you it is easier to catch. **The point is that you get ready for the opportunity.** We believe that there is ample opportunity in the market place to make a significant cash flow profit – enough to support your family. But just like the surfboard you need to get ready. Getting ready in this instance means getting education trained. Education also helps you see opportunities.

With knowledge you are much better prepared to take advantage of opportunity. A lot of people don't see the opportunities and don't take advantage of them because they can't see them—they don't know what is available.

One of the purposes of M.U.S.T. is to teach you on a day-to-day basis what is available. And we do this with live trades. You will never know if Wade Cook is trading a simulation trade or a real trade because he treats both paper trades and real trades the same. **He is very serious about his trading and is one of the very few people that will put all his trades—win lose or draw—on an internet site for the whole**

**world to see.** You will learn as much from the mistakes he makes as well as the good trades he makes. Our commitment is to put the trades on that have a tutorial nature to them so that you can learn. You will not be able to copy the exact trades. And we do not make any recommendations. Just because a trade is right for Wade does not mean that is right for you. But you can learn from his insights.

## Clearing House

We at Liberty Network Inc., also receive e-mail and letters from our students and we have become a clearing house for a lot of different people. Also, Wade is friends with a lot of national instructors and he finds out what they are doing. We try to put as much of their insights as we can on our site. We become a clearing house for good information and this all boils down to a big benefit for you. We realize everyone wants value. There is a world of difference of our site and others. You simply can't get the insights, explanations and tutoring anywhere else. The benefit of being a subscriber of M.U.S.T. is that you can look over the shoulder of one who is in the trenches everyday doing the trades.

REGISTER for M.U.S.T. on www.wadecook.org for only $22.00 a month!

*CALL LIBERTY NETWORK 425-222-3760 or visit www.wadecook.org*

*Prices Subject to Change.*

For Questions or to Order:

Liberty Network, Inc.

1420 N.W. Gilman Blvd. #2131

Issaquah, WA 98027

425-222-3760

**425-222-3764 (fax)**

**Product Sales:** *Toll Free* **866-579-5900**

**www.wadecook.org**

# Appendix 3

My mindset has been of a searching explorer—happy with new discoveries, excited with uncovering ancient wisdom, and thrilled as these words lead people back to the words of God. This has been a constant revelation to me—the Bible is an unending source of knowledge, edification and strength. President Woodrow Wilson said, *"There are a good many problems before the American people today, and before me as President, but I expect to find the solution of those problems just in the proportion that I am faithful in the study of the Words of God. OI am sorry for the men who do not read the Bible every day; I wonder why they deprive themselves of the strength and of the pleasure. It is one of the most singular books in the worlds, for every time you open it, some old text that you have read a score of times suddenly means with a new meaning. There is no other book I know of, of which this is true; there is no other book that yields its meaning so personally that seems to fit itself so intimately to the very spirit that is seeking its guidance."*

It says in Psalms 27, verse one, *"The LORD is my light and my salvation; whom shall I fear?"* To the composer of Psalm 27 and to the author of these special reports, the LORD is personal: *"He is my light."* As Charles Spurgeon said, *"After conversion God is our joy, comfort, guide, teacher and in every sense, our light; he is Light within, Light around, Light reflected from us, and Light to be revealed to us. Note, it is not said merely that the Lord gives light, but that he 'is' light; nor that he gives salvation, but that he is salvation."*

Then we read Bruce McConkie stating this about light, *"defies description and is beyond mortal comprehension. It is in us and in all things; it is around us and around all things; it fills the earth and the heavens and the universe. It is everywhere, in all immensity, without exception; it is an indwelling, immanent, ever-present, never-absent spirit. It has neither shape nor form nor personality. It is not an entity nor a person nor a personage. It has no agency, does not act independently, and exists not to act but to be acted upon."*

The Apostle John says, *"...in Christ was life; and the life was the light of men;"* but adds, *"The light shineth in darkness, and the darkness comprehended it not;"* John 1:4-5. Back to Sturgeon: *"To know God is Light is one thing (1 John 1:5) and to be able to say, 'The Lord is my light' is quite another thing."*

I want and need this light. When I did not feel this type of inspiration I did not write. I desire to be led down the road by this light. Yes, I am weak, but Christ can make my weakness whole. *"And he said unto me, My grace is sufficient for thee: for my strength is made perfect in weakness. Most gladly therefore will I rather glory in my infirmities, that the power of Christ may rest upon me."*

I am humbled by what I have found and continue to search out. I want to keep searching the scriptures: truly *"they are they which testify of me,"*—meaning God. In this endeavor, I have personally found no better attitude or virtue than that of meekness. In humility I search, and then humbly submit my findings to you.

Meekness is not weakness. Meekness helps us maintain our composure. Meekness is necessary for salvation: *". . .God arose. . .to save all the meek of the earth. . ."* Psalm 76:9. Also, another Psalm is very enlightening: *"But the meek shall inherit the earth; and shall delight themselves in the abundance of people."* Psalm 37:11.

I have attempted in these reports to show for appropriate God's words are to our daily walk through life. They fit. Conversely, I have attempted to show that at virtually any and every instance on our lives there is an effective thought from the Bible to help us and guide us. I am just one voice. You will have to do your part. God points us the way. It is up to us to follow. *"But sanctify the Lord God in your hearts: and be ready always to give an answer to every man that asketh you a reason of the hope that is in you with meekness and hear."* I Peter 3:15

Paul taught in meekness. *"Now I Paul myself beseech you by the meekness and gentleness of Christ..."* II Corinthians 10:1. Jesus said, *"Take my yoke upon you, and learn of me; for I am meek and lowly in heart: and ye shall find rest unto your souls."* Mathew 11:29. *"The meek shall eat and be satisfied: they shall praise the LORD that seek him: your hear shall love for ever."* Psalm 22:26.

I want to be taught so much more that I want to teach. "The meek will be guide in his judgment: and the meek will he teach his way." Psalm 25:9. I make no pretenses. God's word is powerful. Wade Cook's words are puny. I only want to help guide a few people back to God's wonderful words. It is in this humbleness of spirit that I pray my few words will find a home, maybe reach out and touch someone to give up a little pride, to abandon harmful ways and return to God. He waits with open arms. This is true and lasting happiness.

> *"But God hath revealed them unto us by his Spirit: for the Spirit searcheth all things, yea, the deep things of God."* I Corinthians 2:10.

As we in meekness continue our quest for the knowledge of God, then maybe, just maybe, we'll say as Job did as he came to find out, *". . .things to wonderful for me. . ."* Job 42:3. It is a lifelong journey. Finding God is worth the effort.

*"Search the scriptures; for in them ye thing ye have eternal life: and they are they which testify of me."*                                                            John 5:39.

## Abundantly Yours,

*Wade B. Cook*

The nighttime gym scene in the movie **Remember the Titans** has a part where the football players started quoting scripture. I loved it, because it was one of my favorite verses. Isaiah 40:31: *"But they that wait upon the LORD shall renew their strength; they shall mount up with wings as eagles; they shall run, and not be weary; and they shall walk, and not faint."*

Years ago I started collecting statues of eagles, but I love God's words more. The promise in this verse is awesome. Inspired by this and a passion for Biblical study, including research into the original Hebrew, Aramaic and Greek words, and a desire to see these Biblical truths brought back into our general discourse and our personal loves, I set about to write these Soar with Eagles Special Reports. I hope you enjoy them.

**#700 Preface:** A study in itself of ancient knowledge and God's will for us.

**#701 Total Harmony:** A discussion of false myths about God. Abraham, the first Hebrew, sets a new standard.

**#702 Gaining Wisdom:** Knowledge to understanding everyday uses: desire first. Learn how to make better decisions.

**#703 7 Ways to Gain Wisdom:** More easy-to-implement formulas for applying knowledge gained. Fun stuff.

**#705 Wisdom and Riddles:** Samson and a great riddle. Hebrew knowledge. Learn how to *project* outcomes, not predict outcomes. New Perspective.

**#706 Noble Living.** A wonderful, uplifting report on nine ways to build a quality life. Excellent.

**#707 Noble Actions:** Living, working for a quality existence. Actions which reflect Godly Values.

**#708 Seeking Peace—Making Peace:** Study Hebrew and its varied meanings. Peace, comfort and more happiness.

**#709 A Pure Heart:** "Incline thine ear..." A Godly heart translated into worthwhile action. Splendid.

**#710 Heart and Soul:** The nexus with God. The lamp unto the body. David's plea! A touching collection of scripture.

**#711 Trusting God:** Building a team. Faith is trust, trust is everything in out relationship with God.

**#712 Dealing with Injustice:** Fight, Flight or Forego to God. Maybe Wade's battles can help you think more clearly.

**#713 A Thankful Heart:** A key to success. Blessing and acknowledgement. Keeping things in proper perspective.

**#714 Attitude is Everything:** Thing High and Fly. Control your thoughts—it's the start of all good things.

## The Following five reports are part of out High-Teens Series (715-719).

**#715 Guard Your Heart:** Only you control your thoughts. A message of Great Importance to all—especially the youth.

**#716 Determination:** Wade's daughter Leslie shares her secret passion—drive, persistence—goal getting.

**#717 The Strength of Youth:** Wade's teen stories. "Double it" and the Second Mile thinking process' Uplifting.

**#718 Ten Laws of Success for Teenagers:** A wonderful expose that will help uplift, motivate, drive teenagers to greater heights.

**#719 The Whole Armour of God:** Don't leave home without it. A report on Ephesians 6. This will give teenagers real things to do better in their lives. Encouraging.

**#720 Influence:** A powerful report on the influence of one. Cautions. Friends, parents, leaders—Please read this.

**#721 A Prayer for All of Us: Jabez:** A detailed study of the four components of Jabez' prayer.

**#722 Wealth: A Generous Viewpoint:** A Biblical and historical look at money and generosity. Really fun.

**#723 A Celebration of Light:** God is the Father of lights. Explore the Light of Christ. Mornings. Sunshine. Health.

**#724 Music to My Ears:** A beautiful collection of thoughts through the ages on music.

**#725 Woman—God's Supreme Creation:** Men will love this report. Finally, a great report which helps women rose above the "wisdom" of the world. Truly inspiring.

**#726 A Virtuous Wife:** A great study of Proverbs 31. Perspective. Beauty. Direct and Godly virtues.

**#727 Motherhood:** You'll want every mother you know to have these beautiful words. Mothers are such a blessing!

**#728 A Time For Everything:** Ecclesiastes 3 comes alive. Build a better, more meaningful life with these insights.

**#729 Friendship Values:** Choosing, helping, building great friendships. Friends as a gift from God.

**#730 Nine Virtues 1-3:** Choosing, helping, building great friendships. Friends as a gift from God.

**#731 Nine Virtues 4-6:** A study of the famous verses in Galatians Chapter 5. A discussion of longsuffering, gentleness and goodness.

**#732 Nine Virtues 7-9:** More in Galatians 5. Knowledge on faith, meekness and temperance. Insightful.

**#733 The Lord is My Shepherd:** Wade's personal testimony and insights into on of the most famous passages of all times: Psalm 23.

Eagles in a Storm: Did you know that an eagle knows when a storm is approaching long before it breaks? The eagle will fly to some high spot and wait for the winds to come. When the storm hits, it sets its wings so that the wind will pick it up and lift it above the storm. While the storm rages below, the eagle is soaring above it. The eagle does not escape the storm. It simply uses the storm to lift it higher. It rises on the winds that bring the storm.

## Appendix 3

When the storms of life come upon us—and all of us will experience them—we can rise above them by setting our minds and our belief toward God. The storms do not have to overcome us. We can allow God's power to lift us above them. God enables us to ride the winds of the storm that bring sickness, tragedy, failure and disappointment in our lives. We can soar above the storm.

Each Special Report is beautifully typeset and is four to six pages long. The price for each is $6.95 with a $2 each shipping and handling, with a maximum S&H of $8. The set for teenagers, #715 to $719, is $22, plus $6 S&H. The whole set of 34 reports can be purchased as a group, handsomely bound, for $99, plus $8 S&H. 1-866-579-5900.